D0456864

heart of my heart

heart of
my heart

365 Reflections on the Magnitude and Meaning of Motherhood

. . . .

A DEVOTIONAL

. . . .

Kristin Armstrong

FaithWords

FaithWords
Hachette Book Group
237 Park Avenue
New York, NY 10017
www.faithwords.com

FaithWords is a division of Hachette Book Group, Inc.
The FaithWords name and logo are trademarks of Hachette Book Group, Inc.

Printed in the United States of America

First Edition: April 2010
10 9 8 7 6 5 4 3 2 1

Library of Congress Cataloging-in-Publication Data

Armstrong, Kristin.
   Heart of my heart : 365 reflections on the magnitude and meaning of motherhood :
a devotional / Kristin Armstrong. — 1st ed.
       p. cm.
   Summary: "Kristin Armstrong shares a year of grace, faith, learning, and love in this
devotional for mothers." — Provided by the publisher.
   ISBN 978-0-446-56169-3
   1. Motherhood—Religious aspects—Christianity.   2. Devotional calendars.   I. Title.
   BV4847.A76 2010
   242'.6431—dc22

                                                            2009037804

For my children, the heart of my heart—
Luke, Grace, and Bella

ACKNOWLEDGMENTS

For the good people at Hachette, especially Rolf, Michelle, and Jana, thank you for caring about me, my family, and my work.

For my girlfriends, because we raise our children together, thank you for your perspective and your prayers.

For my grandmothers, Millie G. and Aune, thank you for the legacy of love and faith that binds our generations.

For my dad, David, and my brother, Jon, because behind every good mom are great men who love her.

For my mom, Ethel, because my understanding of mothering is founded in her goodness, thank you for raising me to love God, children, and words.

For my sweethearts, Luke, Grace, and Bella. With a family like ours, I can be and do anything. So can you.

For my one and only, thank you, Father, for everything.

*T*here are precise moments in life that leave us permanently altered. Moments that seal our hearts and our fates with the realization that whoever we were before is no longer sufficient, having been replaced by someone new.

Becoming a mother was the chrysalis of my womanhood. It was there, in the physical act of labor and holding our son for the very first time, that I was permanently altered, a deep etch on my personal time line, marking very clearly—before and after. My heart existed, beating outside my own body, resting perfectly in the crook of my arm. Luke was living proof, delivered from God Himself, that I mattered, that I had a legacy worth passing down, and that things would be required of me that would take me beyond myself. Since that moment, and the subsequent addition of twin daughters, through the blur of newborns and toddlers, through the sweet haze of preschool, and into the snowballing elementary school years, I have discovered more about myself and my God in the pursuit of discovering my children.

Since then I have had moments overflowing with peace and purpose, and other moments when I wonder how God could ever have entrusted me with an honor and a responsibility of this magnitude. There are moments when I know beyond the shadow of a doubt that God has used me to help hone my children's characters, and there are moments of even greater clarity when I know that God is using them to hone mine.

No one can make me laugh as easily, relax as fully, hope as grandly, love as deeply, fight as passionately, speak as clearly, work as diligently, give as freely, pray as intensely, think as seriously, or play as regularly as my children can.

In raising them, I am being raised up.

Motherhood has motivated me to scrutinize my character and take whatever steps are necessary to address areas of weakness. In the awareness of my frailties, I devour Scripture, experiencing a desire for and reliance on God, knowing that alone I am insufficient for this beautiful assignment. Of all the things in my life, this is one area I don't want to mess up, a gift I don't want to squander, a ball I don't want to drop. Yet I know I sometimes will. It is only through an intimate, daily walk with God that I can summon the courage to even make the attempt. Maybe being a single mother highlights the importance of my Partner.

So here it is, a year's worth of walking. May we grow together, enjoy this adventure, relish this gift, savor this time, and emerge from this year as better mothers. May we learn to love as we have been loved.

Kristin

heart of my heart

"If you bungle raising your children, I don't think that whatever else you do well matters much."

—JACQUELINE KENNEDY ONASSIS

*The only thing that counts is faith
expressing itself through love.*

GALATIANS 5:6

There are a million ways to fall short, to miss the mark, to mess up, to handle it wrong, to miss the point. We can expend our energy in the pursuit of being the perfect mother and come up empty, or we can realize that the only pursuit worth the effort is the desire to be good enough. There are a million ways to be good enough, the first of which is to keep trying. And that's what we're here to do, together, recommitting ourselves each day to the heartfelt goal of doing the best we can with what we have in each moment, in the raising of our children.

It's clear we don't always have what it takes to transition from moment to moment, challenge to challenge, with wisdom and grace. This is not to be taken negatively, but rather as a relief—we simply can't do it on our own; we must stay connected to the Source. He alone makes up for our shortcomings; He alone magnifies our efforts; He alone makes us sufficient. Our children need to see that we have a desperate need to remain joined with the Father. Only by seeing that in us will they learn to recognize and nourish that need in themselves.

We are going to walk together for a whole year. We will emerge as better mothers, more faith-filled women. It isn't as overwhelming as it seems, if we can return to this verse again and again: *The only thing that counts is faith expressing itself through love.* That's it. If we can hold fast to this foundation, the rest of the details will fall into place.

Every good and perfect gift is from above,
coming down from the Father of the heavenly lights,
who does not change like shifting shadows.

JAMES 1:17

Where do we begin?

We begin any task, any challenge, any new year, any worthwhile pursuit in one way—with gratitude. If we begin here, we acknowledge all that God has already done to take us this far. We praise Him for the gifts He has already given us, the ways He has already instructed us, and we reflect on the steadfastness of His promises that He has already revealed to us. In doing this, we align our hearts in the proper position to begin any journey. By thanking Him, we please Him, and our thankfulness serves as a reminder to ourselves of the countless ways He has already proven Himself faithful in our lives. We bolster our own faithfulness when we recall His unfailing faithfulness. We are refreshed and renewed by gratitude. It is a powerful force, able to transform any mood or circumstance.

We approach a new task, or an old task on a new day, with the positive outlook that worship restores to our souls. Whatever you do today, big things and small things, thank God in them and for them. What He has already done, He will continue to do and more as He meets us where we are with exactly what we need—and the truth of His handiwork will manifest itself in our mothering.

*Such confidence as this is ours through Christ
before God. Not that we are competent
in ourselves to claim anything for ourselves,
but our competence comes from God.*

2 CORINTHIANS 3:4–5

I remember my first night home from the hospital, nursing Luke in the quiet of the middle of the night. I was tired, I was fearful, and I felt vulnerable and alone. It was as if the weight of the responsibility of this little life settled into my lap and looked up at me with round and trusting eyes. I wanted to panic, to cry out to God as the wave of hormones tossed my puny life raft on the high seas of my emotions. Who was I kidding? There was no way I could sustain this life, care for this baby, raise this child up into adulthood *every single day* from now on.

You have to have a license to drive a car, fill out a mound of paperwork to adopt a pet from the shelter, study for years to be a doctor, pass the bar to become a lawyer, have credentials to teach, have a permit to set up a campsite, but a baby? The highest calling, the heaviest responsibility, the most timeless task, the ultimate investment can be yours without having to prove a thing.

Is it any wonder we feel ill-equipped? If we feel insufficient, it's because *we are*. Our competence comes from God.

We have been blessed so that we may be a blessing.

Do not be anxious about anything,
but in everything, by prayer and petition,
with thanksgiving, present your requests to God.
And the peace of God, which transcends
all understanding, will guard your hearts
and your minds in Christ Jesus.

PHILIPPIANS 4:6–7

Stop what you are doing.

What do you need? Yes, you, right now. What are you anxious about today? What is the scratchy thing, rubbing a raw spot on the outskirts of your consciousness, breaking your peace? What thought are you holding on to, rolling it over in your mind again and again, like a small stone in your hand? What is stealing your joy, right now? Even if it's vague and attempting to elude you, corner it and name it. Call it out of the shadows, grab it by the scruff of the neck, and take a good close look at it.

And then thank God for bringing you understanding. With thanksgiving, praise Him for being mightier than any of our concerns. Confirm with Him that He is both the source and the solution and that you desire Him to reign in every circumstance and in every corner of your life and thought life. Pray your way through to peace. When our eyes are on God, we are forced to look up and over our circumstances. Like the static on the radio, everything fades when we tune in to the right channel.

He tells us to not be anxious about anything. Are we listening?

But someone will say, "You have faith;
I have deeds." Show me your faith without deeds,
and I will show you my faith by what I do.

JAMES 2:18

It is an important and beautiful thing to tell someone you love them. I tell my children I love them when I tuck them in at bedtime, when I kiss them and usher them out of the car at school every morning, when they leave to go on a trip with their dad, when we end a phone conversation. They will never long to hear those words from my lips. I will never regret not having said them.

But sometimes words get only as far as our ears. Love demonstrated in action whispers directly to the heart. When I pack lunches and cut the crust off sandwiches; when I show up at the recital; when I respond to the feeble voice calling from the nurse's office and clear my day to snuggle; when I practice a spelling list for the umpteenth time; when I ask for (and accept) forgiveness when I handle something poorly; when I cook a special meal to celebrate report cards; when I braid hair; when I repeat memories often enough to forge traditions; whenever I hug when I really feel like yelling...this is love in action.

Love in action is making an offering of oneself. It is the parting of the sea, the closing of the mouths of lions, the feeding of the thousands, the turning of water to wine, the healing of the leper, the suffering of the Cross. Love in action accomplishes mighty things. Love in action changes the world, one heart at a time.

Gather the pieces that are left over.
Let nothing be wasted.

JOHN 6:12

∽

Do you ever feel utterly spent? Like you are trying to make it across the finish line of bathtime and bedtime so that you can crawl into bed and collapse? Do you ever read the same page of the same book every night, only to fall asleep mid-paragraph? I remember when my twins were new and I was trying to nurse them on the same schedule, what began as such tender handling of these precious five-pound darlings was reduced to pajama-scruff-grabbing survival mode, just to silence the squall of double wailing hunger. I, like all new moms, was exhausted, physically, mentally, and emotionally. And yet, somehow, I was able to do it. As new moms, we feed and change and burp and bathe and love. And we get up and do it again. And again.

God takes our meager offerings, limited by our knowledge and our energy, and He multiplies them—just as He did with the loaves and the fishes. He takes the little that we have to offer and He makes it sufficient. With Him we are able to work and parent and maintain our households and our relationships. He takes our offerings and He picks up the pieces that are left over, the fragments of our time, our thoughts, our intentions, and He makes sure nothing is wasted. Just like the leftovers from the loaves and fishes feast (which began, remember, with five small barley loaves and two small fish) yielded twelve baskets of overflow, *after* He fed five thousand people. The point is that when God is in charge of the resources, there will always be more than enough to go around.

Jesus declared, "I who speak to you am he."

JOHN 4:26

If we want to hear what God has to say about the choices we make in our own lives, and the choices we make on behalf of our children, we have to be quiet and listen. God still speaks. I think we sometimes believe that because we haven't personally heard the voice of God from a burning bush, or because an angel hasn't visited us to proclaim the word of God, that God no longer speaks to our generation.

He does speak; it's just so loud down here that it's hard to hear! We have so many things vying for our attention. Between the television, the magazines, the BlackBerry, the Internet, satellite radio, e-mail, the home phone, the cell phone, the iPhone...the din is deafening. And perhaps, with all the layers of sin between Moses' generation and ours, we are separated from heaven by a lot these days. But in spite of all that, the Lord still speaks. The trick is to recognize His voice.

The voice inside your head, the one you can hear when you are frightened or confused, the one that makes so much sense (or no sense at all) that you know it isn't a thought of your own creation? That's Jesus. Or the tug on the sleeve of your conscience, warning you to be careful or be silent? That's the Holy Spirit. Or the slamming of every door of opportunity except for one? That's God.

When we don't know what to do, we have to ask. Then we have to get very still, and very quiet, and prepare to be answered.

*Whoever can be trusted with very little
can also be trusted with much.*

LUKE 16:10

There is nothing glamorous about mothering. With tasks like diaper changing, laundry folding, grocery shopping, errand running, lunch packing, dish washing, meal planning, homework checking, teacher conferencing, and carpool driving, we are constantly in the trenches. We wipe snotty noses, kiss teary faces, clean dirty hands, and hug away tantrums. We chase bad dreams, mark moments, and make memories. We are the historian, the nurse, the chef, the masseuse, the teacher's aide, and the therapist. Often all in the same day. We endure toddler meltdowns, adolescent angst, and teenage eye rolls. We are often exhausted and underappreciated.

But ladies, God sees us and knows our work. If we ever feel a sense of futility or frustration as we do the tiny tasks that make a home and grow a family, knowing all too well that they will soon be undone or need to be redone, we can find hope in the promise that our God is a God of details. The small things matter to Him. He is not simply entrusting to us the menial task of changing a diaper or filling a lunchbox; He has entrusted to us His most precious possessions. We are raising God's children.

When we can learn to consecrate our daily tasks, making them holy offerings to our Father in heaven, everything changes. We infuse love and meaning into each part of our day. We become more grateful and Spirit-filled. God will recognize the shift in the intention of our hearts, and, perhaps, our family will begin to more deeply feel the love behind the little things.

Their children will see it and be joyful;
their hearts will rejoice in the LORD.

ZECHARIAH 10:7

It isn't enough to take our children to church and show them a Sunday God. The God that means "Put on clean clothes, hurry up, get ready, we're going to be late, sit up straight, shush now, don't touch your sister, no talking, stand up when everyone stands up, fold your hands, stop fidgeting, no we can't leave yet."

This is not the "it" this verse is referring to. The "it" refers to a faith-filled heart. "Their hearts will rejoice," the verse says, and "Their children will see it." If our children cannot see our peace and joy that come from our faith in the Lord, then how can we ever expect them to grow up to have hearts that rejoice in the Lord? Our greatest task as mothers is to show our children the love of Christ. When my children grow up and reflect on their childhood, I want them to remember a mom who was full of love and laughter, a mom who was strong enough to handle things yet also soft enough to adapt, ask for forgiveness, grieve openly, experience loss, and demonstrate compassion. I want them to see in me a joy that is independent of circumstances, because it resides in my faith.

Our children need to see us not just as having religion or incorporating faith, but really, truly, deeply, joyfully, loving God and living a life centered in His teachings.

They might hear our words, but they are always watching how we live.

Get up and go into the city, and you
will be told what you must do.

ACTS 9:6

෨ව

Notice Jesus did not tell Saul (at mid-conversion from Saul the persecutor to Paul the believer) to sit and wait for further instruction. Even though Saul was struck down and struck blind for three days, he kept moving, even though he had no idea what was happening to him or what he would be asked to do. Talk about blind faith!

In our own ways, each of us can be rendered immobile by the magnitude of what lies ahead each day. It can be tempting to contemplate crumbling as an option, or hover in a holding pattern. But that is not the way it works for believers. We get up and get moving, and the Lord always meets us where we are and points us in the direction we should go. He supplies our energy and sets our course, but the initial steps to gain momentum are our choice. We have to desire to be useful for His purposes.

This is a decision best made early in the morning, right after our hand fumbles for the Snooze button and we stretch out in bed and make that usual groaning sound. Right there. That's the decision point. Before one word is said, one foot hits the floor, or we have one sip of coffee. While our pajamas are twisted, our teeth are fuzzy, and our hair is messed up, we make the choice. Let's choose wisely.

*I have the desire to do what is good,
but I cannot carry it out.*

ROMANS 7:18

❧

I want to be the kind of mother who:

- Offers only healthy, organic snacks and home-cooked meals.
- Sees and listens to each child, actively respecting their individuality.
- Is accessible and approachable to her children, regardless of subject or situation.
- Accepts responsibility for shortcomings, asks for forgiveness, and seeks to make amends.
- Equips and empowers her children to do their best, in order to honor God with their abilities.
- Is structured enough to provide stability, but spontaneous and free enough to play.
- Illustrates compassion for others with actions above words.
- Asks questions instead of yells.
- Yields to joy, not frustration.
- Raises great and grateful children without taking blame or credit.

Yes, I want to be all these things, and more. I don't always do everything right, but *I can do more things right today than I did yesterday when I lean on Him.* What keeps me from losing heart is knowing where my heart is, which is with God.

May my meditation be pleasing to him,
as I rejoice in the Lord.

PSALM 104:34

God-focused parenting can run counter to the current of our society. Worldly messages can tell us that our children must do this or do that, or be involved here, or go to school here, or read this, or have this. In fact, we can be so bombarded by the messages of the world that the messages of God are reduced to a soft whisper, barely discernible amid the chaos of everyday life.

Is it really important that our children be at piano or swim team practice in the evenings—or is it more important to guard the dinner hour and eat together as a family? Is it more important to go to every single birthday party than it is to keep Sunday reserved for family? To me the essential differences lie in intent and impact.

Our intentions are tied directly to our hearts, regardless of what our actions are. Only we know (of course God knows, too) if what we are doing is based in an intention to please God. And the impact of our actions typically follows our intention. If our intention is to quietly do the right thing and to glorify God with our choices—the impact is enormous. We don't set out with the goal of impressing people, but there is truly nothing more impressive than those who humbly step up and do what needs to be done, or quietly live good lives in the pursuit of holiness. When God is pleased, others are positively influenced.

God did not give us a spirit of timidity,
but a spirit of power, of love and of self-discipline.

2 TIMOTHY 1:7

Do you have certain relationships that bring you down? Do you have certain "friends" or family members who can drop your level of peace, confidence, or enthusiasm in the matter of a sentence? Do these people make you doubt your intentions, your parenting choices, or your direction for your life?

If you know people like this, or if you know people who are currently wilting under people like this, copy this verse on a card and put it in plain sight for as long as it takes to build a wall of courage. Because this wall of courage, fortified brick by brick with the promises of Scripture, is going to become part of the boundary that protects our hearts from the forces set on destroying it. We may not be timid women, but there may be certain people by whom we are tricked into temporarily thinking we are.

Then the power of this verse is unleashed in our lives. We soak it in and realize that we already have what it takes. We are brave, powerful, loving, and self-disciplined. We can set very clear limits about what is, and is not, appropriate when it comes to the treatment we will accept. We define ourselves when we have good boundaries, and our good boundaries help refine those around us. Good boundaries are essential to clean, loving, mutually respectful relationships with our children—now and as they grow.

God has arranged the parts in the body,
every one of them, just as he wanted them to be. . . .
If one part suffers, every part suffers with it;
if one part is honored, every part rejoices with it.

1 CORINTHIANS 12:18, 26

My dad always says, "You are only as happy as your unhappiest child." I wholeheartedly agree. When one of my kids is down, struggling, or has hurt feelings, I cannot feel free and happy; our hearts are tied in certain ways forever.

This Scripture is a perfect illustration of God's church and how we all are interconnected. But the metaphor applies equally to a family. We each are a different part, no one more essential than the other, but we serve different purposes that work together. Think about it, have you ever tried to function with a massive headache? How about a toothache or an earache? Try doing other things when it hurts to think, swallow, chew, talk, or walk. Every part has to be in decent working order to enable us to function properly as a whole.

Our family is exactly like that. When one person is broken, the whole unit is brought down. I remember when my brother got into an accident and our whole family was in a tailspin. Or if someone's grades are faltering, the television goes off across the house while we refocus. If someone aces a test, we all go out to a fun dinner. Everything goes into priority lockdown when someone is in danger—hurt, ill, or struggling. Equally, when one person rejoices, everyone wants to celebrate. If we are really lucky, we have the kind of family that divides the burdens and multiplies the joy.

"Where is your faith?" he asked his disciples.

LUKE 8:25

My purse is a large, bottomless cavern, holding the contents of a full and varied life…my wallet, checkbook, lip gloss, tampons, keys, camera, children's books, sunscreen, Band-Aids, my running watch, ponytail holders, some pens, my journal, a cell phone. When I need to locate something in a hurry, I dig around furiously. "Hold on a sec; I know it's in here someplace." If I'm not careful, my purse could become a metaphor for my life. I love to be well-prepared, for me and for my children, but if I'm so abundantly prepared that *I can't find anything*—am I really prepared at all? I need to pare down and prioritize, in my life and in my heart, putting the most essential items within easy reach. When Jesus asks me, "Where is your faith?" I want to be able to say, "Here it is. I'm standing in it."

I keep this quote from Jon Kabat-Zinn in my calendar: "Voluntary simplicity means going fewer places in one day rather than more, seeing less so I can see more, doing less so I can do more, acquiring less so I can have more."

Create in me a pure heart, O God,
and renew a steadfast spirit within me.

PSALM 51:10

"Mom, can I start over?"

These words melt me no matter how annoyed I am with my kids. If there is arguing, teasing, disobedience, or overall bedlam, these words quench my flagging spirit like nothing else. All my irritation evaporates when I hear the intention of my child's heart. No one, child or adult, means to mess up. Yet we all do it. We drive one another crazy on a regular basis. One of the sweetest gifts from a forgiving heart is the chance for a do-over. I am always happy to offer one, and I'm getting better about asking my children for one myself sometimes.

It's hard to know how to negotiate a comeback after a mood swing, an unkind outburst, or a bad choice. Think about it: How do we feel when we do that? We slink around, too, feeling shame and remorse. When you love someone, there really is no response to this question other than a smile, a yes, a hug, and a fresh start.

I go to God this way: "Father, can I start over?" The intention of my heart is the same: "Can I have a fresh start, another opportunity to do things Your way, a chance to make You proud?" The desire for a pure heart and a renewed spirit is a sign of humility. It's an indicator to God that we know the right way, His way, even if we don't always choose it. I like to think that God's frustration with me melts away with my repentance, just the way it happens for me with my children.

Do not be quick with your mouth,
do not be hasty in your heart.

ECCLESIASTES 5:2

I'll admit that I can have a fiery tongue. I've had to keep ice handy for most of my life. I have said things I regret on occasion, and the cleanup afterward was often unpleasant. This is a terrible feeling when it's between adults, but it's brutally painful when words hit a soft spot in a child's heart. There is no place for angry sarcasm or punitive statements in the raising of children. Belittling them or crushing their spirits has lasting effects. These kinds of remarks are not what I want my children replaying with their therapist from the archives in their minds. I want my words to heal, to help.

So knowing that my filter runs thin when I'm stressed or tired, I have to buy myself some time. I have developed some tactics to create some space to cool off. In the car I sometimes turn up the radio and sing (albeit badly). At home I might disappear into the shower for a respite, hoping to freshen myself up on the inside as well. Sometimes I retreat to my office, or my bathroom, or sit on my yoga mat for a few minutes. Or I do something relaxing like knit or bake. Or I stand at my kitchen sink and reread the Scripture I have taped to the backsplash. In my mini-escape, I go to God. He brings me back to myself and helps me remember who I want to be.

> LORD, *who may dwell in your sanctuary?...*
> *[He] who keeps his oath even when it hurts.*

PSALM 15:1, 4

Love transcends time and supersedes emotion.

Just as a good marriage will at times involve a stronger sense of commitment than of love, there are times when parenting is more pain than it is pleasure. Disciplining a child is not fun, but it's entirely necessary. Sacrificing a selfish desire for the good of the family might come with a pang. Keeping a promise to love someone else more than yourself is sometimes as easy as breathing, other times it feels more like asthma.

Keeping an oath (a promise, a covenant) is an essential part of lasting love. We don't always feel like being generous, being forgiving, or being accountable. Shoot, we don't always feel like thinking about what to make for dinner. But love is forged in moments like this. Don't we want to know that our spouses will choose us even when we feel least worthy? Don't we want our children to know that they are our priorities, even if we feel unappreciated?

God keeps his promises to us... even when we reject Him, even when we choose other things before Him, even when we depart from Him through the shadowy walk of sin. He kept His oath to us, even at the expense of His own Son. Jesus kept His oath through the pain and rejection of the Cross.

We can't just talk about virtues like this, things like selflessness, loyalty, and commitment. We have to live these attributes out here in the light, where our children can see us. By seeing us love beyond ourselves, they will be given a glimpse of the goodness of God.

"Restrain your voice from weeping and your eyes from tears, for your work will be rewarded," declares the LORD.

JEREMIAH 31:16

As mothers, much of our work is unseen. We do the things that are most noticeable when they are left undone. We do the things that usually need to be done again immediately upon completion. We cook, we clean, we pack lunches, we make plans and provisions, we change diapers, we treat illness, we chase bad dreams, we oversee homework, we host playdates, we wash clothes, we unload dishwashers, we tie shoes, we calm meltdowns, we bandage scrapes, we chauffeur between activities, we remember everything and everyone.

Sometimes we go long stretches of time between substantial expressions of gratitude. It can be lonely or frustrating to feel like the invisible servant, with no needs of our own. Sometimes all it takes to keep us going is a moment of truly "being seen" for who we are and what we do.

I had a moment like this one day when I was unloading suitcases and children from the back of my father's car as he dropped us off at the airport when the kids and I were leaving on a trip. "Honey," my dad said to my frazzled self. "I see you," he said. "I really do." My eyes brimmed with tears (happy ones), and I felt totally renewed. I had a lightness in my heart and renewed energy for our journey. All I needed was to feel seen and understood for what I was trying to do. We have a heavenly Father who sees our efforts and recognizes the extent of our sacrifices and the depth of our love. *Our work will be rewarded*, in this lifetime and the next.

We love because he first loved us.

1 JOHN 4:19

I had a call from the mother of one of Grace's friends, the good kind of call that every parent hopes to get.

She wanted me to know that her daughter came home upset about an incident on the playground where another child was excluding her. Her little girl was hurt by this, as you would expect, but she said that she ended up feeling better because Grace stuck up for her. My eyes teared up as I heard this story, thinking of the courage it takes to go against the crowd, especially when they have turned on someone. Later, I asked Grace to tell me about what happened, she shared the same story, and I told her that I might be more proud of her for this than for all her good grades. Using the mind God gave you is important, but cultivating a godly heart is the ultimate. I hugged her tight and told her that she was just the kind of person I would want as a friend. *"I am your friend like that, Mommy,"* she said.

God has done everything to demonstrate His love for me. Because I am filled in this way, I go to great lengths to convey this kind of love and devotion to my children, in words and in action. I love them the way I have been loved, and they are showing signs of growing into the kind of people who love as they have been loved. When we are rooted and established in God's love, our legacy of love grows forever.

*Dear lady, I am not writing you a new command
but one we have had from the beginning.
I ask that we love one another.*

2 JOHN 5

❧

Want to know something that breaks my heart? Literally squeezes the life out of me, ruffles my feathers, and makes me pit out and want to shout out whenever I hear about it?

It's the jealousy, competition, and pettiness that separate women when we so badly need one another. We were not meant to do this mothering gig on our own, people. Our husbands are not enough; in fact, pushing things on them as our sole emotional support is damaging to a marriage. We need the good company of women to keep our sanity, our perspective, and our sense of humor. We have to get our acts together and stick together. As Jesus stated in His greatest commandment, *we have to love one another.*

The only way to counteract this pervasive undercurrent between women is to actively take a stand against it. Be the one who is bold enough to change the course of a conversation. Offer a positive alternative to gossip. Find the courage to have that difficult conversation that is causing separation. Cheer for someone else. Have a zero tolerance policy for mean-girl behavior, and make your rules known by what you say, how you say it, and what you do.

This is a gift to yourself, a great stride forward for all womankind, and a priceless lesson to live out in front of your children. When our daughters see us treat one another with love and respect, they will grow to do likewise, setting similarly high standards for the kinds of friendships they will invest in.

Sometimes when I come across a particularly awesome passage of Scripture, I write it out on a card and insert names to personalize it as a prayer. Then I put the card in my kitchen window and use it as my meditation when I am cooking and washing dishes. This card has been in my kitchen for more than a year now. Change my children's names to your child/ children's names and make it yours. There is no more beautiful gift than personalizing and praying Scripture over our children. As we well know, the heart of a mother for her child is a force to be reckoned with. When we focus that power in prayer, things happen. Don't mark my words, mark His....

For this reason I kneel before the Father, from whom his whole family in heaven and on earth derives its name. I pray that out of his glorious riches he may strengthen you, [Luke, Grace, and Bella] with power through his Spirit in your inner being, so that Christ may dwell in your hearts through faith.
And I pray that you, [Luke, Grace, and Bella] being rooted and established in love, may have power, together with all the saints, to grasp how wide and long and high and deep is the love of Christ, and to know this love that surpasses knowledge—that you may be filled to the measure of all the fullness of God.
Now to him who is able to do immeasurably more than all we ask or imagine, according to the power that is at work within us, to him be glory in the church and in Christ Jesus throughout all generations forever and ever! Amen.

EPHESIANS 3:14–21

Don't be afraid of [the enemy].
Remember the Lord, who is great and awesome,
and fight for your brothers, your sons and
your daughters, your wives and your homes.

NEHEMIAH 4:14

I am normally a fairly levelheaded, mild-mannered person. I don't like to make a scene if I can help it. I would prefer to keep the peace when I can. But there are moments that require us to step out of our shyness and be bold on behalf of our children and to protect our family life.

My mom has always said, "If you aren't an advocate for your child, who will be?" This might mean that we have to speak our truth to a teacher, a coach, or another parent. It isn't always comfortable to make waves or question those in positions of authority. But we know our children best, and our commitment after God is to our families. God tells us in this verse to be strong and fight for our families.

Sometimes fighting for our families means taking a stand against the ways our culture tries to drain family life. Too much homework, overscheduling of activities, television, Internet, video games, iPods, cell phones, and closed doors alienate us from connecting with one another. It isn't easy to turn and go against the current, mandating time together and honoring the sacredness of sharing meals, but it is more than worth it to guard the life within our own walls.

How will our children ever learn to later build and protect their own families' lives if we don't show them?

In six days the LORD made the heavens and the earth, the sea, and all that is in them, but he rested on the seventh day. Therefore the LORD blessed the Sabbath day and made it holy.

EXODUS 20:11

When we lived in France and Spain I noticed that the fourth commandment was an unquestionable part of life. You have no choice but to honor the recommended rest of the Sabbath when every business is closed and everyone is spending the day with their families. A large meal is shared at midday, and families linger together at the table, relaxing and sharing conversation. There is no time frame, rush, or hustle between other activities—this *is* the activity of the day.

Here, Sundays are often plagued with birthday parties, sports, or errands to prepare for the week ahead. We are not honoring the Sabbath day when we fall into bed Sunday night, utterly spent from the weekend's activities.

This past year I have tried to instill a new tradition with my kids. Sundays are our family days. We go on an "adventure" every Sunday afternoon—a picnic, a hike, or a trip to the dog park with our dogs. We go to early evening mass and tuck into our usual row beside my parents and my brother, and my parents take our whole motley crew out to dinner afterward. My dad says it's the highlight of his week and his favorite tradition. For me and my kids, it is a ritual that has become a touchstone, a week that simultaneously ends and begins with God and family.

*Have I not commanded you? Be strong
and courageous. Do not be terrified;
do not be discouraged, for the LORD your God
will be with you wherever you go.*

JOSHUA 1:9

I can't write a devotional without including the above Scripture. This verse became my spear in a very dark and fearful time of my life. I love that it is a command, not a suggestion or recommendation, to be strong and courageous.

As a single mother, I am the one to search the house (okay, with the dog) if one of us accidently left the door open while we were gone. I have to get the creepy bug in the corner and flush it. I have to quiet the chaos and be the voice of calm in stressful or dangerous situations. I have three sets of eyes looking at *me* to lead. (And that fact alone is sometimes terrifying.)

By embracing this Scripture as my mantra, I can model courage for my children. When the moment is right for each of them, I plan to teach them the power of this verse and what it has meant to me. I hope they will make it their own. As much as it pains me to think about it, I won't always be able to be there for them in a crisis. They will have to face peril and heartache, battle fear, and react quickly in the moments that will ultimately define their lives and their characters. I want them to be ready.

I want them to know that the Lord, their God, is with them wherever they go.

Give me wisdom and knowledge,
that I may lead this people, for who is
able to govern this great people of yours?

2 CHRONICLES 1:10

What would you say if God came to you right now and asked you to tell Him the desire of your heart? What if He went so far as to say, "Ask for whatever you want Me to give you." What then?

Solomon, King David's son, had this moment with the Master and did not blow it. God was so pleased with his answer that He gave him a wise and discerning heart, and added a whole load of treats like riches and honor and a long life for good measure. The things to remember are that Solomon (1) asked for exactly what he needed (not merely what he wanted); and (2) he asked for the thing that would equip him to serve others. The desires of Solomon's heart stretched well beyond himself.

When we are confronted or conflicted by the demands of mothering, we would do well to follow Solomon's example. We can ask God for wisdom and knowledge, which is ultimately much larger, deeper, and more useful than asking for an answer or a solution. Constantly humbling ourselves, admitting our weakness or confusion, and asking for wisdom means that not only will we be equipped, but we will stay equipped. God gave us these children as a reward. Of course He wants to help us raise them! We are asking for something He has already made clear that He wants to give. God loves His children, all of us, and wants us to lead our children wisely.

Contend, O Lord, with those who contend with me.

PSALM 35:1

※

I don't know about you, but when someone messes with one of my kids, there is a mama bear inside me that rears her ugly head. I remember when my girls were little toddlers and a nasty little boy on the playground shoved one of them into the wooden play equipment. As her busted lip bled onto my shirt, I held her and looked everywhere for that little creep. The anger that rose inside me was immediate and profound. I found the boy's mother, and she just smirked at me like my bleeding baby daughter had brought this on herself. I had to leave before I lost my filter and my cool.

This kind of pain is nothing compared to bullying boys and mean-girl backstabbing on the playground and in childhood social circles. I have to remind myself to breathe when my child recounts an unpleasant incident involving hurt feelings. I want to head up to the playground myself and say the words that I lacked the confidence to say when I was the kid getting picked on.

But it doesn't work that way. These are not my rites of passage. I have to pray for my children in this regard, and this verse from Psalms is short, sweet, and gets the job done. Children can memorize this verse and call upon it themselves in their moments of hurt or anger. In order for our children to form prayer as their automatic response, they have to watch us call upon Him in our own distress or on their behalf. God will contend with the situation—after all, He wants to build their faith even more than we do.

Create in me a pure heart, O God, and renew a steadfast spirit within me. Do not cast me from your presence or take your Holy Spirit from me. Restore to me the joy of your salvation and grant me a willing spirit, to sustain me.

PSALM 51:10–12

Our God is the God of second chances. Thanks to Jesus, we all can approach God and ask for mercy rather than bracing ourselves for what we really deserve. How blessed are we to have such a God!

I was vividly reminded of the gift of repentance as my son, Luke, made his first confession. In the Catholic Church, we make our first confession prior to receiving the sacrament of First Communion. We make ourselves free of sin in order to receive the body and blood of Christ. Repentance is a big lesson for second graders; adults even have a hard time asking for and receiving the gift of forgiveness.

Luke was so nervous before he went into the confessional that I passed him a note on a scrap of paper. It said, "God loves you and so do I. There is nothing to fear." I saw him take his note out, unfold it, and reread it several times. I watched him go inside and I went limp, suddenly realizing that he had his very own relationship with God. He was growing up. As I was kneeling and praying for him, he slid into the seat next to me with a shy smile on his face.

"How do you feel?" I asked.

"Clean," he whispered and knelt beside me. And I knew he understood.

Sin makes us miserable; praise God, we have a way to move on.

The LORD delights in those who fear him,
who put their hope in his unfailing love.

PSALM 147:11

There seem to be two camps on the subject of fearing God. One camp claims that God is love and there is no fear in love, so don't fear God. Another camp is more hard-core about the fear of God, and every accident or tragedy can be traced back to the wrath of God's displeasure. I grew up in a blended household of Catholic and Lutheran backgrounds, so I have a pretty balanced foundation concerning fearing God. It goes like this:

1. Make no mistake about it; God loves you.
2. Make no mistake about it; God is just, so watch your step.

I am lucky in that my earthly father has always loved my brother and me in a similar combination of love and discipline. He loves us without fail, but there have always been limits on what behavior is acceptable. If we misbehaved, we owned and served the consequences, while the love remained steady.

I think the verse that says God disciplines those He loves (Heb. 12:6) is the key to understanding the fear of God. It does not please Him to punish us, but He disciplines us for our own growth and refinement, out of love. If we can parent our children in this way, it will be an easier transition to unlock the mystery of a healthy fear of God.

By wisdom a house is built, and through understanding it is established; through knowledge its rooms are filled with rare and beautiful treasures.

PROVERBS 24:3–4

When I had an opportunity for a do-over in my life, I wanted to rebuild a life with God at the center. I wanted this for myself, but I was even more motivated to make things right for my children. The rare and beautiful treasures that fill the rooms of a faithful house are things like peace, joy, acceptance, levity, humor, openness, supportiveness, warmth, generosity, protection, rest, nourishment, and contentment.

The initial wisdom imparted by God is what inspires us to build a godly household. But the establishment of that household takes a long time. We deepen our understanding of God as we spend time in His fine company. It's like the difference between the immediacy of being saved and the journey of walking out our sanctification. Or the difference between planning a wedding and sustaining a marriage. Oswald Chambers said that endurance is a sustained effort over time. Establishing our house as a house of God takes endurance. It takes commitment, a dedicated pursuit that goes beyond the initial rush of emotion.

I want to establish a house like this for Luke, Grace, and Bella. I want the rooms to be filled with the rare and beautiful treasures I mentioned above. I want them to be fortified by what they receive at home so that they are able to depart freely and confidently, but that the love and comfort found here also create a timeless desire to return.

As iron sharpens iron, so one man sharpens another.

PROVERBS 27:17

I speak often and reverently about my girlfriends. These are the women I run with, do weekly Bible study with, and raise my children with. We are a community for one another.

They help me keep my perspective, my sense of humor, and sometimes my sanity. They crack up at my children when they are frustrating to me and I have misplaced my joy. They keep me accountable when I state a parenting goal, a new idea to try, or a direction I want to go with my mothering. They ask me the hard questions and wait through my stammering and shuffling for the real answer. They let me know if I seem distracted, out of balance, or hazy in my priorities. They know me well enough to realize when my actions and words are not in alignment with my values. They appreciate my snarky sense of humor when I have PMS. They see my children each as individuals and know their strengths, weaknesses, preferences, and quirks. My children seek them out in social situations and hug them in the hallways at school.

I would not be the mother I am today without their good company. Each of them has different talents and perspectives that add to my overall breadth of experience. We share ideas that worked or didn't work; we grieve the defeats and celebrate the victories that mark the milestones of motherhood. I would not consider facing my next season of trial without them. We pray for one another in ordinary times, and surround one another like a fortress when crisis hits. When the ache of disappointment or loss is greater than words, we sit quietly together and wait for God.

The living, the living—they praise you, as I am doing today; fathers tell their children about your faithfulness.

ISAIAH 38:19

I am sure he meant mothers, too. *Mothers, tell your children about God's faithfulness.*

It is imperative that we do not hide our faith from our children. I am not suggesting that we do this on purpose, of course not, but we might make assumptions that our children know the depth of our dependence on God without explaining our rituals or including them in our journey. My kids know that I get up early and sit with my Bible and a cup of coffee on the sofa and pray. But I am not sure that they know I am specifically taking my questions and concerns to God and hearing His direction when I read His Word or wait on the instruction of His Holy Spirit.

I need to be better about walking this process out with them. I want them to see me struggle, and I want them to hear the words I use when I pray. I want them to know the level of intimacy I have when I approach the Lord, that I am not lofty or expert, just myself.

Then I need to be specific about letting them know exactly how I heard back from God on the matter. Was it a nudge in my conscience that provoked action? Was I directed to a specific passage of Scripture? And then I need to explain how the resolution came about. I need to include them when I return to praise our Father for His faithfulness.

How will our children learn about the journey of faith if we don't walk it out as living examples?

Forget the former things; do not dwell on the past.
See, I am doing a new thing! Now it springs up;
do you not perceive it? I am making a way in the
desert and streams in the wasteland.

ISAIAH 43:18–19

❧

When I learn something new and my former methods are revealed as glaringly incorrect or insufficient, my tendency is to want to flog myself for it. As I grow and look back at how I handled things in the past—what I said, how I treated someone—I often cringe. The last thing in the world I want to do is mess up with my kids, say or do things that leave a mark on their innocence or diminish their confidence. I joke sometimes, "Well now, *that* will definitely require some therapy later." But it isn't funny; I just crack bad jokes at my own expense whenever I want to delay processing the truth. And the truth is that we are going to mess up with our kids; it's inevitable. We are going to say and do things that we don't mean and wish we could undo. We are going to fall short of our good intentions and fail them.

Yuck.

Thankfully we have a redeeming God. The more quickly we can recover from a mistake, own it before God and our children, confess it, accept forgiveness, and get back on track, the less ground we lose. Our children learn from our mistakes and our humility, too. As we learn to go to God in new and specific ways with our mothering, becoming more knowledgeable and diligent we might regret our former ways. But this verse is key: "Forget the former things; do not dwell on the past." We have to let it go and move forward, making the best use of what we know now.

Shake off your dust; rise up, sit enthroned,
O Jerusalem. Free yourself from the chains
on your neck, O captive Daughter of Zion.

ISAIAH 52:2

Having children may be the finest motivation to get right with
God. It is impossible to raise children to inhabit their freedom
in Christ if we are still living in bondage. Every area has to
be redeemed and restored, because if it isn't, it will surely
be brought into the light. And it will likely be brought into
the light at the precise moment we need to teach a lesson on
the subject, leaving us feeling empty and fraudulent. Raising
children requires all we have and all we are. We have to clean
house in a spiritual sense in order to be prepared.

Unconfessed sin, unspoken but necessary conversations,
undone deeds, unhealed addictions, unfulfilled promises, or
unmade changes—all these things chain us to the past and
prohibit our freedom. The door to the prison is open, but we
just sit inside the cell. I do not want any barred territory or
off-limits conversations when it comes to my children. I want
to live in the light with them. I want to be able to answer
their questions and share examples from my journey without
shame or hesitation. Even difficult subjects can be explored
when Jesus has healed us in that area. We can leave a legacy
of freedom for our children and for generations to come, but
first we must be truly free ourselves.

Galatians 5:1 says it is for freedom that Christ has set us
free. Stand firm, then, and do not let yourselves be burdened
again by a yoke of slavery.

Let your light shine before men, that they may see your good deeds and praise your Father in heaven.

MATTHEW 5:16

A lighthouse sits high upon a cliff, well out of reach of the crashing sea below. It is always illuminated from within, and regardless of the weather conditions, its light beckons and guides sailors safely home. It would be impossible to navigate the rocky coastline without a steady beacon on which to fix their course. It would be ludicrous to attempt to make the narrow passage that leads to the harbor in complete darkness.

Just as lighthouses guide, comfort, and help sailors to navigate through the waters, we have to be the lighthouses for our children through life.

We have to be firmly planted in the Rock. We have to transcend the turbulent conditions of the world below and remain steady. At all cost and at all times, our lights must shine. How else will our weary sailors steer clear of danger and fix their gazes on the one thing that does not change?

"You are the light of the world" (Matt. 5:14). Our light comes from God; it is our faith; it is our unwavering belief in an almighty God and Savior. If we allow our light to dim or fade, our precious children are left to navigate treacherous conditions in the dark abyss of a raging sea. Everything we do to grow in faith, every step we take closer to our God, ensures that our light will continue to shine. And this one thing can make the difference between a safe return and becoming shipwrecked or permanently lost at sea.

Remember this: Whoever sows sparingly
will also reap sparingly, and whoever sows
generously will also reap generously.

2 CORINTHIANS 9:6

Parenting, like most investments with a high return, requires patience and a significant investment up front. Think of all the time we spend caring for a tiny baby. Hours upon hours and many sleepless nights are spent caring for a newborn. There are no thank-you notes or kudos for a job well done. The reward for a contented infant is a full diaper or more laundry to add to the pile. But we don't expect to reap at this time; we are sowing.

As children age, we occasionally experience sweet expressions of gratitude. And then, as I hear from older friends, the middle and high school years are short on reaping, rich in sowing. Not much in terms of gratitude, but plenty of requests for money, freedom, and fun. So we try to sow wisely. Moments of connection become the most valuable harvest we reap. We set limits and they try to stretch beyond them. And still we tend to the garden.

When our children are grown and we return to cultivating our own lives, we find ourselves sought after. Large sections of the field we sowed are now ripe. We reap a harvest of friendship, laughter, inclusion, and love. We hold babies and go to birthday parties, share holidays and go on vacations. Our initial investments yield unimaginable windfalls. The currency is joy.

I urge you to live a life worthy of the calling
you have received. Be completely humble and gentle;
be patient, bearing with one another in love.
Make every effort to keep the unity of the
Spirit through the bond of peace.

EPHESIANS 4:1–3

As far as the calling of raising a family, these verses might make up one of the finest family credos around. We have been given the gift of motherhood, and we are called to raise these children well. The task is daunting. I remember when my children were very small and I would occasionally have moments of pure shock, catching a glimpse in my rearview mirror of my backseat full of car seats and little people. It was a temporarily disorienting moment.... *These are mine? How did this happen?* I would simultaneously wonder how I got so lucky and how on earth I was ever going to see this through.

Being a mom has been the most humbling pursuit of my life. I have never cared more about any attempt, any role, any result. I have never loved like this before. So for as much as I want to get things right in the raising of Luke, Grace, and Bella, I manage to mess things up regularly. I say things the wrong way, miss teachable moments, and lose my patience when all I really want to do is love them. But being constantly humbled means I am always seeking God's grace and His redirection. I have to be as patient with myself as I want to be with them. We have to bear with one another's moods, foibles, quirks, growth spurts, outbursts, and phases. We are a family.

Get rid of all bitterness, rage and anger, brawling
and slander, along with every form of malice.
Be kind and compassionate to one another, forgiving
each other, just as in Christ God forgave you.

EPHESIANS 4:32

This verse is a direct rebuke to arguing parents, squabbling siblings, and standoffs with relatives. Stop the madness. We are called to live in peace. This verse does not sugarcoat a gentle hope that we will feel kindness toward one another. Oh, no, it says point-blank to *be* kind and compassionate. Feelings are not even mentioned. And just in case we needed further rebuke, we are reminded of how God has forgiven us. When we stop to think about the magnitude of that, in light of some of the stunts we have pulled, we had better be humbled into submission.

Relationships that last are founded in commitment. We put so much stock in the feelings associated with relationships that when the feelings ebb and flow, we forget that the commitment is still in effect. For believers, relationships are sealed by a third party—God. This is what's called a covenant. This is what enables us to be kind and compassionate, whether we feel like it or not. With God's help, we can get rid of the uglies as simply as we take out the trash. It's not our power that makes this possible; it's God's partnership.

If we haven't already done so, we need to purposefully invite God into each of our relationships and recommit each one. Areas of resentment and unforgiveness are going to have to go, starting today.

*You were taught, with regard to your former way
of life, to put off your old self, which is being corrupted
by its deceitful desires; to be made new in the attitude
of your minds; and to put on the new self, created to
be like God in true righteousness and holiness.*

EPHESIANS 4:22–24

❧

I talk to my kids a lot about attitude.

I probably say things such as "I don't like your attitude, mister." "Somebody needs an attitude adjustment." "Come back and join us when you have a better attitude." Many times the person who really needs the attitude adjustment is me, which is probably why I am frustrated in that moment. A sour mommy is no fun.

We all know that we have to deal with circumstances we would not choose if we had the option—that's life. We also know, or at least have heard enough times that maybe we should know by now, that our reactions to life's ups and downs, our attitudes about those ups and downs, are a choice. I conveniently forget this sometimes, and I act purely as if my behavior is an inevitable, uncontrollable result of something that happened to me. When I'm feeling down, I have to work through the corruption of my old self and make the decision to be made new. The decision is harder than the transaction itself, because God does all the heavy lifting after I finally decide to go His way. He renews my mind and the attitude within, and He helps me inhabit my new self.

I repeat this to myself, out loud or in my head, when I'm feeling stuck: "I will be made new in the attitude of my mind." This has kept me on the high road more than once.

Be very careful, then, how you live—not as unwise but as wise, making the most of every opportunity.

EPHESIANS 5:15–16

There are opportunities hidden in everything, if our eyes are adjusted to see them.

A challenge is an opportunity to grow. A lie is an opportunity for truth. A wound is an opportunity for healing. A loss is an opportunity to prepare a space. A mistake is an opportunity to learn. Pain is an opportunity to give or receive comfort. An illness is an opportunity for pause. Fear is an opportunity for courage. A rebuke is an opportunity for reflection. A failure is an opportunity for a second chance. An argument is an opportunity for communication. Weakness is an opportunity for strength. An insult is an opportunity for forgiveness. A dead end is an opportunity for direction. A betrayal is an opportunity to welcome something new. Sin is an opportunity for repentance. A crushing blow is an opportunity to believe. Devastation is an opportunity to trust.

I cannot tell you how I long to be wise in this way. I want to be aware and careful how I live, not missing these divine appointments for growth. What if news was just news, and we didn't waste time trying to define it as good or bad or make sense of it at all? What if we could condition ourselves to immediately search for the lesson? This would be living a life that makes the most of every opportunity.

If I have any hope at all of teaching this to my children, I have to first learn it for myself. I have a lot of work to do.

Be strong in the Lord and in his mighty power.
Put on the full armor of God so that you can take
your stand against the devil's schemes. For our
struggle is not against flesh and blood, but against
the rulers, against the authorities, against the
powers of this dark world and against the spiritual
forces of evil in the heavenly realms.

EPHESIANS 6:10–12

Spiritual warfare is an area in which I have a lot of room to grow. I have had an awareness of the existence of evil for as long as I can remember, but it is only in recent years that I have realized that I have a responsibility to do something about it.

But I will tell you this. My passion to protect my children has kindled the fire of my desire to become a formidable warrior. Our weapon is the Word of God and our faith in it, our power comes from God Himself, and our strategy involves prayer.

Think of it this way: Have you ever gone through a season of your life when it seemed like everything was going wrong? When things you could normally handle with ease felt insurmountable? These things are signs of a spiritual attack. It can happen to our children, too. They feel left out at school, they don't fit in, their grades begin to drop, and they start to slip away. The enemy has found a mark. How mad does this make you? Hopefully it makes you mad enough to enlist. Find some other soldiers and study the Word to find your weapons. Practice wielding your authority. Train to become fit for the moment when it is going to matter the most.

Children, obey your parents in the Lord,
for this is right. "Honor your father and mother"—
which is the first commandment with a promise—
"that it may go well with you and that
you may enjoy long life on the earth."

EPHESIANS 6:1–3

Well, this makes "because I said so" seem sort of lame, doesn't it?

I believe that our children have to accept our authority. I don't mind if they question me, if it's a real question, not rooted in belligerence or disrespect. Sometimes their questions actually help me. But ultimately, whether they agree or not, whether they like it or not, they have to obey. And it isn't because we say so, it's because God says so, and He is the boss.

This is where we reap the fruits of having shown our children that we go to God's Word for the answer. We can't just bust open the Bible to Ephesians chapter 6 because we want to prove our point on this subject, close the argument, and move on. We have to lay a firm foundation of going to God for wisdom in every area so that it has proven validity over time. We have to honor God as the center of our household and create an atmosphere of reverence so that our children grow to understand and love His authority.

If they can comprehend that God disciplines those He loves, then they have a better chance of accepting our discipline as coming from a place of love as well. He wants us to obey His commands because His ways lead to life. A good life, filled with peace and prosperity in this world, and an eternal position in the next.

*Be joyful always; pray continually; give thanks
in all circumstances, for this is God's will
for you in Christ Jesus.*

1 THESSALONIANS 5:16–18

Small children have a lot to teach us about joy.

They are captivated by the small details of life: a marching line of ants, birds hopping across the lawn, walking barefoot in the sand, chasing waves, fireflies and puppies, the silky feel of paint on fingertips, touching paper. They find delight in everything. What happens to us when we get older? Why do we quit playing? Why are we always in such a rush?

Life is fleeting, and if we aren't living with intention, we're missing it. Our God is a God of beauty and of intimacy; He tucks sweet surprises in our path all the time. He delights in His creation and longs for us to appreciate it as He does. Being joyful is not connected to the condition of current circumstances. It is a personality trait, and as such, can be cultivated. The verses above give us a good clue as to how we can go about cultivating a joyful spirit—by gratitude, giving thanks in all circumstances. I do this when I feel stressed out and I'm driving someplace, feeling my thoughts ping around my head without the benefit of paper to release them by writing them down. As I drive, I think about all the things I'm thankful for and I say them out loud. I just let my mind fly and I get on a roll. By the time I get to my destination, I am a new woman. I am hopeful, thankful, overwhelmed by God's goodness.

Prayer plus gratitude equals praise, and praise is the quickest route to get to joy. Try it today. I dare you.

The rod of correction imparts wisdom, but a
child left to himself disgraces his mother....
Discipline your son, and he will give you peace;
he will bring delight to your soul.

PROVERBS 29:15, 17

Giving clear and consistent discipline to my children is one of the more unsavory aspects of motherhood, even if it is an essential ingredient. I do not enjoy taking away privileges, canceling outings, and being "the strict one." I'd much rather hug them, love on them, play with them, take places, and be fun. But without discipline, kids can't grow up to be that fun. Without discipline, any household can turn into *Lord of the Flies*.

Discipline does not mean you keep your child on a leash; it just means you give them a nice, safe, fenced yard to play in. When they know their limits, they can enjoy more freedom. Eventually there is less tugging and more playing. Just as we become wiser and better people when God disciplines us, our children grow from our correction. We want our kids to grow up into good people, loving, compassionate, people whom other people enjoy and respect.

Without discipline, these things won't happen. Without discipline, pint-sized brats grow up and become supersized jerks. When kids go through life without tying behavior to consequence, they are oblivious forever. We all know at least one person like this, someone who does whatever they please and thinks that rules apply to everyone but them. They are oblivious to the pain and inconvenience they cause people, because no one ever corrected them.

*Above all, love each other deeply, because
love covers over a multitude of sins.*

1 PETER 4:8

Love looks at the intention of a heart, not the occasional mishandling of a moment.

When we know we are loved, deeply and truly loved, we give someone the benefit of a doubt, because we know they would never intend to do us harm. If we don't understand their tone, words, or actions, we ask them about it, because we genuinely want to know where they are coming from or what is really going on behind the scenes.

I ask my children for forgiveness often. When I use a snappy tone, shush someone because I'm "busy," overreact, or any myriad of things I mess up on a regular basis, I try to circle back. When I get the feeling in my spirit that something didn't settle quite right, I will return to the subject with my child. I let them know where I fell short of being the kind of mom I want to be and ask them to forgive me. Thank God, they always do. I want them to see me as my imperfect self, and experience the regular exchange of forgiveness (both asking for and receiving) that is required in family life and all significant relationships. If they see me humble myself, they won't be so mortified to do it themselves.

Owning our sin and expressing regret over our shortcomings is a total relief. It's a relief to be free of them and it's a relief to release someone we love. Respecting other people's feelings is a natural outpouring of a heart that has been respected. This begins at home.

God is not unjust; he will not forget your work and the love you have shown him as you have helped his people and continue to help them.

HEBREWS 6:10

In all the tasks involved in raising our children, we are working for God and showing Him our love.

He sees and remembers our work and will reward us for how we handle this great responsibility. Our everyday tasks can take on new meaning when we consider whom we are working for and aim to please Him. I think of this as consecrating my tasks, making them holy. And it completely changes the way I view tasks and the love and energy I put into them.

When I pack lunches for my kids, typically a rushed and mundane event in the morning, I now try to think about blessing each of them with food to sustain them and how the reminder of home in the middle of the long school day could be just what they need in that moment. When I grocery-shop or plan meals, I try to think about how I can make mealtimes special for us, something we look forward to and a time we honor as a family. Because of this, even though it would be tempting as a single mom to consider just serving grilled cheese as they sit at the counter, I still make the effort for a real family dinner. We sit together at the table, pray before our meal, talk, laugh, and attempt to practice our manners. I want to honor God with this ritual. When I'm folding clothes or something rather boring, I take the time to pray. The time passes quickly, and my thoughts are in order just like my piles of clothes.

How can you consecrate your tasks today?

No discipline seems pleasant at the time, but painful.
Later on, however, it produces a harvest of righteousness
and peace for those who have been trained by it.

HEBREWS 12:11

My own seasons of discipline have not been pleasant. Being pruned does not feel good. Being tested and purified by fire is not warm and cozy; it burns. But oh, how these seasons have strengthened me. Ultimately, when the seasons were far enough in the past to yield the benefit of perspective, I realized that great peace and blessing have come from the painful lessons. All discipline leads to obedience, which leads to freedom—if we choose to embrace the process with faith.

It pains me to discipline my children. I ache for their disappointment and regret and wish that I didn't have to follow through. But I have to do it. Not only that, but I have to do it in such a way that they understand I am not making this happen; I am not causing the pain of this moment. It was their choice or their behavior that led to this result. So I hug them and tell them I will miss them at the movies and I wish they were able to go, and I leave. And I feel like crying more than they do. But they own the lesson, and that is the entire point. They are not the victim.

I can begin to understand how God feels as He invokes my punishment; He doesn't like it either. It must hurt His heart to rebuke me and make me suffer my consequences, but He does it out of love so that I will learn and grow. He wants my brokenness to be healed.

In the same way, I want righteousness and peace for my children.

*After taking the cup, he gave thanks and said,
"Take this and divide it among you. For I tell you
I will not drink again of the fruit of the vine
until the kingdom of God comes."*

LUKE 22:17–18

Every year the season of Lent is probably my greatest time of spiritual growth and renewal. I love the themes of solemnity and sacrifice. It is a welcome break from the pace and the striving of the world to have a season of spiritual housecleaning. I love to experience the season with my children, to talk about either giving up things in order to put God before their own pleasure or doing things to please God.

One year we wrote down what was on our hearts for Lent and we burned those papers, using the ashes to make crosses on one another's foreheads. That must have made a huge impact on my children, because they still talk about it. Or maybe it was just cool to burn something, I'm not sure. What I do know is that the traditions we make as a family have a major effect on the spiritual formation of our children. They learn how to honor holy things when they grow up experiencing reverence.

What areas are you going to work on for Lent this year? What can you do with your family that will make this special time one of growth and renewal for everyone in your home? This is a time to be purposeful about the spiritual direction of our children. Take these forty days to step it up.

With the tongue we praise our Lord and Father, and with it we curse men, who have been made in God's likeness. Out of the same mouth come praise and cursing. My brothers, this should not be. Can both fresh water and salt water flow from the same spring?

JAMES 3:9–11

Taming the tongue is a lifetime pursuit. Words are powerful and need to be handled with care, having the ability to both heal and hurt. If we aren't careful, in our exasperation we can say things and use tones with our children that we would never consider acceptable with our friends or strangers. And yet these are the people we love the most.

Unthinking remarks are exactly that, without thought. Meaning, they wouldn't come out if we stopped to think. Even in His perfection, Jesus had to take time away to replenish Himself. Surely we need to do the same.

When frustration levels rise and we are tempted to react instead of lead, we need to take a grown-up time-out. Whether it's stepping outside to sit on the porch for a second, a moment of solitude in the bathroom, a hot shower, a walk around the block, or even a quick prayer in the next room—it doesn't matter what, how, or for how long, it just matters that we learn to pause. Once we can perfect this technique in terms of a physical departure, however brief, we can more quickly and easily locate this quiet place on the inside, which is where it counts. This is our well, and it contains Living Water.

*The prayer offered in faith will make
the sick person well; the Lord will raise him up.
If he has sinned, he will be forgiven.*

JAMES 5:15

Our greatest channel of power, our ultimate alliance, our true vehicle for change in the care and raising of our children is prayer. When our children are sick or struggling, our prayers over their feverish foreheads or our pleading for their protection and direction may be the thing that saves them. God is the one who can grant access to the best care, the wisest counsel, and the quickest remedy.

I know God hears me when I go to Him on behalf of my children; He knows well the depth of a mother's love. He will equip us to intercede with the power and authority of Christ. This is a great responsibility. We cannot take it lightly. We cannot neglect our development in this area only to be leveled when crisis hits, rendered useless to ourselves and our loved ones. Intercession and the depth of faith behind it must be practiced in ordinary times.

Not only must we nurture our lives of prayer individually, we must also find and foster relationships with other women who will join us as advocates in prayer for our children. When a group of believers is gathered in His name, our power is magnified and the voices of our prayers echo loudly in the chambers of heaven.

*Your beauty should not come from outward
adornment.... Instead, it should be that of
your inner self, the unfading beauty of a gentle and
quiet spirit, which is of great worth in God's sight.
For this is the way the holy women of the past who put
their hope in God used to make themselves beautiful.*

1 PETER 3:3–5

It isn't easy to grow into our beauty in this day and age, as we begin to notice the signs and shifts of age coming before we even feel like full-fledged grown-ups. It isn't easy for our daughters as they navigate the confusion and pitfalls created by media messages, peer groups, boys, and fashion.

I want to teach my daughters that their beauty is part of their design from God and has nothing to do with what they put on or how they present themselves. Instead, beauty is something that is revealed when they are being their authentic selves. I can't toss out morsels of wisdom on this subject and meanwhile go on to complain about my body, or groan at my reflection in the mirror. If I am not good enough in my own eyes, how will my girls ever see themselves clearly?

I have to live a healthy and authentic life, with my beauty and my confidence based in God. I have to treat myself kindly and be an encouragement to other women. If I put more emphasis on the cultivation of my inner self than on the losing battle to alter or preserve my shell, my girls will have an up close example of beauty that hopefully will speak more loudly than the voice of the world.

*Command and teach these things. Don't let anyone
look down on you because you are young,
but set an example for the believers in speech,
in life, in love, in faith, and in purity.*

1 TIMOTHY 4:11–12

By listening to our children, we help them develop their
voices. In order to instill the confidence that their voices have
value, children first have to experience their voices being heard
and respected at home. If we want our children to have the
courage to speak out if something is wrong, or to speak up if
they have a better idea, we need to let them know that we back
them up. Their confidence grows because we believe in them,
and they begin to believe in themselves.

Confidence like this stems from believing in an almighty
God.

There will be people—maybe teachers, maybe coaches,
maybe even someone from church—who look down on or
minimize our children because they are young. Consider, then,
why Jesus asks us to have faith like a child. Jesus knew that the
faith of a child is pure and uncomplicated. Regardless of how
they are received by those who don't understand, we want our
children to know that they are old enough to make a difference, and that they are never too young to set an example for
others. The expression "out of the mouths of babes" reminds
us all that sometimes the most profoundly honest and preco-
ciously wise statements come from children. They see things
and people with uncanny accuracy. They have a lot to teach
us. Are we listening?

Dear children, let us not love with words or tongue but with actions and in truth.

1 JOHN 3:18

⁂

Words are important. It's good to say things such as *I love you, I miss you, Please forgive me, You are important to me, I'm happy to see you.* These words are balm to the soul. But words, like promises, are empty if the motive behind them is selfish or the actions surrounding them are inconsistent.

Love in action and in truth is undeniable. Saying *I love you* is one thing, but showing it consistently over time is another. Just like the friend who may not know what to say but has the courage to show up and walk into the vortex of our pain, being there for someone is silently loud.

As a single mom with three children, I sometimes feel a tug-of-war for my attention. Everyone needs to feel like the only one, at least once in a while. I started a tradition where every so often I surprise one child with an alone overnight or weekend. My parents make this gift possible for me by taking the other two children while we're away. Even one night away, just the two of us, opens up conversation and creates intimacy that would not happen otherwise, and the connection remains long after the weekend is over. I know it's a treat for them because they blossom in my undivided attention, opening up to me like a flower. When we return home, we have a renewed appreciation for each other, and a special closeness that lingers.

There is no fear in love. But perfect loves drives out fear, because fear has to do with punishment. The one who fears is not made perfect in love.

1 JOHN 4:18

⁂

I did not grow up in a household where fear ruled. I did not have to worry about repercussions when speaking my mind, even if I disagreed with my parents. It may not have changed a thing, but I could always share my opinion. Even when I messed up and knew I was busted, I was more upset with myself for having disappointed my parents than I was truly scared of their reaction. They definitely disciplined me, but it was to help me, not hurt me.

I realize that some people will cringe when they read this Scripture because they grew up afraid, walking on eggshells, not knowing when a parent might erupt, lash out, or leave. I ache for you if this was your initial knowledge of love, and I pray that the Lord has come into your heart in a major way, healing those areas of brokenness and setting new standards and definitions of love.

The beauty of Christ is that we are a new creation in Him, and with Him we have the power to do things differently. If you still flinch in response to anger, if you route immediately to a place of shame, if you are freaking out at the idea of being a parent and making the same mistakes with your children, or if you are in a relationship with a man that echoes the fears of your childhood, take heart. You are stronger than you think. You have an alliance with the Almighty, and all things are possible with Him. You can do it differently. You can be made perfect in love.

Dear children, keep yourselves from idols.

1 JOHN 5:21

※

I think the main idol of these present times is the electronic screen. I can see it in myself sometimes, and I can really see it in my children. "Noooooo, don't turn off the TV, five more minutes!" "No, don't turn off the video game; I'm almost to the next level!" How about the way we carry our BlackBerry devices and iPhones around everywhere? We are constantly checking to see who has called us, reading new e-mails, or sending texts. We cannot be separated from them; I reach for mine as soon as I get into the car; it has clearly become a habit, or perhaps even an addiction. It's as if going from one place to another without multitasking is a major waste of time.

We have become so obsessed with immediate response times that we expect someone to respond to us right away, and we put that same expectation on ourselves. When I finally did get a BlackBerry, I was consumed by how convenient it was. I used it all the time. Soon I realized it was becoming an idol to me and I had to make some changes.

For Lent one year, I gave up using the phone in the car—that was a major change. I had some of the best conversations with my children. After Lent I decided to keep this idea in some form by a new rule: no phone calls in the car unless I am alone. These rules sound so ridiculous, but that's what happens when we make an idol out of something. What are your idols?

*Dear friends, build yourselves up in your most
holy faith and pray in the Holy Spirit.*

JUDE 20

How do we build ourselves up in our most holy faith? I know *when* we need to build ourselves up: right now is ideal. Too often we turn to our neglected or faded faith in a time of crisis, only to wish we had spent more time cultivating and strengthening it in ordinary times.

I look at my spiritual training and my physical training in a similar way. I don't want to wait until I'm laid up in the hospital to wish I had taken better care of my health. I want to address it now, while I can do it without the pressure of a problem. I want to build my strength, my endurance, my speed, and my flexibility.

Our spiritual conditioning is built over time as well. I need to be strong enough to carry my cross when it's my turn, and help others bear their burdens. I need to be able to react quickly and be light on my feet, getting back on track if I take a wrong turn, or sprint to the scene if someone needs me. I need to be flexible when God requires me to change or bend beyond my usual comfort zone. I want to fuel myself properly in a spiritual sense as well, by feeding on the Word of God and nourishing myself with healthy, satisfying relationships.

It's no mystery to me that these areas are entwined. When I neglect one area, the other suffers, and when I am well trained in one area, the other blossoms as well. If you consider that our bodies truly are the temple of the Holy Spirit, this makes perfect sense.

As God's chosen people, holy and dearly loved,
clothe yourselves with compassion, kindness,
humility, gentleness and patience. Bear with
each other and forgive whatever grievances you may
have against one another. Forgive as the Lord
forgave you. And over all these virtues put on love,
which binds them all together in perfect unity.

COLOSSIANS 3:12–14

I have this Scripture taped to my bathroom mirror because this is where I get dressed every day. As I get ready for my day, I want to be purposeful about considering how I present myself to the world in the ways that really count. This verse is an excellent way to start the day, to align my heart with God and His purposes, and remember who I want to be. Just as we choose our clothing each day, we can choose to adorn ourselves in beautiful and lasting spiritual fabrics like compassion, kindness, and patience.

I can fill my pockets with heavy burdens like unforgiveness and resentment, or I can move unencumbered through my day. Am I going to stick that heavy rock in my bulging pocket for yet another day or am I finally going to lay it down? The initial choice is hard, but after that, God does all the heavy lifting.

Forgiveness is the best beauty treatment around. It's better than any makeover. And finally, the overcoat. You know how some jackets just seem to work no matter what the season? This is what it means to put on love over all these things. Love makes the outfit. When you're wrapped in it, you are always ready to face the world.

The sacrifices of God are a broken spirit; a broken and contrite heart, O God, you will not despise.

PSALM 51:17

When my children make poor choices with their behavior, I discipline them accordingly. When my discipline is met with back talk, sass, eye-rolling, or flat-out rebellion, what was just a minor frustration suddenly becomes inflamed. It's now bigger than a simple mistake. The discipline has to kick up a notch to account for the disrespect. It's kind of like when you get pulled over by a police officer when you're driving, and he tells you that you were going five miles over the speed limit. A quiet and respectful apology might set you free, especially on a good hair day, or you might just have to pay a fine. Start an argument about your speed, rationalize the importance of your destination, huff and roll your eyes, or call the officer names, and you are sure to get a ticket for your speed, and likely another one for your sass, and maybe even arrested if you go too far. No one likes that kind of attitude.

In order to model humility and repentance for our children, we have to take this posture before God when they are watching us. We have to own our mistakes outright. We have to go to the people we have offended and do what we can to make things right. We take our broken spirit to God and ask Him to forgive us. Just the way we ache when one of our sweethearts turns a teary face up to us and sobs their regret over a mistake, our softened hearts are quick to forgive and so is God. No one likes to see their child hurting.

Let him who boasts boast in the Lord.

1 CORINTHIANS 1:31

Young children of a certain age are so confident and free. They say what they think and have no shyness about it. "I'm so pretty in this dress." "I'm awesome at basketball." "I'm so smart, watch what I can do!" "I'm the best in the world at this game." When our kids are small, we think this is adorable and probably secretly wish that we felt so good about ourselves.

Childlike confidence can turn into adult-sized arrogance if a heart has not been matured in faith. I want my children to have healthy self-confidence, knowing their skills and strong points, but their ultimate confidence cannot be self-confidence. True confidence comes from belief in an almighty God. The fine line between keeping a child from pridefulness and maintaining their self-esteem is drawn in humility. Humility is not being mousy or playing small; humility means knowing who we are in relation to God. Humility is a carefully cultivated garden whereas pride is a runaway weed. Narcissistic adults are children who were allowed to grow up thinking they were the center of the universe.

We are working on this at my house, all of us. When we get good grades or have a great football game, our prayers first thank God for our talent, then thank our teachers for their teaching, our coaches for their instruction, our teammate for the great assist, and our family for backing us up. Nothing great is ever accomplished alone. And more will never be entrusted to those who forget to credit the source.

> *To do what is right and just is more*
> *acceptable to the LORD than sacrifice.*

PROVERBS 21:3

During this time of Lent, I like to consider more than only what I'm giving up—no meat on Fridays, and sometimes no coffee, or wine, or sugar, or complaining. It's good to sacrifice; it's always a valid effort when we work on our self-discipline. But in addition to giving something up, have we thought enough about what we are giving?

I know I need to work on this, for myself and with my family, during the weeks before Easter. We can honor God with our actions as we show Him our love and gratitude.

We can serve the poor, feed the hungry, help at the animal shelter, write letters to people we love who aren't expecting it, write letters to soldiers or prisoners who really aren't expecting it; we can call friends and family we've lost touch with, we can visit a nursing home, we can "adopt" an orphan through a ministry program, we can donate items to a children's shelter or a home for unwed mothers, we can use our time and talents to spread the gospel of peace and compassion. When we do these things with our children, they see that giving up something for Lent doesn't just mean doing without, it also means doing. Love is a feeling, but it is also an action.

Consider it pure joy, my brothers, whenever you face trials of many kinds, because you know that the testing of your faith develops perseverance. Perseverance must finish its work so that you may be mature and complete, not lacking anything.

JAMES 1:2–4

⁂

I can't say that I am mature enough to be joyful when a trial arises in my life, but I have progressed beyond curling up into a fetal position with a blanket over my head, whining incessantly or crying to my friends. Okay, I still cry to my friends sometimes. But I have begun to rely on God. This is huge.

Instead of going directly into "Why me?" mode, I am beginning to be more interested in the lesson. *What are You trying to teach me here, Father? I am open and willing; please help me.* Once I switch gears and get my head out of the circumstances and fix my gaze on God, I get some breathing room, or at least enough perspective to see as far as the next step. The testing of our faith is in trusting the next step to be illuminated, and perseverance is when we continue to walk along His path. This is a lifelong journey, to be sure.

I really do want to move to the level of joy. I know people who live there. I want to actually celebrate when the next trial appears. I will start by praising God first, then asking Him for my lesson. After all, if He sees me as a worthy candidate for more training, maybe He has an assignment in mind for me.

Do not forget this one thing, dear friends:
With the Lord a day is like a thousand years, and a
thousand years are like a day. The Lord is not slow in
keeping his promise, as some understand slowness.

2 PETER 3:8–9

On a very humble level, I think mothers can understand this. Someone told me that when your children are small, the days feel like years and the years feel like a day. It's so true! I remember when my kids were babies and our world was about diapers, nursing, and not sleeping. When I was tired and feeling alone in my postpartum haze, my hours belonged to the feeding and nap schedule and the days were long. Or maybe the nights were just short; I can't remember. But when I look back on that now, with all three of my children, those years were a tiny blip on the radar of my motherhood. I can't even remember whatever I might have stressed over, and I wish I could feel the weight of my babies in my arms again and inhale the perfect smell of their soft skin.

God loves us like that. It's almost hard to imagine, but He does. He looks back on the time with His people, and, to the Ageless One, each civilization is a blip. Yet He knows each hair on our heads and the way each of our days will play out before we even get out of bed. His perspective is so vast. We sweat over our time frames, our plans, and our agendas, and He controls the tides, the turning of the earth, the climates, the seasons, and the plot of every character ever invented. Every door ajar is one He opened; every detour sign was placed by His hand. If I could just trust His promises and make peace with His timing.

David said to Nathan, "I have sinned against the LORD."

2 SAMUEL 12:13

God used Nathan to convict David of his sin of having an affair with Bathsheba and his cunning plot to have her husband killed so he could possess her. Nathan told him a story that mirrored his own sin, only the characters were fictional. David was outraged at the travesty committed by a man in the story, until Nathan pointed out that he, David, was that man. Ouch.

All of us are at risk for being blind to our own sin, and sometimes God sends us a Nathan; other times we have to be a Nathan. This is why it is so important to have a close group of godly girlfriends as our support system and our accountability monitors. Sometimes we have to be accountable to one another, other times these relationships become our practice zone for stepping out in the world. I have gently spoken to an incensed woman in an airport bathroom, raging at her child, because she was about to go too far. I was terrified to intervene, but it was my turn to be a Nathan. "Can I help you?" I said. "I know it's hard. What can I do?"

My words made her realize how she was treating her child. Her eyes filled with tears and she whispered, "Thank you." I wanted to cry, too. We have to help one another. We need less Pharisees and more Nathans in this world, and we can start with ourselves.

Our Bible study group uses this as a code; it's humorous but quick to get our attention: "Hey, it's me, Nathan. I need to talk to you..." When you have built a relationship of intimacy and trust, a rebuke is an act of love for God.

God is faithful; he will not let you be tempted beyond what you can bear. But when you are tempted, he will also provide a way out so that you can stand up under it.

1 CORINTHIANS 10:13

It is so hard to delay gratification. It's hard for children; it's hard for adults, too. This is an excellent verse to teach our children early on, so that it has years to sink in. For young children, the temptation may be to let their anger take over. Maybe this means throwing a fit or lashing out in violence at a sibling. Just as a child learns how to move from wearing diapers to using the toilet, the key is to recognize an urge and control it, before it happens. There is always at least a tiny sliver of time between impulse and action, and this is what we want to learn to recognize. This verse goes right to that spot.

If we can train ourselves in the simpler things, like closing our mouths before a nasty remark comes out, then we are learning to ask God for the way out. He will provide a way, every single time. If we can train our children to do this with meltdowns, outbursts, and hitting at a young age, we will have a better chance of helping them to triumph over the temptations that come with a much higher cost . . . alcohol, drugs, sex, and deception.

Sometimes just telling myself that God will not let me be tempted beyond what I can bear is enough to keep me clean. Our children have to know this verse by heart. We can't always be with them in the moment of indecision, that tiny sliver of time, but God can. That's why they need to know where to turn.

Knowledge puffs up, but love builds up.
The man who thinks he knows something
does not yet know as he ought to know.

1 CORINTHIANS 8:1–2

Women can be such pains. We need one another so much, and yet we are so quick to judge one another. We judge who breast-feeds and who bottle-feeds, who uses cloth diapers and who uses disposables and what this says about our commitment to the planet, who works and who stays home, who has a nanny, who allows their kids to see PG movies, who eats organic and who has a pantry full of food laden with preservatives and high-fructose corn syrup. It's endless and endlessly annoying.

Let's get one thing straight: we don't have an expert in the world. Every mother is still learning and just trying to do her best, and this looks different each moment. I wrote this book about mothering and I'm doing it not because I know anything, but because I have so much to learn. And considering that the most valuable lessons come from making mistakes, we have no room to judge. We nag our kids to share from the moment they can grip a toy in their chubby, drooly fists. But we aren't always sharing with one another. We need to share what we know, where we're struggling, what has helped, what has hurt, what worked, and what didn't. The minute we think we have the hang of this, we need to get down on our knees with our faces to the floor and let love build us up.

The unbelieving husband has been sanctified through his wife, and the unbelieving wife has been sanctified through her believing husband. Otherwise your children would be unclean, but as it is, they are holy.

1 CORINTHIANS 7:14

Some of you reading this book may know the ache of loving a nonbelieving husband, or carry the weight of a child who has abandoned their faith. Some of you may have a friend who knows this ache. Life in a home that is not united in the Lord is not easy to navigate. It's hard to fix problems together with different sets of tools. It's hard to see the same thing without a shared perspective. It's hard to make plans when our goals are not the same.

It can be easier, however, when we realize that we are not responsible for changing or converting anyone. We are not responsible for how often our spouses or grown children are seen at church, or what people think of our families. We are responsible for living and loving in such a way that our lives themselves become invitations. Our faith is big enough to cover our families. I love how this verse reminds us that our children are already and always holy.

Women, particularly groups of women, who are persistent in prayer for a loved one's salvation have witnessed miraculous transformations in faith. We offer the most powerful intercession when we let go of our expectations and timetables and invite God to whisper to a wandering heart. We simply ask and then get out of the way. We believe, and then we trust.

When God gives any man wealth and possessions,
and enables him to enjoy them, to accept his lot
and be happy in his work—this is a gift of God.

ECCLESIASTES 5:19

I love the significance of the little tucked-in phrase *"and enables him to enjoy them."* Many people have wealth and possessions and yet have no ability to enjoy them at all. Thinking that their lack of fulfillment is somehow related to insufficient quantity, they continue to strive and collect, pouring their treasures into a leaking vessel. They are missing the catalyst called contentment, the ability to enjoy and appreciate our blessings.

My mom has a framed needlepoint that hung over the kitchen table of every house we ever lived in. It says, "Contentment is not the fulfillment of what you want but the realization of how much you already have." Whatever we have or don't have, the gift from God is to be able to accept it with a grateful heart. Paul said it this way in Philippians 4:11: "I have learned to be content whatever the circumstances."

Some seasons of motherhood can be dotted with periods of restlessness or vague resentment at a loss of identity or more limited freedom. No one likes to talk about this, but I don't mind being honest. Because the sooner we can be honest about our striving or our restlessness, once we recognize it and own it, the sooner we can ask God for what we really need. We need the gift of contentment. We need Him to enable us to enjoy our lives, to accept where we are right now, and be happy with the work He has given us.

Naked a man comes from his mother's womb, and as he comes, so he departs. He takes nothing from his labor that he can carry in his hand.

ECCLESIASTES 5:15

꙰

My childhood priest used to always say, "Give me your calendar and your checkbook and I'll tell you what your treasures are." Try it. Comb your Quicken and your BlackBerry with Father Arnold's eyes and tell me what he would see. Does your life, not as you see it or hope for it, but as it really is, reflect your true treasures? If we can take nothing from our labor that we can carry in our hand, we had better make sure our treasures are the kind that can be stored in the heart.

The season of motherhood is at once eternal and fleeting. What I mean is, once you have a child you are a mother forever, but the time we have to really bond, spend time with, and make a difference in the lives of our children is short. It can slip through our fingers while we are mistakenly taking care of things that seem so important at the time. I ache for older people who spent a lifetime investing in the wrong things, only to find that the account that yields most is bankrupt.

We don't automatically get a relationship with our adult children just because we birthed them; we earn that reward over many years. We might appear naked when we come and go from this world, but what a treasure it is to be swaddled in love as we arrive and clothed in love as we depart. We must live wisely.

You will seek me and find me when
you seek me with all your heart.

JEREMIAH 29:13

When I was little and looking for something, I would ask my mom where it was. She would tell me, and I would search for it, not be able to locate it, and holler back, "I can't *find it*." She would say, every single time, "Open your eyes, dear." And I hear myself saying the same thing to my children. I go to the pantry and hand them the box of Rice Krispies, which is sitting on the middle of the bottom shelf, exactly where I said it would be. So many times in our laziness we look with our eyes closed. We want someone else to hand to us what we are seeking.

We do the same thing with our faith. We whine and say things like, "I can't see God these days." "He's silent." "He doesn't talk to me the way He talks to other people." "The Bible seems so obscure. I can't understand it." "I'm not getting much out of church right now." "My kids just aren't interested anymore." "It's so hard now with sports and stuff on Sundays." God doesn't move. We do.

He is always the same, always faithful, always speaking to us, always listening, always watchful over us, always loving us, always right where we left Him—right by our side. He expresses Himself in and through everything, all around us. If we can't find Him, perhaps we need to open our eyes. God reveals Himself to those who seek Him with their whole hearts. A halfhearted attempt is exactly that, half of a whole heart. And that's not going to cut it. If we can't find God for ourselves, we can't possibly share Him with our children.

Each one should test his own actions. Then he can take pride in himself, without comparing himself to somebody else, for each one should carry his own load.

GALATIANS 6:4–5

I cannot begin to tell you how much I appreciate the difference in my travel experiences with my children today as compared to years ago. I remember schlepping a stroller, Pack 'n Plays, an overstuffed diaper bag, suitcases . . . it seemed incomprehensible that three small people could generate such a load. I would be exhausted by the time we hit airport security.

Today my kids are older and life is easier. I tell them to each pack their bag to take on the plane. I have a bag and a suitcase and they each roll their own carry-on. I marvel at our independent little pack as we roll through the airport, thinking how far we've come.

The way people travel says a lot about them, and I want my kids to carry their own load, at the airport and in life. It's tempting to do things for our children, because we think it's faster, less hassle, or we do it more neatly. Children who don't learn the natural order of sowing and reaping by carrying their own load will never thrive on their own. We interrupt the instructional nature of natural consequences when we do things for them, cover for them, or bail them out. There are enough adult children who still live at home, are in debt, unemployed, addicted to something, watch daytime television, and still won't bring their dirty laundry downstairs. I don't want one on my sofa, and neither do you.

Do not let anyone judge you by what you eat or drink.

COLOSSIANS 2:16

This verse is helpful in knowing where God stands on issues about food and drink. Teaching children from an early age that the body is the temple of the Lord is imperative. This matters from a standpoint of sexuality, when they will endure pressure to go too far. This matters when they have to decide whether or not to accept the beer at the party, and possibly drive home. This matters when young girls are overwhelmed by the pressure to be thin and take drastic, unhealthy measures to wither away.

When we allow public opinion to be the judge of what we eat and drink, then we have made an idol out of our peers. Idolatry is not God's favorite. It isn't even so much an issue of rebelling against parents as it is about blatantly ignoring God, and no one throughout the entire Bible ever fared well by doing this. When we harm our temples, we hurt Him. Remember when Jesus got so angry at the people who were treating the temple like a marketplace and He started yelling and flipping tables upside down? Enough said.

We have to talk to our kids, keep the conversation continuous and open, and pray with them through the tough spots. And if it becomes too much to bear, we have to be prepared to help them find respite in a safer spot someplace else.

After the wind there was an earthquake, but the Lord
was not in the earthquake. After the earthquake
came a fire, but the Lord was not in the fire.
And after the fire came a gentle whisper.

1 KINGS 19:11–12

We can get so used to life in the vortex of our chaos that we become immune to it. We endure so much constant noise that we forget our souls crave quiet. We can grow deaf to the voice of God.

Like warm pockets of water when swimming in a cold lake, there are slivers of quiet to be found for the one who truly seeks them. There is a reason Scripture gives Jesus' example of seeking God early in the morning (Mark 1:35); He knows we need Him first, and with fewer distractions. I love my house in the morning. My Bible waits on the table next to the sofa. Before I do or say a thing, I am silent. I rest my hands in my lap or fold them in prayer and I breathe deeply until I can feel the peace of the Lord. If there is a word or a verse on my heart, I use it as my mantra, meditating on it until I find balance within.

Now I am ready to greet God and meet the day in prayer. The more quickly I can train myself to find that peaceful and quiet place, the more easily I can return to it throughout the day. Before a meeting while waiting in the lobby, in the pickup line at school, even in the full-blown action of my house in early evening, God is still speaking to me. He whispers encouragement, peace, insight, and love. Even when my life is noisy, I still have to be able to get quiet enough to hear Him. Stillness is a practice, outside and within.

We have different gifts, according to the grace given us.

ROMANS 12:6

❧

Jealousy is an ugly beast, unattractive in its expression but far more foul in its infestation within. It can ruin moods, teams, families, friendships, marriages, churches, and communities.

Children battle jealousy in their way, and we adults battle it in ours. We may as well own up to it in front of our children and teach the important lessons while we learn them. When we are too busy looking at other people, we miss what God is trying to do for and with us. I like to tell myself, "You can spend time thinking about what she's doing when you are completely done with your growth in every area." That usually gets me back on track pretty quickly.

When we take our gazes off God and our minds off gratitude, and start paying more attention to everyone else and what they have and what they're doing with what they have, we start to wilt. We all fit in someplace in God's spectrum. There will always be those who seem to have more than us and those who seem to have less than us when it comes to talent and treasure. When we waste time making comparisons and calculations, trying to figure out our spot on the spectrum, we are missing the opportunity of our own callings. God has certain tasks assigned specifically to us, to make use of our gifts in perfect harmony with His timing. When we are off our marks, pouting or making trouble because of jealousy, we don't receive our assignments on time, and we don't have the faith and focus to complete them for His glory. We miss out and the kingdom misses us.

In him we were also chosen, having been predestined according to the plan of him who works out everything in conformity with the purpose of his will.

EPHESIANS 1:11

In a spiritual sense, there is no greater honor than adoption. As Christians, we are not God's original chosen people—the Jews are. But we are also chosen, predestined to be part of His family and to be treated as sons and daughters. He loves us exactly the same. He disciplines us exactly the same. He forgives us the same. He makes sacrifices for us as our Father. He gives advice, as Fathers do. He makes provision for our futures, so we will always be taken care of. We have a spot at His table forever. When holidays come, we know exactly to whom we belong. On Sundays, when it feels like everyone is busy with family, He is expecting us.

There is an undeniable blessing to be born into a family, but being chosen to join is almost even sweeter. For those of you reading who have adopted your children, officially or unofficially, I want to express my love and my heart for you. For those of you who have a healed heart because someone has adopted you, God bless you. For people who do not know the love of family, it seems like a world that belongs to other people, a vision that can be seen apart, as through glass. But when we open the door of family to other people, especially children, and show them the same love as we would give our own, we are truly loving others as Jesus calls us to love.

He who fears the Lord has a secure fortress,
and for his children it will be a refuge.

PROVERBS 14:26

I want my family's home to be a fortress. No matter what the world sends our way, whatever mistakes we've made, what kind of day we've had—when we walk through the front door of this house, I want my family to find peace. Our home is a place where we can share our faith, cry and laugh without reservation, express anger, heal, extend and receive forgiveness, and be silly and let our hair down. I will go to great lengths to create this refuge. I pray for protection around our fortress daily, I create firm boundaries with our schedules and our family time, and I have specific standards for how people will be treated within these walls. Everyone deserves a place to feel safe.

Our homes are excellent physical examples of the spiritual fortresses created by our faith. Unlike our homes, from which we depart each day and enter the rest of the world, the refuges of our faith moves with us. When we build our faith fortresses together as families, brick by brick with shared wisdom and experiences, we maintain our connection and enjoy secure protection throughout each day. It is a way of returning home and finding comfort, no matter where we happen to be at the moment.

As much as I'd like to, I can't be there for my children every time they come to a crossroads or each time they suffer pain. I can't be there but their faith can. This is the refuge I want for my children, that they may dwell "in the shelter of the Most High" and "rest in the shadow of the Almighty" (Ps. 91:1).

She is clothed with strength and dignity; she can laugh at the days to come. She speaks with wisdom, and faithful instruction is on her tongue. She watches over the affairs of her household and does not eat the bread of idleness. Her children arise and call her blessed; her husband also, and he praises her.

PROVERBS 31:25–28

The Proverbs 31 woman has it going on.

Some women have trouble with the way some sections of the Bible define women and their roles. The idea of being submissive to your husband may feel like a large pill to swallow with a dry mouth, if you define *submissive* in other than a godly way. But Proverbs 31:10–31, labeled with the heading "Epilogue: The Wife of Noble Character," clears up any contemporary misunderstandings about how God sees the power, responsibility, and capability of a woman.

The Proverbs 31 woman is not some mousy hausfrau. She is strong; she works hard both inside and outside the home, makes important decisions, and has the full confidence and respect of her family. She is efficient, dignified, shrewd, faithful, wise, and loving. She and her husband each bring their best, and together they make a successful partnership. Their children are blessed to grow up in such a household.

She clearly isn't anxious about the future. She trusts God to prevail on behalf of her family, and she has a spirit of joy. I bet her good mood is contagious. Take the time to read this chapter in its entirety during your quiet time today and see where God is calling you to grow.

There is a time for everything, and a season for every activity under heaven: a time to be born and a time to die, a time to plant and a time to uproot…a time to tear down and a time to build, a time to weep and a time to laugh, a time to mourn and a time to dance…a time to embrace and a time to refrain, a time to search and a time to give up, a time to keep and a time to throw away… a time to be silent and a time to speak, a time to love and a time to hate, a time for war and a time for peace.

ECCLESIASTES 3:1–8

Juggling different aspects of our identities is an inescapable part of motherhood. I want to be the best mother I can be to Luke, Grace, and Bella. I also want to have a thriving career. I want to keep growing in my faith. I want to nurture my friendships. I'd also like to meet the man that God has specially picked out for me and the kids. But these things aren't happening all at once. They *can't* happen all at once. I couldn't handle them if they did!

If I can reflect back over a year of my life and see evidence of progress in all the areas that matter to me, that has to be good enough. God takes the long view; remember, His perspective is eternal. We operate with minutes, hours, days, while He is more of a seasonal guy.

We can really focus on only one thing at a time if we are giving it our all. If we look at what matters most to us in terms of seasons, then we can take peace in the fact that eventually it will all unfold as it should. This Scripture is so beautiful when interpreted by a mother's heart. It brings us a quiet confidence to know that everything has its time.

If one falls down, his friend can help him up.
But pity the man who falls and has no one to help
him up! Also, if two lie down together, they will keep
warm. But how can one keep warm alone? Though
one may be overpowered, two can defend themselves.
A cord of three strands is not quickly broken.

ECCLESIASTES 4:10–12

These verses speak to my heart about family and friendship with such clarity and reverence. A few images come to mind: My children and I spent the night in a tent outside my parents' house, with pillows and blankets and both our dogs. The temperature dropped significantly during the night, and when I woke up early in the morning, our entire brood was warm in one big, entangled, snoozing pile.

Another image, when my daughters and I went camping with their Girl Scout troop and one of the mother-daughter activities was to scale a fifty-foot climbing wall. I remember being drenched with sweat, shaking with fear and effort, and hearing my little girls yelling encouragement and calling out directions of where to reach my hand or place my foot. I made it, all the way to the top, because they were beneath me.

We need one another. It's important to cultivate situations and plan adventures where we work together with our children and have to rely on one another. Maybe it's a campout, maybe it's a ministry trip, anything that takes us outside our comfort zones and thereby makes us vulnerable enough to express our need. A cord of three strands can represent our family unit—parents, children, and God. Together, no matter what happens, we are not easily broken.

A good name is better than fine perfume.

ECCLESIASTES 7:1

I went to a great parenting class last year at my children's school. We discussed the difference between discipline in terms of punishment and discipline in terms of teaching. Our instructor would often encourage us to ask our children in the midst of bad behavior choices, "Are you being who you want to be right now?"

The way I answer this question in the heat of a moment matters to me, and I think it is starting to matter to my children. If, instead of giving into frustration, I remain neutral and ask questions like, "Are you the kind of person who uses violence to solve problems or do you use your mind to work things out?" Or, "I know you're tired of homework, but are you the kind of person who gives up before a task is complete?" After they pause long enough to answer my question, I follow up with, "Can you think of another way to handle this situation that does match with who you are?"

Going through this thought process allows them to own their choices today, making it more likely that they'll follow through. Defining ourselves together along the way is different from me waiting until they are teenagers and then trying to cram my values down their throats in response to a major problem. At that point I can possibly withhold enough privileges to mandate a certain response, *but I can no longer affect whether they care.* And that's the part I'm more interested in. The way we see ourselves takes a long time to evolve, so we may as well approach it intentionally.

I have seen something else under the sun: The race is not to the swift or the battle to the strong, nor does food come to the wise or wealth to the brilliant or favor to the learned; but time and chance happen to them all. Moreover, no man knows when his hour will come.

ECCLESIASTES 9:11–12

Not one of us is immune. Trials come in all flavors, in all seasons, to everyone. We never know when it's our turn. We wake up on that day, thinking it will be an ordinary day like most others, and then something happens that changes everything. A phone call brings news that takes our breath away and buckles our knees. A plus sign shows up on the stick—or doesn't. A husband says he needs a break, to take some time to think about "what he really wants." A pediatrician wants to do another blood panel; something isn't quite right. A longtime boss gives you two weeks' notice.

It doesn't matter how much we pray or how well we try to live, at some point our hour will come and we will be tested. That much is certain. It is also certain that during our testing, God will not leave us or forsake us. As for everything else, well, some of it depends on the test and some of it depends on us. A big predictor of our performance on a test is how we react when it comes. Do we spend weeks wailing and cursing God at the unfairness of it all? Do we attempt to avoid or outrun it? Or do we save valuable time at the beginning by simply turning to face it, making an assessment and a strategy. Maybe this is as simple as, "Okay, this stinks" (assessment); and "God, I need Your help" (strategy). And then we get down to the humble, hard work of dealing with it.

Do not leave your post; calmness can lay great errors to rest.

ECCLESIASTES 10:4

≥≥

No matter how much we are freaking out on the inside, moms are expected to be unflinching in the face of an emergency. We can have the luxury of a meltdown later, when the urgency has passed.

On the first day of our summer vacation, we went straight to the beach. The girls played happily in the sand, and Luke found a friend to boogie-board with. I watched them, feeling the rare moment of total mommy serenity. Then a big wave came out of nowhere, and I scanned the shore for Luke. He was there, on the sand, but moments later he ran up to me, sobbing. He had hit his chin on a rock, and there was so much blood it was hard to see, but it appeared that his tooth had cut all the way through his skin.

I remember the moment clearly, swallowing my fear like a lump and arranging my face back to neutral before he could look me in the eyes. All I had time to utter was, "Lord, help me...." It was enough. Luke turned his frightened face up to me and saw strength waiting for him. Blood makes me woozy, so this was clearly God taking over. My voice was calm as I reassured him; my actions were swift and steady. Somehow I managed to keep pressure on the bleeding cut, gather the girls and our things, and find an urgent-care facility.

Later that night, after everyone was asleep, I turned on the shower, stepped in, and started to cry. My strength left me, but it was okay—all I had to do was go to bed. When danger strikes or chaos arises, we are wise to stay at our posts, remain calm, and wait for instruction.

*A bird of the air may carry your words, and
a bird on the wing may report what you say.*

ECCLESIASTES 10:20

※

The most important thing about good character is having the diligence to be consistent.

Our words matter. They are an extension of our hearts and they craft the stories that give life to our characters. If your friends can't stop gossiping even after you have taken a stand against it (with subject changes or a blatant request), then it's time to consider refining the company you keep. There is no way we can tell our children how bad gossip is, how hurtful it feels, if we are still doing it! This is something to model for our children more than we talk about it, particularly the ability to silence gossip with grace. This is an art form, and I have been lucky enough to watch some artists work. I am in awe. Some women can shift the entire climate of a gathering with their clean, fresh air. I want to be like that; I want my children to know their mother as a woman like that, not afraid to take a stand and step it up.

Our children can also be the bird that carries our words. As any preschool teacher will tell you, they hear some very interesting personal reports from the homes of their children. If we are consistently living clean and speaking with a pure heart, we won't ever have to worry who is listening.

*When the wine was gone, Jesus' mother said to him,
"They have no more wine."...His mother said
to the servants, "Do whatever he tells you."*

JOHN 2:3, 5

I am typically long-winded in my prayer requests. I go to my Father, explain the background, state exactly what I need and then go on to explain how I think it would best be accomplished. It is usually my meager mind that gets me into these predicaments, so why do I think I can direct the Creator of heaven and earth on how to get me out of them?

Mary knew exactly what she was doing. There was a situation at the wedding in Cana, she noticed it, and went to Jesus because He could solve anything. She did not blather like I would: "Hi, honey, sorry to bother you. The wine is running out, and the party is just getting going and I'd hate for everyone to have to go home early. Could you go get those six stone water jars over there? Take those and fill them with water and work a little presto-chango magic on them, will you, sweetie?"

Mary didn't even *ask* for anything. She simply stated the situation: "They have no more wine." She didn't go on and on, beg Him, or tell Him how to take care of business. I want to be so bold and trusting that I can go to God and tell it like it is. "My son has a fever." "Our flight has been canceled." Then I want to wait peacefully, knowing that He will work it out His way, in His time, and the result will be better than anything I could come up with. All I have to do is whatever He says next.

Why do you look for the living among the dead? He is not here; he has risen!

LUKE 24:5–6

Easter is the culmination of everything for us Christians: It is the pinnacle of our faith, the ultimate act of sacrifice and redemption and glory. And we get to relive the rich symbolism of it every year, with the forty days of Lent followed by Good Friday and the empty tomb on Sunday. Every year I get to go deeper with my children, digging our conversation into more fertile ground.

Every year Easter means more to me, both in terms of the journey of my own faith and in the faith of my children. Watching them reach higher levels of understanding and appreciation for what has been done for them deepens my own faith alongside theirs. I want them to understand that we have a God who *brings the dead back to life*. He restores people, and He also redeems the dreams, relationships, hopes, and visions that we thought were dead.

When I think of the stone rolling back to reveal the tattered scraps of linen and no body, I am in awe. I like to think of the stone rolling back on areas of my own life that I have sealed off as hopeless, opening up to fresh air, light, and new life. There is an undeniable Easter afterglow, warm and promising. If Jesus conquered the grave, imagine what is possible for those who believe.

What does it mean to you that He has risen? How do you convey this meaning to your children? What do you want them to know about the significance of being Easter people?

Jesus called the children to him and said, "Let the little children come to me, and do not hinder them, for the kingdom of God belongs to such as these. I tell you the truth, anyone who will not receive the kingdom of God like a little child will never enter it."

Our children have a thing or two to teach us about faith. Children are uninhibited in their worship; they truly delight themselves in the Lord and don't care what that looks like or who is watching. They are quick to believe, not muddled by years of doubt and discouragement that get in the way. They have an easier time getting the message without getting hung up on the delivery. They are naturally attracted to the light, and want to walk in it.

My children easily accept concepts that I struggle with. It's almost as if their grasp of the truth is more intimate than mine, an inherent part of them rather than something to grapple with. When Jesus says, "Come," they recognize His voice and just go.

I took my son, Luke, on a truck run for Mobile Loaves & Fishes, a ministry that delivers food to the poorer areas in Austin. Luke was in the thick of things, handing out drinks, sandwiches, and candy, happily chatting with his customers as if he did this every day. He blew me away. When I go on a truck run, I must bring some baggage along with me. My son just brought God. I packed him dinner to eat on our way home, and he gave it away to the last man in line when we ran out of food. "It's peanut butter and honey with the crust cut off, sir. You'll love it."

The Kingdom of God belongs to such as these.

From everyone who has been given much,
much will be demanded; and from the one who has
been entrusted with much, much more will be asked.

LUKE 12:48

Just as you can't possibly know about marriage by planning a wedding, you know very little about motherhood by having a baby. I remember holding Luke in the hospital, and those hazy, sleep-deprived months afterward. I remember thinking how hard it was to do this mothering thing, how tired I was, how much effort it took just to get out the door with all our supplies. Ha.

Mothering to me meant nursing, changing diapers, rocking, and trying to get him to sleep. He couldn't move or speak at that point, yet somehow I thought I had my hands full. I laugh about that today, thinking about what mothering means to me now; with a houseful of children with their own activities, assignments, ideas, emotions, and needs. Making sure they are clean and fed is the least of my worries. But I had to start someplace.

This Scripture perfectly describes the evolution of a mother. We received the ultimate gift, the highest honor, when God gave us a child to raise for Him. He entrusts us not only to keep this little person alive and safe, but also to cultivate their mind, their emotions, and their faith. It's a lot to ask because it's everything, an entire person. But it's also a fraction of what we receive, especially if we manage with God's grace to do it right.

Yes, much will be asked and demanded of us. But it will never be more than we can manage, since God Himself paired us specifically and perfectly to fit together as mother and child.

"I am the Lord's servant," Mary answered. "May it be to me as you have said." Then the angel left her.

LUKE 1:38

I think of Mary a lot in my day-to-day mothering. I stared at her statue for years at Mass, as my toddler children drove me to distraction every Sunday, wondering how she did it with such grace when I was hanging on by a thread. I have sat at the bedside of each of my sick children, praying that Mary would comfort us both. My relationship with Mary opened up when I became a mother. When I think of the kind of faith I want to build and exhibit for my children, I think of handling news or meeting challenges the way she did. "I am the Lord's servant. May it be to me as you have said."

I remember seeing the movie *The Passion of the Christ* and watching Mary, amazed at her strength. I could barely look at the screen, and she was on her hands and knees mopping up her son's blood. She didn't even leave when He was up on the cross, His life ebbing away before her eyes, even though her own heart was breaking into a million pieces. She looked up at Him with such anguish. "Flesh of my flesh, heart of my heart...," she began, and it was there, right there in those words at that moment, that I believe the entire essence of motherhood was captured.

Heart of my heart... I love my children like that, and Mary understands better than anyone.

*So they gathered them and filled twelve
baskets with the pieces of the five barley loaves
left over by those who had eaten.*

JOHN 6:13

I think of this miracle at least several times a week, more than that if I am feeling more stretched than usual. We all know the story: Jesus fed a crowd of five thousand people with five barley loaves and two fish. This was truly amazing; I can't even figure out how many pizzas to order for a birthday party.

When my to-do list is spilling onto multiple pages and my kids seem to need more and more of my time and energy and it still is barely enough, I stop what I'm doing and read this chapter again. If Jesus could do that with bread and fish, He can surely do it with me—one mother. In my morning prayer time, or a desperate shout-out later in the day, I ask Him to multiply me, to make me sufficient for everyone. I ask Him to take what I have to offer and bless it as He blessed the loaves and fishes, making enough of me to go around. That prayer has made a difference every single time. He either expands time or amplifies me. Whatever it is, it works. Suddenly I can go about my regular tasks and I don't run empty.

Even more incredible, in the same way the disciples were able to collect twelve baskets of leftovers, I find that when God multiplies me, there is something left over for me. I can somehow collect a bit of myself afterward and offer it back to Him. When, at the end of a long, busy day I find a few moments to myself, I just smile and say, "You did it again. Thanks."

Jesus replied, "You do not realize now what I am doing, but later you will understand."

❧

Any believer who has ever been through a dark or confusing time can appreciate the magnitude of this statement. Like driving in fog or getting caught in a crashing wave at the beach, nothing is ever clear when we are in the thick of it. When God takes us to a place we wouldn't necessarily choose, His reasons are never easy to understand in the moment. Only later, with the wisdom and perspective of time, might we comprehend a little bit of His working behind the scenes of our lives. Most things we won't understand until we are beyond this lifetime. I wonder sometimes when things don't make any sense to me if maybe certain things have to happen in my life just because they impact a long chain of circumstances that will make a major difference to someone else later on.

In a similar way, our children ultimately have to trust that we have their best interests at heart when we set certain standards or enforce certain rules. *No, no more sugar. It's bedtime. We don't watch that program; it's inappropriate. Homework first, then you can go. Your teammates are counting on you. We go to church on Sunday as a family. I don't care if everyone else is going, they are not my child; you are. Are her parents going to be home? You have to call and check in when you get there, and again when you are leaving. Because, I love you, that's why.*

Because I love you, that's why. That's the part we have to trust. If we can understand that much now, the details will fall into place and make more sense later.

This is what the Lord says: "I will extend peace to her like a river, and the wealth of nations like a flooding stream; you will nurse and be carried on her arm and dandled on her knees. As a mother comforts her child, so will I comfort you; and you will be comforted over Jerusalem."

ISAIAH 66:12–13

There have been, and there will be, days when we as mothers just don't know what to do. Whether we are hanging on to the last shred of our patience, constantly on the verge of tears, or at the end of all the coping skills we know, it happens. And when it does, the Lord is there.

When we think of all the times we have comforted a child through sickness, meltdowns, broken hearts, hormone roller coasters, growth spurts, disappointments, and betrayals, it is such a comfort to remember that God loves us like that. We are His daughters, and when we start to fall apart, He will comfort us *as a mother comforts her child*. He will carry us in His arms. He knows love like that; He is the Author of that love. A love that is intimate, compassionate, sacrificial, devoted, passionate, fierce, and eternally comforting.

When the weight of the responsibilities and pressures become almost too much, let's always remember that we are forever children in God's eyes. We always have a safe place where we aren't expected to know the answer, we don't have to say the right thing, and it's already understood that we aren't strong enough. What a relief.

I will give you a new heart and put a new spirit in you; I will remove from you your heart of stone and give you a heart of flesh. And I will put my Spirit in you and move you to follow my decrees and be careful to keep my laws.

EZEKIEL 36:26–27

I have gone through a couple of seasons in my life where I put my faith on the back burner and left it to simmer. I didn't stir it. I didn't check on it. When I finally recognized that I was starving, I lifted the lid and it was a charred black sludge.

I have experienced the total transformation of a heart of stone into a heart of flesh. My hardened heart thought I didn't need God, that I could handle life on my own. My hardened heart was never really happy, never really sad, never really excited, just there, going through the motions and calling it life. Thankfully, God is the finest transplant surgeon around.

When He gave me a heart of flesh, it began beating immediately. I feel things deeply now, highs and lows, joy and sadness, the intensity of living an open and authentic life. I can be hopeful, and remain so even when things don't go my way. I want to obey, even when it means my desire is delayed. I want what God wants for me, even when I don't know what it is yet or when He plans on revealing it.

I thank God that this transformation happened for me while Luke, Grace, and Bella were small. I know He used them to soften my heart, and I am so grateful to Him and to them. They keep me real. They do something sweet and then high-five one another when they make me cry, because they discussed beforehand how they knew I would. I love the way they know my heart.

It is for freedom that Christ has set us free.

GALATIANS 5:1

Too many women are trapped in relationship patterns of controlling and pleasing. These patterns may manifest themselves in a relationship with a parent, a child, a friend, a spouse, or be a pervasive pattern in every relationship.

It's a dance pattern. It requires two willing partners, their theme song, and years of practice. The steps are the same: One partner, hand on the shoulder, wields the perceived power, using his or her emotional presence to manipulate, guilt, and shame. The other partner, hand on the hip and moving backward, retreats, placates, absorbs, and disappears. It's a terrible two-step, a waltz from hell.

Christ did not set us free so that we would live lives of bondage. He came and conquered so that we would be truly free. Not just from the penalties and separation of sin, but joyfully living our freedom in all the moments of our lives. He came to change our tune. It's this kind of life that invites other people to faith.

If you are still trapped in this dance, if you are living an approximation of freedom, if you have given your power away or taken someone else's, it's time to change. If you are really ready for a new song, ask the Lord to use His might to break this pattern. Based upon your willingness and your faith, the freedom can come in degrees or blow through your life like a gale. The freedom is already ours, hard-won and timeless and waiting; we just have to occupy it.

*Each [woman] should give what [she] has
decided in [her] heart to give, not reluctantly or
under compulsion, for God loves a cheerful giver.*

2 CORINTHIANS 9:7

It's time for a little honesty here, my friend. I hate meetings. Committees give me a rash. Houseguests can really put me out. I have donated money just to avoid a luncheon or gala, and I have not been one bit cheerful about it. I sometimes hand money to homeless people just because I have made eye contact and feel guilty.

While many of the things we do can look pretty and kind on the outside, we know and God knows the motives of our hearts, and that is where this verse hits home. If we are giving on the outside, but inside we are cringing, muttering, or pouting, we have to stop and assess. We have two options in this case: either choose not to give because our gift is not really a gift, or take some time to look at our motives and find out where and why we are stuck. Giving, when our hearts are right, is a great joy. It feels good, and just like the old cliché, when it's right it's far better than receiving. Even when the giving is substantial enough to be sacrificial, like mothering, perhaps, it feels good even when it hurts.

We won't teach our children about generosity by our actions alone; they know us too well. They feel whether our hearts are present or not, whether we are cheerful about giving or not. Generosity is more than an effort to be generous; it is the reflex action of a healed heart.

An honest answer is like a kiss on the lips.

PROVERBS 24:26

I read a quote the other day (unfortunately it was nameless, so I can't thank the source) that said, "If the truth hurts, then it's probably working." It hurts to tell the truth sometimes, and sometimes it hurts to hear it. But no matter how it hurts, truth is a relief, and it's always better than a lie. A kiss on the lips is an intimate gesture, signifying the depth and closeness of a relationship. In the same way, telling someone the truth is a way of showing love.

Children ask a lot of difficult questions. My kids have asked me tough questions about Santa Claus, sex, salvation, two mommies, tampons, the tooth fairy, why they can never play at so-and-so's house, drugs and alcohol, and the demise of my own marriage. I am never expecting the question when it is lobbed to me out of left field; usually I am looking for clovers and have taken my eyes off the ball. And then there it is, their question flying straight at me, their innocence landing with a thud in the curve of my glove. And it is up to me.

This verse reminds me that by virtue of my intimate relationship with my children, and my desire to maintain it, I owe them the truth. The truth is the truth, and while it may go into greater levels of detail as they age, it is always the same at the core. In those moments, I stop what I'm doing, stall for a second to breathe deeply and exhale a prayer (*Please don't let me mess this up, mess them up; help me choose my words…*). And then I answer the question.

My yoke is easy and my burden is light.

MATTHEW 11:30

Have you ever had one of those experiences where it feels like the weight of the world is suddenly upon your shoulders, that you can barely breathe, staggering under the massive load of it all? I think it is a little reality check from the Lord, to make sure we are aware of exactly how much He is carrying around for us. We carry it for a bit, nearly collapse, then He takes it back and we are amazed and grateful. When we really stop to think about the full responsibility of raising a child or children, of maintaining a marriage, of making a living, of fitting it all in and making it work—we crack.

Because, ladies, we were never intended to do it by ourselves.

When we are living in proper alignment with God, He does all the directing and load bearing and we carry what He hands over to us. This changes from circumstance to circumstance. Sometimes we don't carry anything at all. When it gets too hard, He takes everything and we float along after Him. The strength and sweetness of Jesus in the midst of great pain is one of the biggest faith builders in a lifetime. Once you have felt it, you never forget.

The next time you feel the full, unassisted weight of your load, don't freak out. Praise Him instead. Thank Him for all the times He carries it, and often carries you. The power of praise will automatically begin the exchanging of yokes, putting the weight of your world back onto His mighty shoulders.

Immediately, something like scales fell from Saul's eyes,
and he could see again. He got up and was baptized.

ACTS 9:18

We all have areas of blindness, things around us we don't see clearly enough to understand. We also have blind spots in our own characters that can cause serious danger. Pride is one of them. It renders us absolutely clueless about ourselves and our affect on other people.

We need to pray often and humbly for the scales to be removed, which are like spiritual cataracts that keep growing back. When I can feel an energy shift or a rupture in a normally cohesive group, I often ask God, "Help me here; what am I not seeing?" Sometimes He reveals things that make me gasp. At least I then have the opportunity to try to adjust or make amends.

Sometimes He uses our friends or family members to be His nudge. Many times He uses our children to reflect the image of our behavior back to us. One time during a crabby afternoon commute, my cell phone mistakenly dialed my home phone. Our car trip was recorded on our home voice mail. When I heard my kids sass me I was sad; but when I heard my harsh reprimand I was ill. I had no idea how sharp and impatient my voice sounded when I was acting like a shrew. I know that it was no mistake that our ugly afternoon was recorded. I needed to hear myself with fresh ears at a time when I was willing to listen. I would never use that tone with my friends, and I love my children even more. What's wrong with that picture? It changed me. I saved the message, and resaved it for months. I am not perfect, but I am much more aware; and I am grateful to God for removing my scales.

He who was seated on the throne said,
"I am making everything new!"

REVELATION 21:5

The other night I was cleaning up dinner dishes and my kids were fighting. I let things go for a while, trying to let them work it out and not involve myself as a constant referee. When it became clear that they were not on a trajectory for resolution, I had to intervene. I reminded myself to think like a teacher, not like a dropout from an anger management class. I prayed for guidance and for peace. It was so loud that it was hard to get a word in edgewise. I clanged two pot lids together like cymbals and said calmly, "Put your shoes on, grab a dog, and meet me by the front door."

"Huh?" They were curious; it was after six p.m. and time to read and finish homework, not walk. I said nothing for a while; they shrugged and made faces at one another. We got out of our cul-de-sac and I said, "We are each going to say one nice thing about everyone here, including the dogs. I'll start." I went through each person and both dogs, one by one, and said something I loved about them. Bella went next, and what she said made us all stand up straighter. Luke and Grace realized we were serious, and each of them took a turn from the heart. I tried not to cry; I had no idea they really saw one another with such insight and love. We walked home on a little trail by the park, and there was no more arguing. No one remembered what they were so angry about in the first place. Before I went to bed, I praised God that He had intervened and made everything new.

A gentle answer turns away wrath.

PROVERBS 15:1

Sometimes the noise in my house and my car gets so loud that it takes effort to be heard. I have fantasized, in fact, about having a privacy window in my Volvo like they have in limousines to give the client privacy. In my case it would be about giving the driver peace. When I need to quiet or correct the masses, it's tempting in my frustration to try to raise my voice louder than the din. This rarely works, and if it does, my voice sounds more like a sergeant's than a mom's.

I notice when I volunteer at my children's school that a teacher never gets louder in order to be heard above the noise of the classroom. In fact, she gets quieter. Her words impact what's going to happen next, and the only people who will know are the ones who are listening. She speaks softly to make her point and lets the consequences of not hearing the information take care of the rest. It doesn't take long before the class quiets themselves in order to hear what she has to say.

I decided to try this approach at home. At first it was strange to speak so quietly in the face of chaos, "You will need to work it out, or the television will have to be turned off for the rest of the evening." No response because, of course, no one could hear me. *Click.* I turned off the television. Next time, they had an easier time hearing me. I tried it again when I had to deal with a difficult adult. My voice got softer in contrast to the rising emotions; and our conversation did not spiral out of control. A gentle answer not only deflects wrath (and noise and chaos); it defuses it. Try wielding your softness as your power.

You drench its furrows and level its ridges;
you soften it with showers and bless its crops.

PSALM 65:10

Family life is far from neat. If you look at it like a garden, it definitely has its share of weeds, landslides, drought, floods, unplowed territory, and dormant fields. A garden is a work in progress; it is a labor of love. It is never truly complete, because its needs change with the climate and the passing of the seasons. Some sections are in a state of preparation or rest, others in a field of bloom, others are ripe for the harvest. Mothers tend to spend the most time working in the garden; watering, weeding, fertilizing, and tilling the soil. Sometimes the work is so hard it leaves us with blisters or an aching back.

We have to remember that we are not working in this garden alone, especially during some seasons when the work feels futile or overwhelming. God is with us, making the terrain even and well-watered, and the soil rich. The garden of our family is nourished by faith, with the seeds of God's Word planted where they get the most light. The labor in our garden is pleasant toil, leaving us tired and satisfied at the end of the day. Our work is holy and our harvest is tangible; we can enjoy the fruit that grows.

> *Commit to the Lord whatever you do, and*
> *your plans will succeed.*

PROVERBS 16:3

This verse applies to the big things in life as well as to the minutiae of every day. Several mornings a week I run with my friends. Before we return to our cars, we pray out loud as we finish our run, each person taking a turn. I always ask God to forgive our sins and ordain our day, using our time and talent for His glory. I love the sacred act of committing our day to Him together, before the sun has even come out.

When I start my days this way, it seems like things flow for me, and I can accomplish what needs to be done and still have something left over. Often I find I am called and able to meet a need that I could not have anticipated or allowed for if I were operating under the limitations of my own schedule. I notice things that might otherwise escape my attention when I'm too busy scrambling.

I recommit my heart to God every morning, asking Him to strengthen my faith. I recommit my children and my parenting to Him every morning and again every time I feel stressed, confused, or start to stumble. We initially commit our children to the Lord when they are baptized. This is a formal statement to the body of Christ as a church, but for me, I need to continue to reaffirm His position and power. It's important for me when I worry about their safety to remember that they are His children before they are mine. He can protect them better than I can. He is love, so He knows what each child needs more intimately than I do and how to offer it in a way that it is best received.

May my meditation be pleasing to him,
as I rejoice in the Lord.

PSALM 104:34

❧

I used this verse for many months as a guide to limit my desire to please. By releasing myself from the obligation to please people, I could more easily focus on the ultimate goal of pleasing God. I kept this verse on a three-by-five card by my kitchen sink and read it so many times that I began to absorb it into my character. Now I take the card out only when I feel challenged or attacked in this area. I say the verse to myself when I am stuck walking through a gossip minefield. I say it to myself when I am worried about making a good impression. I say it to myself when my children are arguing. I say it to myself if I am tempted to read or comment on something that is none of my business.

If our hearts are in the right place, our desire to please God always overrides our desire to please people. This verse simply snaps us back to attention.

It's easy as mothers to get sucked into conversation that makes our heads spin. *Where are your kids going to school? Are you breast-feeding? Oh, you're not taking piano? Doing swim team? Learning Spanish? Playing soccer? Football? Sending your kids to camp? Doing this mission trip or that? Where do you work? Did you hear what happened to so-and-so? Is that organic?* The ways to get tripped up into fueling gossip or feeling inadequate are endless. So we have to choose beforehand. Is our desire to please God? Knowing the answer to that question becomes our baseline, and our backbone.

Better a dry crust with peace and quiet than
a house full of feasting, with strife.

PROVERBS 17:1

As parents we have to make tough decisions and serious sacrifices. We have to determine what is worth the effort, and what comes at too high a cost. We struggle to balance our roles and juggle the responsibilities between maintaining a house and making a home.

As a single mother, I have to be careful to ask God first before making choices that place a burden on my family. If I am gone all the time trying to earn a living, but the people I'm trying to support feel neglected—what's the point? There is such a thing as "enough." God is the only one who can offer the perspective or the power to make the choices that bring peace and maintain balance.

I can tell if I am going to God first and asking Him to direct me because when a yes comes from Him, everything falls into place. My kids are content, I don't miss the things I can't get back, and I am not stressed out. When I work His way, I am sufficient for each assignment and am not depleted when I return to my real life at home. When I go about it my own way without asking God first, I am scrambling to make ends meet, feeling like I'm rushing and shuffling my kids, and I am exhausted. No one wins—not me, not Luke, Grace, or Bella, not my work, not God. I cannot glorify Him when I am hanging on by a thread. My kids are happiest when my heart is at rest and present with theirs.

Ants are creatures of little strength, yet
they store up their food in the summer.

PROVERBS 30:25

Have you ever bought an ant farm for your kids and watched the ants quickly set up a society? They are tiny, yes, but they are bigger than we are when it comes to organization, efficiency, camaraderie, and obedience. Whether they have to scale a giant tree, carry leaves that are many times their size, relocate an entire colony, or find water in the midst of a drought, they join forces and make it happen. They take care of one another.

Ants are a perfect example for us, and our children, if we want to visualize the merits of family life. We are going to come across challenges that are too big, too heavy, too tall, or too far for one of us to manage on our own. But by working together we can do things that far surpass our stature.

When I was a child, my family moved thirteen times. There was no way my father could have accepted and excelled in these new jobs with IBM if he had been all alone. There is no way my mother could have handled relocating and resituating our lives over and over again without being fueled by the love of her family. There is no way my brother and I could have handled that many moves without our parents' making life seem like a grand adventure, to be experienced and enjoyed together. This team spirit and sense of adventure became part of me, and I bring that to my mothering today. When my kids and I have an obstacle or an adventure ahead, we seek God's guidance and march forward together. What is impossible apart is possible together, and *all* things are possible with God (Matt. 19:26).

A righteous man is cautious in friendship.

PROVERBS 12:26

I am lucky to have a close group of friends in my immediate community, and I am blessed to have a handful of friendships that have been part of me for the majority of my life. My Bible study group in Austin is made up of eleven women, including me. They are precious to me and essential to my daily walk with the Lord. My lifetime friends include Peggy, whom I have known and loved since birth, Christi since third grade, Saskia since college, and Paige since I became a mother. When I have something weighty on my heart, or I need someone to tell me like it is, I have safe places to go.

I have prayed since my children were born that they would have friendships like these. But these relationships have evolved slowly over time, trusting by degrees and loving through the layers that finally reach the heart. Once a friendship settles there, it is mine for life. I want my children to be open with their hearts, but also wise and discerning (Prov. 4:23). I want them to choose relationships with reverence. We have to pray about the people our children choose to spend time with; part of their character is forged by the company they keep.

Jonathan said to David, "Go in peace, for we have sworn friendship with each other in the name of the LORD."

1 SAMUEL 20:42

The deep friendship between David and Jonathan was one of the most beautiful examples of covenant friendship of all time. Their connection was summed up perfectly in these words: "He loved him as he loved himself" (1 Sam. 20:17). Knowing love like that is profound. It changes the landscape of our hearts and the way we look at any relationship from that point forward. Even when they were forced to part because David had to flee from Jonathan's jealous father, Saul, they departed in peace because their relationship was founded in the Lord.

When we have relationships based in Christ, we don't have to fear separation of time or distance because the friendship is cemented in the unchanging One. David and Jonathan understood this, and they had freedom because of it. In verse 4 Jonathan said to David, "Whatever you want me to do, I'll do for you." With a covenant friendship, this is understood and never taken advantage of or taken for granted.

I want relationships with each of my children that are founded in the Lord, and therefore have a core that is unchanging in our ever-changing world. I want our relationship to be based in God, so that we are not responsible for owning one another's feelings. We are responsible only to act in accordance with our loving hearts. If my primary relationship is with God, then my cup is filled by Him. Every other relationship is a gift, a sweet extravagance, an overflow. When we love like that, we can always come and go in peace.

Splendor and majesty are before him; strength and joy in his dwelling place. Ascribe to the LORD, O families of nations, ascribe to the LORD glory and strength, ascribe to the LORD the glory due his name. Bring an offering and come before him; worship the LORD in the splendor of his holiness.

1 CHRONICLES 16:27–29

No matter where we go, our families reside in the dwelling place of the Lord. How blessed are we to have a shelter to house us with strength and joy!

What kinds of offerings are we making in return?

I am working on trying to be more purposeful with my children in making offerings as ongoing worship. Going to church on Sunday is not the only offering. Scripture says God wants us to offer ourselves as a living sacrifice. Our children can understand this if we embrace it ourselves and live our lives accordingly.

Good report cards can be offered back to the Lord as gratitude for a fine mind, a strong work ethic, and good teachers. Our day can be an offering to God, praying in the morning that we would be an instrument of His peace. Our efforts in sports or fitness can be an offering to God in gratitude for our bodies. Taking Popsicles to a friend with strep throat can be an offering of thanks for our health. Babysitting for a friend and holding her baby is an offering of thanks for the gift of life. Loving one another is an offering to God in response to His love.

Our lives can be a constant expression of worship. Our children will learn to look at life that way if we explain it as we live it. Be purposeful and live out loud.

David said to Solomon, "My son, I had it in my heart to build a house for the Name of the LORD my God."

1 CHRONICLES 22:7

We all start with such good intentions.

David could not have been more loved and favored by God. He had every intention of building a house for God in the center of Jerusalem. He had a heart for God, and it seemed he would accomplish every single thing he set out to do. But he let his guard down and sin found a foothold, pulling him off track and derailing his good intentions. David ultimately admitted his sin and repented, and the Lord was merciful. David had to pay for his sin with painful consequences, but he never lost faith. Although he got to be part of the planning process for the house, it was his son Solomon who remained true to his intentions and had the honor of building God's house.

This tells me that our children learn from, and can be truly blessed by, our mistakes. As my children grow in age and understanding, I will be able to be honest with them about my journey and the snares of sin that took me off God's path. I want them to know so that they can be like Solomon, and learn from the places I've been without needing to learn from their own visits. When we share our lessons with others, especially our children (in appropriate ways), their growth redeems our time spent in the pit.

What do you have in your heart to build? Share your dreams, and your pitfalls, with your children because they may have to pick up where you leave off.

Bear with me a little longer and I will show you that there is more to be said in God's behalf.

JOB 36:2

Mile twenty-five of a marathon. A dark patch in a marriage. A rebellious teenager. The last half hour of a long road trip. Another lousy date. A rough counseling session. The last exam before graduation.

It's easy to lose heart and lose hope when we are almost there. Have you ever heard God whisper, "You're almost there," to you? If you haven't, you will. It is one of the most tender, uplifting moments in our walk with God. He has the perspective from above; He knows how much longer our endurance has to last because He allocated just enough to carry us through. When we can't see the finish line, it is tempting to give up, thinking we can't keep up the pace any longer. But when He whispers that the goal is just around the next corner, we can summon all we have left and pull through.

Can you imagine if a woman in labor, racked with pain and fear and coated in sweat, said, "Okay, enough. This hurts. I'm done." That could never happen, because if she's made it that far, her baby is going to be born, like it or not. It's exactly the same with other things in our lives that have to be born. Are we just going to say we're done and check out?

If God is asking you to bear with Him a little longer, hang in there. He has more to show you. Please don't give up. You are almost there.

*May the words of my mouth and the meditations of
my heart be pleasing in your sight, O LORD,
my Rock and my Redeemer.*

PSALM 19:14

Before I sit down to write or step up to a podium to make a speech, I pray this psalm. While I enjoy writing, giving speeches is not in my comfort zone. I can feel my heart thudding, trying to escape the confines of my chest. My breath shortens and I feel light-headed. My palms are cold and clammy and I pray my armpits aren't sweaty. My spit turns to pancake batter and no amount of water seems to thin it out. I wonder every single time why on earth God puts me up to this torture. I take a deep breath (or try to), pray Psalm 19:14, and let the Holy Spirit take over. So far, I have survived every single time.

If this verse works in crisis situations like a speech, I wondered, how would it work in the regular challenges of motherhood, like a chaotic school morning trying to get everyone out the door? Or a difficult conversation that was about to take place? I decided to try it.

The verse works like a quick trip to the chiropractor; *click, click, click, click,* and the structure behind my character realigns with God. Once my heart is in the right spot, my words seem to want to follow. Try it for yourself. Commit this verse to memory and pray it when you can feel your pulse giving you a warning. Before a word comes out, you will have rededicated yourself to our Redeemer. He will translate the rest.

Before this faith came, we were held prisoners
by the law, locked up until faith should be revealed.

GALATIANS 3:23

⁂

Law says, "Obey, or you will suffer the consequences." Faith says, "Your heart will change, and you will want to live in obedience."

God doesn't want our begrudging compliance. He wants obedience rooted in love; a desire to please that goes far beyond mere avoidance of punishment. This is why faith changes our hearts. Our motivation resides here, and our decisions spring from our intentions. The motivation of avoiding pain yields a different outcome than desiring intimacy. God first invites us into a relationship with Him, then He explains the rules as we go. This is the way I want to parent.

I want my children to love and respect me, and I want our relationship to deepen in intimacy as they grow. I want them to want to obey me because they trust that I hold their best interests close to my heart. Without that component, I am simply making and enforcing rules like a dictator. Fear of punishment will work for only so long, and then children will simply choose deception because they might avoid getting caught, at least some of the time. This is no way to live or raise children.

When my children are grown, I want them to desire a relationship and connection with me. I want adulthood to move our relationship to the next level, not represent a long-awaited escape. This is not only a bounty to enjoy later; this is a harvest to be cultivated today.

*You were running a good race. Who cut in on you
and kept you from obeying the truth? That kind of
persuasion does not come from the one who calls you.*

GALATIANS 5:7–8

❧

I have a ceramic tile in my office that says, "Run your own race." It is leaning against a photograph of me, smiling huge, after crossing the finish line of a thirty-one-mile trail race. If you think I'm one of those crazy talented athletes, think again. I am just like you. I never thought I could do anything like that race. At one point, I couldn't even run three miles. My endurance was built up by experiences over time, not by any special gift.

The "Run your own race" quote is precious to me. Anytime I start to pay too much attention to people around me (particularly in a running race), I lose confidence and lose heart. I get distracted. I go faster than my pace to try to match someone else's, and I don't have what I need to make it to the finish. That thirty-one-mile race was different. I looked at it like a journey, not a race. My mind was set on crossing the line, not on my watch, and I had a list of all the reasons why I simply would not give up.

Don't let other people cut in on you and break your stride. Don't try to match anyone else's pace; their goals might not be the same as yours. Stay focused on your own race. Pay attention to where you are and how you are doing; don't waste time and energy looking at everyone else, making incorrect and unproductive comparisons. Our children need to learn this vital lesson as early as possible so they can run the race marked out for them.

In his heart a man plans his course;
but the LORD determines his steps.

PROVERBS 16:9

On the morning we were supposed to race in a half-marathon, Paige was suffering from the onset of plantar fasciitis. We were sitting on our hotel beds while she was trying to stretch, and she came across this Scripture. It spoke volumes to us that morning, not knowing what would happen when we got out on the course. Paige might have it planned in her head that she was going to run thirteen miles, but God might have had something else in mind for her.

We can put our desires before God, and if they are also His desires for us, we can feel totally confident that He will help us get there. But how our adventures play out along the way is not ordained by us. We have to trust Him to get us there. The Lord is going to determine our steps, every hour of every day, as we walk along in this journey.

We have no idea when we pick up our feet where they are supposed to land; the key is to follow the light. God is always in the light. He illuminates each step, through His Word, through His people, and through His manipulation of circumstances as He opens and closes doors. When we don't know where the light is, we need to stop until we're sure. This is an important principle in learning how to navigate our own faith journeys; and a crucial responsibility when we are leading children as we go.

The crucible for silver and the furnace for gold,
but the LORD tests the heart.

PROVERBS 17:3

If you have ever been through a season of testing, you know the "Ouch" I'm referring to. It is not a pleasant experience to be pruned. It is not a treat to walk through fire. A pit is not a pretty place. But oh, the view on the other side!

When the onset of such a season comes upon you, it will feel like a mistake at first. Like a bad surprise or an inappropriate gift you want to return. The sooner you can grasp that, yes, this is your time, the sooner you can get on with it. We have an initial, simple, yet enormous decision to be made at the onset of a trial. Are we going to turn to God or are we going to go into the dark? If we choose to turn to God, then He is invited to meet us in our testing. And what happens there is a gift that cannot be received *any other way*.

We learn the basic components of faith—love that leads to trust. After we can trust, we can comply. By this, I mean, we can agree with His purposes for us (even when we don't understand them yet), and we can learn what He intends for us to learn during this season. The lessons come, the decisions are made, and we learn about obedience. It is there that we find peace. Peace leads to freedom, and before we know it we are out on the other side of the experience, our feet on solid ground.

If you have not been through one of your seasons yet, I want to encourage you. Be on guard, be watchful, be ready. But do not be afraid.

He who conceals his sins does not prosper, but whoever confesses and renounces them finds mercy.

PROVERBS 28:13

My parents always had a thing about integrity. "Just tell the truth, and it will never be as bad as if you don't," was their philosophy. Once, in high school my class was taking a test and my teacher stepped out of the room. The class started talking and goofing off, and when she stepped back into the room she was furious. She yelled at us and said, "If you were one of the people talking, raise your hand right now!" I had said something to a friend, so I raised my hand. The room had been full of chatter, but I was the *only one* who raised my hand. She used me as the example and slapped a detention on my desk.

I came home from school and told my parents what had happened. My dad had steam coming out of his ears. He wanted to talk to my teacher. The next morning, he told her, "We have spent a lifetime teaching our daughter about integrity. She was the only one who had the courage to tell the truth, and you chose to punish her. You made a very poor decision and I wanted you to know." My teacher was shaking in her boots. She quickly apologized and said I didn't have to do the detention. "Of course she does, she was talking during a test. That's not why I'm here. This conversation was about you." And he turned and went to work.

Twenty years have passed, but I have not forgotten that. My earthly father is like that. My heavenly Father is like that. Speak the truth, confess your sins, and we can move forward together.

*[The Lord] satisfies your desires with good things
so that your youth is renewed like the eagle's.*

PSALM 103:5

Sometimes I go long stretches of time being the organized, efficient, homework-and-chores taskmaster mom. I must appear to my children like a prim woman holding a clipboard and a watch. I can take this for only so long. And then, as my kids will attest, the kid inside Mom has to come out. And she does.

One day I hollered at the kids for getting in the pool in their school clothes. I came running outside, yelling about how much trouble they were in, all the way to the edge of the pool...and mid-rant, I did a cannonball, in my clothes. One night we stopped at this cute cupcake place on our way home from dinner. My frosting-covered kids were playing tag next door in a big grassy lot and I stood there watching them, feeling so mom-like with my heavy purse on my shoulder and my keys in my hand. I kicked off my shoes, dropped my purse on the grass, and chased them around for twenty minutes.

I don't want my kids to miss out on knowing me just because I have to take care of them. Why would I share my wild sense of humor, goofiness, and spontaneity with my friends and hide the fun parts of me from my kids? If they can't see me let my hair down once in a while, I may as well cut it off. My mom says, "Count the day lost when you don't laugh with your kids." Yes, parenting is work, but it's also a chance to be a kid all over again. Don't miss it.

A stingy man is eager to get rich and
is unaware that poverty awaits him.

PROVERBS 28:22

When we fear going without, our tendency is to hoard. This is true in a financial sense, and it is also true in an emotional sense. A financially stingy person never reaches for the check, always looks for the cheap solution, and never contributes to charity or helps someone in need. They are too self-centered and too materialistic to be generous. An emotionally stingy person withholds compliments and affection. They don't want to get involved in situations that might require intimacy or compassion. They are too busy to listen. Their heart is too closed off to be generous.

In both cases, the desire to hoard, withhold, and guard has the opposite effect of the desired outcome. We don't end up having more—money, energy, love, or happiness—because when we keep things to ourselves, we end up with far less. Those suffering from emotional and spiritual poverty are the poorest people of all. God calls us to be cheerful givers, and He has established spiritual principles to ensure that generosity is blessed and rewarded. Give, and you have more to give. Skimp, and you have less for yourself.

Our children will grow up with generous hearts if that is what they have known and experienced. They will freely give of their resources if they come from a family who doesn't hoard their own. It's important to teach our children that we are blessed by being a blessing.

He tends his flock like a shepherd: He gathers
the lambs in his arms and carries them close to his
heart; he gently leads those that have young.

ISAIAH 40:11

What a beautiful image of God's heart for mothers! He brings all of us along together, protected and watched over, to greener pastures. He gently leads us because we have young ones in our care. How sweet that we are *specifically* mentioned here.

Leading "gently" implies that there is no tugging, prodding, shoving, threats, or manipulation involved. We have to know the voice of the Shepherd, the specific feel of His hand, if we are going to follow a gentle lead. We can't be living so loudly that His voice is drowned out. We can't be pulled in so many directions that His touch is indistinguishable. In order to be gently led, we have to develop a certain sensitivity to our Shepherd. Our obedience and discipleship spring forth from love and respect, not through force.

Where is God trying to lead you right now? If you get quiet enough to hear His voice, if you separate yourself from the chaos, can you feel the guidance of His hands? Find some time today to be alone with the Lord. Ask Him how He wants you to tend to your flock. Tell Him how much you want to follow Him, staying close by His side. Pray for those who need to be carried right now. Who are they? What is it they need? Ask Him how you can best intercede on behalf of His lambs. If you need to be carried right now, draw closer to Him and make your needs known. He longs to comfort you and carry you. He longs to hold you close to His heart.

All beautiful, you are, my darling; there is no flaw in you.

SONG OF SONGS 4:7

As hard as this is to accept, without shame or self-deprecation, this is how God sees each of us. If we are ever going to convince our children of their own beauty, we have to accept and embody our own. What is more beautiful than being a child of God? By allowing God to transform us into His likeness so we can truly see ourselves as beautiful, we can offer our beauty back to the world.

I want my daughters to grow up knowing that they are beautiful, that they are enough, exactly as they are. I want to communicate this fact to them in a way that goes beyond skin-deep, in a way that will reach their cores. I want to root this inside them in an unconditional way that will remain with them as gangly teenagers, postpartum moms, if they are feeling middle-aged and lumpy, or feeble, old, and gray. Beauty is a gift from God, unearned and unmatched. Accepting and acknowledging it with grace and humility, regardless of our outer appearance, is a mark of a faithful woman.

I want my son to grow up knowing his own worth and his own beauty, as a boy and as a man. I want him to have eyes that see the true beauty of a woman, so he can recognize and appreciate the depth of a godly woman. If, as his mother, I don't embrace my own beauty, how will he learn to honor the beauty of his wife?

We have to be able to accept God's love, His definition of us and His viewpoint, if we are going to be able to pour His love out in a way that lavishes others. Let yourself sparkle.

*I am the LORD, your God, who takes hold of your right
hand and says to you, Do not fear; I will help you.*

ISAIAH 41:13

In the period surrounding my divorce I had panicky moments,
feeling sweaty and light-headed, unable to get a deep breath. I
don't call them panic attacks, because panic wasn't attacking
me; rather, it was the enemy and his disguise was fear. *How am
I ever going to survive this? How am I going to raise these kids?
How can I change my vision when the picture I wanted is gone?
How am I going to handle everything all by myself?*

Aha! The answers were revealed, as they often are, buried
within the questions: I am not going to handle anything all by
myself; I can't and I don't want to anyway. I am going to get
through this with God's grace. If you are in a place where you
feel overwhelmed—maybe with a crying baby, or a whining,
disobedient toddler, maybe a wayward teen, maybe walking on
eggshells with your son—or daughter-in-law—listen to what
God says to you: "Do not fear; I will help you." Offer Him your
right hand and let Him lead you. He is the Lord, our God.

Fear does not come from God, so reject it. Pull off evil's
disguise and call his bluff, just like the kids at the end of every
Scooby-Doo episode. "Why look, it's Farmer Ted!" Except that
it's evil, and it needs to go back in the dark where it came
from.

I will lead the blind by ways they have not known,
along unfamiliar paths I will guide them;
I will turn the darkness into light before them
and make the rough places smooth. These are
the things I will do; I will not forsake them.

ISAIAH 42:16

I know a little girl who has recently been diagnosed with Batten disease. This disease presents itself first with the onset of blindness, then mental deterioration, and ultimately death before a child reaches his or her teens. There is no current cure or method of postponement. As a parent, when you get news like that about your beloved daughter, what do you do with that? How do you cope? How do you look for peace when your daughter's vision is growing dim and hazy and you know how the story ends?

Her parents are beautiful, faithful people. They handle her path of blindness by admitting their own. God is leading all of them along this unfamiliar path. He is lighting their steps, helping them to see the positive even in the darkness. He smoothes out their rough places, or carries them when the terrain is simply too rugged to traverse.

How do we handle it when God gives us darkness? Children handle grief by still managing to find joy in the midst of it. They turn their freckled faces up to the sun. They go high on the swing. They draw pictures, sing songs, and laugh with their friends. The point is that they don't stop living. They don't shut down the way we do. They aren't crippled by fear, and what-ifs, and oh-nos. They are blind to tomorrow and they let God lead them today.

*Anyone who loves his son or daughter more
than me is not worthy of me.*

MATTHEW 10:37

❧

I have a friend who, until recent years, struggled in certain areas in her relationships with her grown sons. She was always trying to figure out how to stay connected to them, how to be close to their wives and children, how to spend more time together. One day, God asked her if she cared more about what her son thought than what He thought. She was speechless. How could she, a godly woman, have made an idol of her children? This was a blatant violation of the first commandment, a serious sin. Ouch.

She repented and regrouped. She started over in her heart, with God laying the groundwork in her relationships with her children going forward. What she found was precisely the connection and the closeness that she had been longing for! When God assumed His proper position in her life, all other relationships were unable to take more than their good and godly share.

She allowed the Lord to help her navigate the complicated waters of mothering adult children. Even with my younger children, I have to be very conscious not to let my love for them assume first place in my life. I have to be extremely clear that I am getting my emotional needs met by God first. Otherwise, I might unknowingly put an unhealthy burden on them that I would regret later.

Our role is never over; our growth never ends. My wise friend reminds me of this often. Being a good mother is a lifetime pursuit.

*You hypocrite, first take the plank out of your own eye,
and then you will see clearly to remove the speck
from your brother's eye.*

MATTHEW 7:5

This verse is a powerful slam against judging others. We have so much work to do on ourselves that we should almost be too tired to examine other people's shortcomings.

As our children grow, or if they are already grown, we find we are no longer able to just talk the talk. They soon will see if our talk and walk match, stride for stride. We can't correct them in areas where we aren't living clean ourselves. We can't expound on the poison of gossip if we are slinging mud around every time we pick up the phone. We can't talk about responsibility if we drink three cocktails with dinner and then drive our family home. We can't talk about generosity when we speed past the homeless man on the corner and make a remark about laziness. We can't talk about the importance of our faith and show up at church only on Christmas and Easter.

It might be an interesting exercise to take some time to journal about your values, the most important things you want to pass down to your children. Then take some time in prayer and ask God to reveal if there are any areas where you are living out of alignment with those values. Once He shows us where our talk and walk conflict, we can own it and make it right. Then we will have something to teach our children, at every age.

Do not give dogs what is sacred; do not throw
your pearls to pigs. If you do, they may trample them
under their feet, and then turn and tear you to pieces.

MATTHEW 7:6

This is a hard lesson to teach, because it's so hard to learn for ourselves. We want to be generous and loving people, and we want our children to grow up to be people like that. But the fine line has to do with guarding our hearts as the wellsprings of life (Prov. 4:23). We have to ask God for discernment as to how and where we invest our hearts, and the care we take to keep our thoughts and bodies pure.

I don't want my children to be reckless with their hearts, souls, minds, or bodies. I want them to save and savor their finest gifts for the people and the passions that are of God. I know how it feels to throw my pearls to pigs. I have wasted thoughtfully chosen words on people who are not in a place to listen. I have wasted my affection on totally unworthy recipients. I have revealed my soul to a few people who were never meant to have even a glimpse of a woman like me. I have, at times, given myself away.

And the Lord has redeemed all of that. He has shown me a new way of tending to my heart, neither closed off nor wastefully open. Our pearls are precious, ladies. Let's guard them and polish them, sharing them appropriately. Let's show our children how precious their hearts are. Only by learning reverence for what is sacred will they understand the value of pearls. Only by being surrounded by people of goodness will they ever know how to recognize a pig.

*Small is the gate and narrow the road that
leads to life, and only a few find it.*

MATTHEW 7:14

I am horrible with directions. I may have been somewhere fifty times, and I still have to ask again how to get there. I print out directions off the Internet before I travel, to and from destinations, because I can't remember where I came from or follow directions in reverse order. It's really sad. It used to give me plenty of shame and anxiety. Now I just roll with it, and if my kids are with me, Luke can usually get us back home (he's ten).

So you can imagine how unsettling this Scripture verse is for someone who can hardly find her way around her hometown. Sometimes I wonder if I am doomed. If I have trouble finding major highways, how on earth will I ever find a small gate and narrow road?

I took up trail running, partly to give my knees a break and partly to overcome my fear of getting lost. I worried I would be left in the woods for days, vultures circling above my body. But the opposite happened; I started to pay greater attention to my surroundings. I noticed the funky tree trunk where I needed to stay to the left. I began to see things I would have simply overlooked in the past.

Maybe our faith journeys are like that; the more we practice, the more we learn to recognize trail markers. We have to know what to look for if we have any hope of finding our way home.

Likewise every good tree bears good fruit, but a bad tree bears bad fruit. A good tree cannot bear bad fruit, and a bad tree cannot bear good fruit. Every tree that does not bear good fruit is cut down and thrown into the fire. Thus, by their fruit you will recognize them.

MATTHEW 7:17–20

As we can see, it's imperative to make sure we are good trees. We have to accept our pruning from God and continually monitor our branches and leaves. Our roots must run deep into solid ground and be able to find living water no matter the climate or conditions. The fruit we bear is indicative of the health of our trees—our ministry, our work, our charity, our relationships, our children.

For anyone struggling right now with a troubled child of any age, maybe a child into drugs or alcohol, maybe a child with a behavior or discipline problem, maybe a child suffering from a mental or emotional issue, maybe a child who has blatantly departed from the faith, an adult child who cannot sustain his or her marriage or be a good parent to your grandchildren; whatever the case may be, take heart. You are a good tree, and this means that your children are good fruit. No matter what the circumstances look like right now, it is not over. God has not finished writing your family's story. The ink is not dry; the pen is still moving across the pages of time. The plot and the characters can, and will, change. But this does not change: A good tree cannot bear bad fruit. Be encouraged and be hopeful.

Jesus said to the centurion, "Go! It will be done just as you believed it would." And the servant was healed at that very hour.

Some people quit smoking cold turkey; other people chew Nicorette gum for years. Some people forgive and get on with it, some need to see a therapist for years. Healing is always available to us. It just looks different for different people. Regardless of what needs to heal, the catalyst is belief. We have to believe we can live without cigarettes. We have to believe we can live without resentment. We have to believe in an almighty God who makes all things possible.

What an amazing statement: *It will be done just as you believed it would.* This could mean, "My child failed algebra, just as I believed he would," or it could mean, "I got that promotion, just as I believed I would." I don't know about you, but it makes me want to be more intentional with my thinking. When we give voice to negative thoughts or beliefs, we give them power. When we speak healing and life and faith, we give those positive things power too.

What is going on in your life right now that needs healing? What looms out there that seems so big you secretly wonder if God can handle it? Confess these things to God, including areas of unbelief, and ask for His healing. This verse clearly gives an example of cooperation with the Lord. He heals; that is His part. We believe; that part is ours. The servant was healed at that very hour. We can be, too.

He replied, "You of little faith, why are you so afraid?"
Then he got up and rebuked the winds and
the waves, and it was completely calm.

MATTHEW 8:26

Storms freak me out, and I live in Texas where we have some big ones. I don't mind the rain. I don't mind the boom of thunder, or the answering crack of lightning. I don't mind the dramatic temperature changes. What I can't abide is the wind.

I am not sure where, how, or why this fear originated, but when I see bending trees or hear the howling sound outside my windows, I wig out. The wind in my chimney makes such a haunted sound that even my earplugs provide no relief from the sleeplessness it causes. My friends even text-message me in the middle of the night: "Windy out. You okay?" Clearly I am not okay, when I'm reading their text underneath my covers by the glow of the screen. I often wish my kids would wake up and be scared enough to come downstairs and sleep in my room. But they aren't afraid; they don't even wake up.

I asked a therapist about it once, and she laughed and told me it was a control thing. I wanted to be in control, and the howling outside reminded me I wasn't. Oh, dear. It's a trust issue, of course. My trust in the One who controls the wind should trump my fear every time. Whether the tempests in our lives are natural or spiritual, we need to have faith that Jesus can calm the storm. We can be at peace in our tiny craft of life, even as we are tossed around on mighty seas. We are never lost; we are never beyond radio contact; we are never beyond the reach of His hand to save us.

*The rain came down, the streams rose, and
the winds blew and beat against that house; yet it did
not fall, because it had its foundation on the rock.*

MATTHEW 7:25

My parents raised me to have a foundation of faith. I grew
older and slipped in and out of seasons of reverence, but when
the first significant storm came in my life, though it was terrifying, my house did not fall. In fact, as the storm raged outside and shook my house, my faith held steady and then grew,
making everything else I cared so much about before seem
useless and insignificant. This is what I want to provide for
my children. I want to lay such a solid foundation on the Rock
of Christ that no matter what storms blow through their lives,
I know they will be structurally sound and protected. We have
no guarantees that we will be here when those storms come for
our children, either nearby or still here on earth, so we must
work hard now to account for that possibility.

We can find greater peace in the knowledge that even if our
children have seasons of waywardness or lukewarm faith, we know
the foundation is there and cannot be changed. Even if a storm
tears a house apart by its boards, it is possible to rebuild on a strong
foundation. A strong foundation is taught, is explained, is spoken,
is shown; but most of all, it is lived. The choices we make every
day become the cement of that foundation. Let's make it level
and thick. Let's make it something we would be proud to put a
handprint in, bury a cross in, or carve the initials of our families
in when the top layer is still wet. How else will our children ever
remember who they are if everything else is ripped away?

I thank Christ Jesus our Lord, who has given me strength,
that he considered me faithful, appointing me to his service.

1TIMOTHY 1:12

I was burrowed in bed one Mother's Day morning, sheets pulled up over me, our dog at my side. I was under strict orders not to get out of bed without permission. I could hear a ruckus going on in the kitchen, Luke barking orders and subsequent grumblings from the sisters who were getting overruled. There was a lot of banging, thudding, and other questionable noises.

My door burst open. "Happy Mother's Day!" All three angled themselves to carry a teetering tray. On it was a flower, a cup of coffee, a plateful of toaster waffles swimming in syrup, and a glass of orange juice dangerously close to being knocked over. Grace was carrying the newspaper in her other hand. Bella had a book she made me at school: "I love my Mom because..." They proceeded to bring in other gifts, mostly items from around the house carefully selected and wrapped many times over in Christmas paper, hermetically sealed in duct tape. Luke made me coupons.

As I looked around my bed, covered in children, newspaper, strips of duct tape, and bunched up balls of wrapping paper, it occurred to me (not for the first time) that I might be the luckiest woman on the planet. My life isn't perfect by any means, but having these children is more than I could ever want or ever deserve. They have made my life and molded my heart in a way that would otherwise be impossible. I praise God on Mother's Day and every day that He considered me faithful and appointed me to Luke, Grace, and Isabelle.

*Because of the man's boldness he will get up and
give him as much as he needs.*

LUKE 11:8

In this verse, Jesus is talking about the hungry midnight snacker who goes to his neighbor's house in the wee hours looking for some bread. He keeps knocking, and eventually the man gets up and feeds him. The man isn't feeding his neighbor just because he is hungry; he is feeding his neighbor because he was bold enough to pound on his door in the middle of the night.

Jesus is telling us that persistence pays off, particularly in prayer. He goes on in chapter 11 to remind us that if we will give good things to our children, imagine what God will give to His (v. 13).

But if we are going to approach the Master of the universe and kneel before His throne of grace, we can't just mumble something quickly and rush off. We have to be persistent in prayer, confessing our sins, praising His might, and making petitions that are in line with God's will. If He doesn't answer right away, we can't have such feeble faith that we automatically assume our request has been returned, stamped "denied." We have to continue to knock and hold all our expectations in faith.

The old cliché says, "If at first you don't succeed, try, try again." It doesn't say, "If at first you don't succeed, throw in the towel and pout, then quickly settle for less." God wants to bless His children abundantly. Let's pray with our children for what we need, and for what we want. Big dreams require big faith.

We live by faith, not by sight.

2 CORINTHIANS 5:7

Have you ever gotten ready for something important and spent so much time worrying about how you look that nothing looks good anymore? And you leave the house late and in a huff, a pile of clothes on the floor of the closet? Have you ever made a hasty judgment about someone based on appearance, only to admit later that you were foolishly wrong? Have you ever fallen for someone because you thought they were cute, and later learn that they aren't even nice?

Appearances are deceiving. Our eyes see what we want them to see, because we want our impressions to match our expectations. But if, as believers, we give too much credence to our sight, we miss out on the gift of discernment from the Holy Spirit. Things may indeed look one way, but they may actually be very different. If we learn to live by faith, we can process what we see in a spiritual context. We can ask God to make up for our lack of vision and supply us with His own perspective or framework. We can be free from making assumptions about ourselves, other people, and situations. What we view as bad news might be the best thing that ever happened to us. What seems like good news at first might be danger in disguise.

We have to ask. And we have to teach our children to ask. They have to ask us if they aren't sure, and we have to direct them to God.

"Martha, Martha," the Lord answered,
"you are worried and upset about many things,
but only one thing is needed. Mary has chosen what is
better, and it will not be taken away from her."

LUKE 10:41–42

All multitasking control freaks need to copy down this verse and stick it up around the house, on the dashboard of the car, in the calendar, by the phone. My friends and I even say to each other, "Easy, Martha…" when we can see someone is losing perspective. Martha is miffed because she and her sister, Mary, are hosting the Son of God and she is doing all the work while Mary chills out in His company. She expects Jesus to reprimand her lazy sister, and He compliments Mary instead!

As women, particularly mothers, we do too much! We have to-do lists that dwarf Santa's December master list. Mary is busy enjoying the Lord's company, and He says *she has chosen what is better.* What can we learn from that? Two thousand years later, and we are still struggling with the same things. Not only are we still too busy striving and doing (instead of being and learning), but we are still making catty judgments about others who we think have it easier than we do or are slacking off.

The Lord still invites us to sit at His feet. We think we are too busy solving things on our own to take time out when, in fact, the time spent in His presence is the path to peace every time. If you don't even consciously know when you're spinning, ask a friend to remind you, "Easy there, Martha."

Do not let the sun go down while you are still angry,
and do not give the devil a foothold.

EPHESIANS 4:26–27

✺

We have to let our children acknowledge and experience the full range of human emotions. After all, we don't want them to grow up to be numb or emotionally constipated. Anger isn't as enjoyable as joy, but it still has to be welcomed and understood. However, it is not invited to stay the night. Whatever it takes, whether it is an argument with your husband, your mother, your child, or between any family members, it has to be worked out before bed. Often, I have used this Scripture as my trump card—we absolutely have to find some form of peace or forgiveness before bed. Even if we don't completely agree, it's okay; we can still hash that out or simply accept it tomorrow. But the bad feelings that lead to division and isolation, those must go before we turn in for the night.

If we don't, as this verse describes, the enemy will have a foothold. If you have ever been so upset that you can't sleep, you know exactly what this feels like. As the sleepless hours tick by, the problem grows and the hurtful feelings multiply. By morning we are so exhausted we have lost hope and perspective. We are doomed to another day of anxiety, emptiness, and disconnect. This is exactly what the enemy had in mind.

We must return to a place of love before bed. "When you lie down, your sleep will be sweet" (Prov. 3:24).

The LORD your God has enlarged your
territory as he promised you.

DEUTERONOMY 12:20

When we do well with the assignments we have been given, God rewards us with more and bigger assignments. Our preparenting lives were boot camp before we were given the awesome responsibility of motherhood. God watched how we handled other relationships and other situations before He entrusted us with one (or more) of His children. Our territory not only encompasses our roles and responsibilities; it is also our circle of influence. As we handle certain conversations, issues, or circumstances with grace, God sees that we are working for His glory. He is pleased and gives us more to do.

If your plate is full, instead of being overwhelmed, be grateful. Consider that your plate might be full (unless you have overloaded it yourself with busyness, which is a different story) because God is equipping you to make a difference in many directions. He will never give us more assignments than we can handle gracefully. He is not a God of confusion; He is a God of clarity, possibility, and truth. The way we raise our children equips them to then go out and have their own growing territory. The way we live our lives and raise our children is evangelism without words, spreading the message of God's love across the earth.

Woe to you who are complacent in Zion.

AMOS 6:1

Complacency is getting so comfortable that you forget to lock your doors. It's buying elastic-waist pants instead of stepping on the scale. It's assuming your husband knows you love him. It's being used by technology instead of using it. It's accepting a C when you are an A student. It's going to the same restaurant every single time. It's a perpetually dirty car. It's Internet porn instead of intimacy. It's not flossing then avoiding the dentist. It's a debit card without a budget. It's putting up with bad manners because it's easier than constantly correcting the children. It's prepackaged, preservative-laden food. It's going to a job every day that you hate. It's making your neighbors look at a shaggy, unkempt lawn. It's going through the motions and leaving your heart behind.

Nowhere is complacency more dangerous than in our faith. Being lukewarm spiritually leads to blindness, rationalization, loss of integrity, and sloppy choices. Complacency is the laziness in small things that leads to big problems like troubled children, marital affairs, or being laid off from work. It's thinking that spirituality is a substitute for faith. It's thinking that you feel boxed in at church, without considering the possibility that the box might actually be a hedge of protection.

> *Go; I will help you speak and will teach*
> *you what to say.*

EXODUS 4:12

It's very intimidating when we realize our words have impact, so we better make them count. I feel this way, totally humbled and unworthy, when I step up to a microphone to talk to a group of women about their faith or their fitness. I feel this way when I'm about to be interviewed and I want to make my words count for God's glory. I feel this way when I need to discipline or have a serious conversation with one of my children, knowing that my words are going straight into their memory banks and they will forever remember how I handled this situation, for better or for worse.

I joke that this is the "fraud complex." Like eventually people are going to find out that I have absolutely no business doing what I do. Honestly, I would rather feel like a fraud with a seeking and humble spirit than feel like I had all the answers and be a fool.

Sometimes a situation has the benefit of time to pray and prepare. Other times it is thrust into our laps with no lead time at all. In moments like that I whisper out loud or in my head, *"Be with me."* And I know it's simple, but I feel God's presence in response. He is always with me, but maybe I just need to make sure I feel Him. God does not put us in places so we will fail. When we are walking closely with Him, He sets us up and sees us through. He will choose our words, be our filter, guide our timing, and open the hearts of the recipients. We have to trust this enough to be able to just go.

I consider that our present sufferings are not worth comparing with the glory that will be revealed in us.

ROMANS 8:18

❦

When people remind me or ask questions about my IVF treatments, I can barely remember that I got pregnant that way. What was so all-encompassing to me at the time—all the shots, treatments, waiting, disappointment, and elation—is barely a blip in my memory today. Same with labor and delivery. I know it hurt, and I know the recovery took a while, but so what?

Remember back to when you had a tiny newborn and your whole day was made up of nursing or bottles, diapers, and snippets of sleep? We all thought that's what being a mom *felt like*, what being a mom was all about. Or how "hard" and exhausting it was when we had a tiny baby in a sling or in an infant seat—*hard?* They couldn't move! They couldn't argue or escape! That was such a tiny little slice of time compared to raising and knowing a person. I love to reflect on those things and remind myself that I had no idea what stretched out before me. What I understood and what was really going on were two totally different things; I can see that now with the perspective of time passing.

I remind myself, my friends, and my children of this very thing. What seems like suffering right now will be only a blip on your memory radar at some point, a mere strand in the tapestry of your life. It's hard to see our way beyond suffering when we are mired in the thick of it, but we have to lift our eyes up and away. There isn't any pain or suffering that can diminish the glory of God within us.

*If any of them do not believe the word, they may be
won over without words by the behavior of their wives.*

1 PETER 3:1

Won over without words. How beautiful to think we can live
in a way that offers a silent and open invitation to believe.
This passage refers to unbelieving husbands, but it can easily
be applied to skeptical children, relatives, friends, or cowork-
ers. If we live lives marked by joy, contentment, and serenity,
regardless of circumstances (a true mark of real faith), we
make people curious about us. *How is she able to handle that?
Why isn't she upset? Is she always in a good mood? How come
she isn't always in a rush? How does she have time to listen? She
makes it look easy.*

Of course we can make it look easy when we have the
Lord to do the heavy lifting on our behalf! We are not responsible for other people's belief or unbelief. We can take no credit
for faithful children. We can take no blame for children who
have departed the faith, if we have done everything possible to
lay a firm foundation. We are to do our parts, and let God do
His. Our expectations and our timing are not the barometer
for belief; God holds the hearts of those we love. Faithful children (and husbands) recognize God's voice as He calls their
names, already written in the Book of Life.

If we can evangelize through our choices, our actions, our
peace, our energy, our compassion—we are living as Christ
intended. Jesus invited people into His presence, and as His
disciples, we are asked to do the same.

A man reaps what he sows.

GALATIANS 6:7

The finest method of discipline is the one that God uses, allowing the natural consequences of an action to teach the lesson.

Bella was really sassing me the other day. We had plans for a playdate and I had told Bella that I was not going to tolerate any more sass, and the next step was consequences only, no words. She sassed me on the way to gymnastics. Afterward, Luke and Grace piled into our friend's car and headed to the playdate. Bella got into my car alone. "Where are we going?" she asked.

"You and I are going home. Only Luke and Grace are going to be able to go." She was incredulous. She screamed and cried the whole way home. When she finally quieted down, I hugged her and said, "I'm sad for you, too. I'm sad that you made the choice to be disrespectful to me again. I hope you make a better choice next time so we can have some fun." There is a big difference between being punitive and teaching that choices have consequences.

I explained to Bella that God handles things the same way with me. I read a warning in the Bible. Should I then decide to go my own way and step outside His direction, the consequences are mine to bear. But if I decide to obey and follow Him, good consequences like peace and blessing are mine as well. She understood. Sometimes the best parenting is simply getting out of God's way.

You will know that I am the LORD; those who
hope in me will not be disappointed.

ISAIAH 49:23

This verse does not say that those who hope in the Lord will be disappointed only sometimes, or that those who hope in the Lord will be disappointed only when something goes wrong. It says that if we hope in Him, we will not be disappointed. So what's the trick? We all get disappointed; life has its ups and downs. What does this mean?

The more I read this and pray for understanding, the more I realize that maybe it's hard for me to comprehend because I am not there yet. I do know some people who are never disappointed. No matter what life slings at them, they instantly adjust and accept and are grateful. They never allow a spirit of disappointment or discouragement to creep in; they just don't tolerate it. They keep hoping, placing their trust in our sovereign God again and again. They don't miss a beat. And the people I know who are like this are not happy-go-lucky because they have had perfect and easy lives. They are real people with real challenges, walking out real faith journeys. Their lives are beautiful adventures with God.

Imagine living like this. Imagine parenting like this. Imagine the contentment, the joy, the ease. It's possible for us, too. Believe it or not, we choose whether we are disappointed or hopeful.

*We are God's workmanship, created in
Christ Jesus to do good works, which
God prepared in advance for us to do.*

EPHESIANS 2:10

Stick this verse in the face of an insecure or overwhelmed spirit and watch fear wilt. So much for our excuses; all the work set before us was preordained by God. He planned for us to do this, and He prepared us to do this. We are His workmanship.

God knew that you would have this job, these responsibilities, this husband, this family, these friends, and these children to rear. He gave all of us the gifts to use and the outlet for their splendor. The next time you feel burdened or uncertain, remind yourself, "God prepared this for me in advance. He already knew I could do it. According to Him, it is already done." Our children can likewise be comforted by this verse. When they have a big presentation or report, an important game, an exam, a part in a school play, or an interview, they get nervous, too. They need to know that they are already enough, they are ready, and they are handpicked and prepared by God for such a moment as this.

I had a babysitter when the girls were little who would always say, "Everything is unfolding as it should." My life at the time with toddler twins was pretty chaotic, and I wasn't sure things really were going according to any plan. But every time she said that I felt better. Consider that your life today is unfolding exactly as it should.

*Honor your father and mother, so you may live
long in the land the Lord your God is giving you.*

EXODUS 20:12

We honor our parents because that is what we are told to do. But we also honor our parents because that is what we have seen and learned to accept as our "normal." When I was growing up, my parents made every effort to stay connected with their parents. We talked on the phone every week. We spent holidays together. We made long road trips to visit them. We spent summer months at my grandparents' lake house. I learned the value of family by watching it honored over time.

Even today, we travel with my children to see their great-grandparents. My parents live fifteen minutes from our house and know everything about our schedules, classes, sports, and so on. They show up at everything, or even just stop by the cafeteria and bring lunch to the kids. They can take over if I have to travel, and I don't even have to explain the workings of our family life. My children are blessed to experience the loving ties among four generations.

My point is that it isn't enough to hold the fourth commandment over our children's heads and demand obedience. We have to show them what this means by honoring our parents and grandparents as well, by staying connected and sharing our lives. We can't be upset if we're lonely when we're old if we never showed our children how to love older people when we had the chance.

I tell you that if two of you on earth agree about anything you ask for, it will be done for you by my Father in heaven. For where two or three come together in my name, there am I with them.

MATTHEW 18:19–20

We know how important it is to pray for our children, but these verses remind me of how important it is to pray *with* our children. When we gather together around the dinner table, or on the floor in the living room, holding hands and talking to God together, He is among us. In the car on the way to school, when we ask God to protect us and guide us, and open our minds to learn, He is right there. When someone has a rotten day, and we join together and ask for comfort, He shows up. When the kids are fighting, we can stop the madness by asking for peace to blow through our house like a mighty wind.

My prayers for my children are mighty. But when my children join me, bringing their pure hearts and unfettered faith, we can really move mountains. I share prayer requests for people my kids don't even know and I ask them to join me in prayer. A couple of nights ago when I was tucking Grace in, she asked me how Desiree was doing with her cancer. Grace doesn't even know Desiree, but she remembers to pray for her! Our children's hearts are so close to God, and so unclogged with the debris that we adults have. When we fail to include them in our prayer lives, we are missing an incredibly powerful source and they are missing out on the experience of learning how to intercede.

Jesus looked at them and said, "With man this is impossible, but with God all things are possible."

MATTHEW 19:26

❧

Without God, our perspective is puny. Our thoughts are meager. Our hopes are limited. Our ideas are stale. Our strategies are weak. Our options are few. Our views are cloudy. Our strengths are feeble. Our efforts are futile. Is it any wonder that when we are struggling to solve things with our own tools, we stagger under the weight of the impossible?

God knows no limits. His solutions involve things we couldn't even imagine. He can line up so many extraordinary events in succession, involving strangers and adjusting time, opening doors we didn't know existed and slamming those that lead to dead ends. Let's not waste time by making plans or trying to control outcomes; instead let's begin by praising His omnipotence and aligning our hearts to cooperate with His strategy. Trust is the key. When we don't know what He's up to, it's not easy to lay the issue on the altar and leave it there. But it is precisely that trust that allows us to open up to divine resolution and not settle for the human kind.

Bring it all to Him…the big hopes, the big dreams, the deep healing, the impossible fantasies. The "what-ifs" and the "if-onlys" are His specialty. Making a way where there is no way is exactly what He loves to do, because it leaves no doubt, in the minds of believers and nonbelievers alike, that something extraordinary just occurred. There is no way the glory can go anywhere other than to the Source. This makes God smile.

"But what about you?" he asked.
"Who do you say I am?"

LUKE 9:20

If we don't have a clear answer to this question, how can we ever properly introduce Jesus to our children? We had better be totally clear about who Jesus is to us, because our children will ask, and our children will watch us as the answer to that question is revealed.

Who is Jesus to you?

Is He a Sunday thing? Is He the Messiah? The Son of God? Part of the Trinity? The way, the truth, and the life? The Healer? The baby in the manger? The Teacher? The Light of the World? The Restorer? The Redeemer? The Giver of life? The Lamb of God? The body and blood in bread and wine? The Alpha and the Omega? The Living Sacrifice? The fulfillment of Scripture? The answer to prayer? Peace Himself? Love personified? Hope revealed?

If your definition of Jesus is founded in a personal relationship with Him, then there is no wrong answer. Children always seem to know when we are speaking from our hearts, so when we speak of Jesus, we had better start there.

Your eye is the lamp of your body. When your eyes are good, your whole body also is full of light. But when they are bad, your body also is full of darkness. See to it, then, that the light within you is not darkness.

LUKE 11:34–35

We have to protect our children's eyes so their minds and spirits remain full of light.

So much danger lurks in this world. The Internet, YouTube, Facebook, cable TV, magazines, books, movies, cell phones, and music can all be used for good. These things can also be used as channels of darkness. Exposing young eyes to inappropriate material can have lasting and damaging effects. We have to protect what enters the lives of people who have been entrusted to us. This is no time to be lazy. We have to watch what they're watching, read what they're reading, monitor technology and communication, and put televisions and computers in common areas. We have to be knowledgeable enough and bold enough to put a foot down when something does not match the values of our families.

We also have to be mindful of our own eyes. Because if we aren't intentionally searching for good things that bring light, we can let darkness enter by default. And the more desensitized we become, the more we can rationalize what is okay for our children, and the next thing we know, the current of the world has taken our entire ship off course. We can't navigate for our families if our own moral compasses are faulty. The less darkness we permit, the more shocking and distasteful it will remain. We must train our eyes to always seek the light. There is always a better choice.

Every good and perfect gift is from above, coming down from the Father of the heavenly lights, who does not change like the shifting shadows.

JAMES 1:17

Every single one of us has discovered more about either who God is or who He is not from our life experiences with our earthly fathers. Two things stand out to me when I think about my dad. One is that he was and is always there for me, without exception and without condition. He has never broken a promise to me, or to my children. And when he gives me a gift, it is always the highest quality available, never an approximation. He once brought me back a beautiful handbag from Paris for my birthday. I was stunned. I thanked him, and he said, "You should never settle, sweetheart. You aren't a knockoff kind of girl."

It was and is a beautiful bag. I still carry it today when I get dressed up. But more than that, it was a message from my father (and my Father) that I was precious and valuable and worthy. I would be making big decisions in the years that followed, involving my career, marriage, and children, and Dad wanted me to know and always remember how he saw me. I haven't forgotten. Today if I am tempted to settle in any category of my life, I hear his words in my head.

Let us be wise and purposeful in the messages we give our children about who they are to us, and who they are in Christ. Let's give them memorable illustrations about how we see them. Let's remember that they will have a tape that plays in their heads and our voices are on it; let our words speak life.

This is what I'll do. I will tear down my barns and build bigger ones, and there I will store all my grain and my goods. And I'll say to myself, "You have plenty of good things laid up for many years. Take life easy; eat, drink and be merry."

LUKE 12:18–19

❧

Ah, yes, the parable of the rich fool. A story of complacency at its finest; add consumption, materialism, and spiritual blindness, and you have an update on modern life all around us. Until the recent downshift in our economy, we thought this booming lifestyle would continue forever. We started to take it easy. We lost our edge. Our country and our times became Parable of the Rich Fool, Part II.

Luke 12:20 goes on, "But God said to him, 'You fool! This very night your life will be demanded from you. Then who will get what you have prepared for yourself?'" It's just like that for us. We have no idea when our day is coming, be it our day to die or our day when life as we know it totally changes. What then? If we have spent all our time working to amass things rather than living a rich life with God, we will have nothing to show for our time, or nothing to draw from when we need more than barns full of grain and goods.

Without being overly morbid, it's good to be conscious about the legacy we want to leave for our kids. Are we spending more time building a financial base than a spiritual base? When times are tough, which account will our children really need to draw from? Let's make sure they won't be overdrawn.

Everyone who exalts himself will be humbled, and he who humbles himself will be exalted.

LUKE 18:14

For the past few days my kids have been a handful. Testing me on limits, pushing my buttons again and again the way an impatient person (usually me) repeatedly hits the elevator button, thinking doing so will somehow speed up its arrival. There was a point where I got so exasperated last night that I finally just had to throw my hands up and laugh. Of course, I am floundering with my parenting right now; I'm in the middle of writing a manuscript for mothers! If I attempt to go to work, writing in my office each day (or in the pickup line at school, or outside gymnastics), and I am coming from any place other than on-my-face-humility, both my parenting and this book are doomed to be useless.

If any one of us thinks that we totally have it together, that we always know the right answer, the right thing to say, or the perfect advice to give—we are in big trouble. Even when we think we are getting the hang of this mothering gig, the phases change, the children grow, we change, circumstances change, or a new challenge presents itself. It's called growth, and there is no end.

We have hope of being far better mothers when we liberally season our experiences with humility. We need to stick together, not waste time acting like we're perfect and don't need help or community. We need one another, and, more important, we need God. But it's hard to get His help when we are posturing like we've got it all on our own. There is only one expert, and He is exalted. The rest of us should be humble.

"Neither this man nor his parents sinned," said Jesus, "but this happened so that the work of God might be displayed in his life."

JOHN 9:3

When Jesus and His disciples passed a blind man in the road, they asked Jesus about the cause of his blindness. Was it his parents' fault or his fault? Jesus clarified that rather than being punishment for any sin, the man's blindness was for God's glory.

I have good friends with children who have Down syndrome and cerebral palsy. When each couple first received the news about their baby, there was naturally a period of shock, uncertainty, and adjustment. I can't read this verse without thinking of these beautiful children and where their families are today. It is so abundantly evident, in both children, that the glory of God was always meant to be displayed in their lives. They could not be a bigger blessing to their families, and to every single person who has the honor of knowing them. And their mothers are two of the most amazing, faithful, strong, and generous women around. Of course God would have a gift in store for them; they are equipped to recognize and celebrate the glory of God that is present in their children.

We all would benefit from this lesson in perspective. When something happens that provokes the initial reaction of "Why me?" or "Why us?" stop and think. Maybe this circumstance is a gift, and you have been chosen to receive it because you are very special; you have been anointed. When things happen so that the work of God might be displayed, it is an honor beyond measure.

*The thief comes only to steal and kill and
destroy; I have come that they may have life,
and have it to the full.*

JOHN 10:10

I am aware of spiritual warfare and our need for protection,
and I want to be diligent in prayer, bold in my belief, and
purposeful in my actions. I want to acknowledge that there is
a thief, an enemy, without giving him too much of my energy.
I would rather focus my energy and attention on our God who
saves. But I refuse to go about blindly, thinking that the stealing, killing, and destroying in this world are simply "bad luck"
or "unfortunate circumstances" instead of a flat-out attack.

An important part of raising children is protecting them.
We make our children hold hands when they cross the street.
We tell them not to get into cars with strangers. But do we
also specifically pray a hedge of protection around each child,
every day? Are we consciously and conscientiously asking
God to guard their bodies, their innocence, their hearts, and
their minds? We must be mindful that the timeless struggle
between good and evil continues to play out today, on both a
physical and a spiritual level. It's all around us. The more discernment we have in recognizing good and evil, the stronger
advocates we become for our children.

God wants us to have life and have it to the full. As our
Father, He wants to protect us, prosper us, bless us, heal us, and
love us. There will always be shadows, deception, temptation—it
is unavoidable. But God's protection for believers prevails.

The LORD your God is with you, he is mighty to save.
He will take great delight in you, he will quiet you with
his love, he will rejoice over you with singing.

ZEPHANIAH 3:17

I needed this verse today, and, as often happens, I opened the Bible right to it. God is so sweet the way He spoon-feeds me. My kids left this morning to be with their dad for three weeks, kicking off the start of summer. It was such an emotional buildup, these final weeks of school, so much noise and busyness and now, suddenly, silence. I am working on being able to love and let go, love and let go. It doesn't feel natural, but it is inevitable for all of us, single moms or not. I have had a sticky paper stuck on my desk now for two months. It says: Dare to believe. Dare to be empty. Dare to let go.

I didn't know it was sitting there all this time to prepare me for today. I have felt close to tears most of the time for the past two days. Then today, when my kids drove off, waving and blowing kisses out the car windows, I waited for the stabbing feeling of loss...and instead, miraculously, found peace. I was smiling and blowing kisses, waving and running across the front yard until they drove out of sight. Then I took our dog for a walk, still waiting for misery to descend, but instead I felt light.

God did indeed quiet me with His love today. I pray so hard about transitions, and yet I'm always surprised when He carries me through them. When will I ever learn? When will I ever understand that God takes great delight in me, and my children? He is mighty to save. He saved me today.

*The LORD will guide you always; he will
satisfy your needs in a sun-scorched land.*

ISAIAH 58:11

It's important that we are clear about how and where we get our needs met.

I had a reality check last week along these lines, and it's embarrassing to even put it on paper, but I need to do it so I don't forget. Something happened with Luke and I got my feelings hurt. My reaction surprised me; I felt so vulnerable and immature. I went into my office and pretended to work, knowing that I needed some time to sort through those feelings so I wouldn't dump them in Luke's lap. I was hurt the way I would be hurt by a friend, and I felt pouty about it.

I had to turn to God, confess my mess, and repent for not going to Him as the primary means of satisfying my needs. I am the mother and Luke is my child. I am supposed to be present for him, so he can rely on me. When we get out of alignment, we irresponsibly put the burdens of our needs onto our children, husbands, parents, siblings, or friends. All our relationships are reciprocal to some degree, but the immature feelings I had were a sign to me that I was out of line. When I am connected to my Source, all my other relationships fall into proper place and perspective. They are a sweet dessert, not my main nutrition.

Single moms need to be even more mindful of this, without a husband in the picture to provide another layer of accountability. It's humbling to admit to having our feelings hurt by our children, but if we can talk about it and move it quickly into the light, we can be restored by the Lord and His unwavering grace.

We fix our eyes not on what is seen,
but on what is unseen. For what is seen
is temporary, but what is unseen is eternal.

2 CORINTHIANS 4:18

I struggle with keeping an eternal perspective. I can get so mired down in the minutiae of my day-to-day living that I suddenly find myself trapped by what is seen. I can see the pile of laundry, the pile of bills, the pile of homework, the pile of deadlines, the pile of details to attend to. I see myself as a mom, and as a writer. I know whenever I start to feel cagey that I am overdue for a perspective shift.

Usually this means I have to get outside, alone or with my dog, walking or running, or simply sitting on my back patio and looking up at the trees. "Lord, remind me. What am I doing? Who am I to You?" Sometimes it happens right away, and sometimes it takes some time, but eventually peace washes over me in such a way that it feels almost physical. The worries of here and now loosen their stranglehold on me, and I feel God responding with His Spirit.

Nothing has changed outside, in the details of my life, but I am changed. That rush of peace reminds me that these are just details, the things that add up between today and tomorrow, and they will sort out and get taken care of in good time. But more than that, I am reminded that I am here not just for these things; I am here as a child of God. The value of who I am and the things I do is not measured by what is seen. I am trying to live a life where my accomplishments and my treasures, the essence of my work and my purpose, are held in a heavenly storehouse.

I have learned to be content whatever the circumstances.

PHILIPPIANS 4:11

I write this verse on the first page of any new notebook I buy. I never know when I buy a new notebook where my life will be by the time the pages are full. That's why I have the ritual of starting each new notebook with just this quote, on page one.

I figure if I can focus on contentment regardless of the circumstances each day, I can be certain that I am always growing in peace and in faith. Some days when I write in my notebook, things are great and I'm crossing off the to-do list with ease, receiving calls bearing good news and opportunities, and brainstorming with flowing creativity. Other times, however, the same things sit on my list for weeks, because I'm too lazy or overwhelmed to take initiative. Sometimes I avoid returning calls because I already know I probably won't like what the person has to say.

Sometimes deadlines or speaking engagement topics sit idle, with no scribbles of ideas or outlines beneath them—just the date glaring back at me from an empty page. Life is uncertain. My entire list could be wiped clean and all my deadlines canceled until further notice in a matter of a moment, if something were to happen that took priority over all else.

I don't want to take this for granted. I don't want to neglect the cultivation of contentment in ordinary times, because I may have to lean heavily on it in extraordinary times.

Judge nothing before the appointed time;
wait till the Lord comes.

1 CORINTHIANS 4:5

Staying spiritually neutral, not assigning positive or negative values to circumstances in life, is not easy. Just as my yoga instructor encourages us to acknowledge distracting thoughts and let them go, we have to be able to do the same with circumstances that take our eyes off the Lord. We will never understand why some difficult seasons are required, or how one loss allowed for a future gain. The more we try to figure it out, the bigger our headache becomes. When the Lord comes, everything will be made perfectly clear.

I like to imagine private movie theaters in heaven. Lights flicker and the tape rolls. Some scenes make us laugh out loud, some scenes make us cheer, some make us ill with regret, and others make us sob—tears of sadness, relief, joy, understanding. As we watch the drama that was each of our lives, we realize that we are not alone in our little viewing room. Jesus is sitting there, quietly watching with us. Anytime we want to pause and ask Him questions, He is available. He can explain everything. He will show us clips from other people's stories so we finally know how things fit together. He will point out scenes that made Him so proud, and He will forgive other scenes that broke His heart.

In the midst of living out my story today, I stop sometimes and shake my head, telling myself, "There's one for the movie." I can't wait to understand.

He who guards his lips guards his life.

PROVERBS 13:3

Young children have no filter. They say whatever they think, regardless of circumstance or company, whenever the thought enters their minds. My daughters have asked explicit questions about tampons in the checkout line at the grocery store. They have told the preschool teachers in the pickup line about their father's choice of pajamas, or the lack thereof. They have said loudly in the middle of church how they have to go "number two, right now!" Sometimes it's embarrassing, sometimes it's hilarious, but one thing is certain: It's always unpredictable.

These things can slide somewhat when you are a young child. But the same lack of filter for an adult can be inappropriate and unacceptable. Yet filter-less people are roaming around everywhere! Just because we think something doesn't mean we have to say it, right? But things slip. The only real way to guard our lips is to start taking thoughts captive immediately, without giving them free rein to roam in our minds. If we replace ugly thoughts with healing ones immediately upon discovery, praying to God to set us right, our chances are better than relying on our filters alone. Filters get clogged. They get dislodged. They can't always be trusted. Only a clean head and a clean heart can ensure that our spoken words reflect who we want to be with God's grace.

*Afterward, as you know, when [Esau] wanted
to inherit this blessing, he was rejected. He could
bring about no change of mind, though
he sought the blessing with tears.*

HEBREWS 12:17

❧

I heard someone describe a storeroom in heaven, filled with blessings, stacked high like a pile of unopened presents. These are supposed to represent all the things that God wanted to give us but we missed out on. Maybe we were too busy. Maybe we walked right past it. Maybe we were distracted by our pain or the things we thought were so important. Maybe we were angry with God and wanted nothing to do with Him for a while. Maybe we thought a gift was intended for someone else.

Certain things are specifically intended for us, at certain times. Once we miss them, we usually can't go back and claim them. Sometimes they can no longer be found; other times they have been repurposed for someone else. The point is, like the old saying goes, "You snooze—you lose." If we aren't being present, if we aren't staying connected to God all the time, we are going to miss some of the beautiful things He has in store for us and for our families. It's not that God won't bless us again, but it won't be the same blessing He originally intended. I'd rather open the gifts as I find them than find a pile of unopened presents waiting for me on the other side.

Peter replied, "Repent and be baptized,
every one of you, in the name of Jesus Christ
for the forgiveness of your sins. And you will receive
the gift of the Holy Spirit. The promise is for you
and your children and for all who are far
off—for all whom the Lord our God will call."

ACTS 2:38–39

How beautiful to consider that the gift of the Holy Spirit dwelling within us is a promise not only for us, but for our children. I don't remember my baptism as a tiny baby. But I have had private baptism moments since then, invitations from God to cleanse and renew in His presence.

One was an early morning rainstorm, when I felt pulled from my bed and drawn to my back porch. As I stood there and slowly woke up, I realized that God was calling me. I walked out into the rain, in my pajamas, arms outstretched, knowing that I was free. Another time I was running along the beach praying for change in my life. I felt God tug at my heart, wanting to know if I was ready for change. I stopped, stared at the ocean, heard His whisper in the crash of the waves, and ran into the spray. Somehow, even on that popular stretch of beach in the early morning hour, I was amazingly alone. It was a moment with our Father that I will never forget.

The call to repent and be baptized isn't just a ritual at church, though this is a beautiful and profound experience. Sometimes if we are paying attention, we can hear God inviting us to be alone with Him. There is nothing wrong with needing more than one fresh start in a lifetime.

*So do **not** fear, for I am with you; do **not** be dismayed,*
for I am your God. I will strengthen you and help you;
I will uphold you with my righteous right hand.

ISAIAH 41:10

The kids and I went on a hike with my friend Terra and her two children, Logan and Lake. We wound our way up the mountainside, then came back down, the children running ahead as we walked. When we came to a rocky path that descended into a creek where some other children and dogs were playing, our kids wanted to join the fun. They scampered down the steep hill like goats, as did Terra, even with Lake in a backpack, and I followed gingerly behind them.

The mountain stream poured between two boulders and made a little waterfall into a pool below. The kids thought it was an ideal waterslide, but I was anxious. How cold is that water? How steep is that waterfall? How deep is the pool? Are there any rocks beneath the surface? Will they be able to climb out? I was full of worries, yet I didn't want to poison my children's sense of adventure with my fear.

Never more at home than when she is outside, Terra loves running, hiking, kayaking, and camping. Strapping baby Lake onto me, she slid into the icy water and wedged herself between the boulders so the kids could climb into her lap. They all slid down together in a giant splash, then she helped them climb up the rock face on the other side. Blue-lipped and chattering, they were totally exhilarated and happy. A memory was made in that moment. Terra acted on behalf of the Lord for me and my kids that day, saying, "Fear not, I will help you."

Watch—and be utterly amazed.
For I am going to do something in your days that you
would not believe, even if you were told.

HABAKKUK 1:5

We all have areas in our lives that are not going the way we planned, or don't look the way we imagined they would. Maybe it's a hollow marriage, maybe a difficult child, maybe an empty job, maybe a sick parent. These things aren't easy. But what if we take this verse to heart and consider that the way things look today is not the final picture. What if we really believed that God was in the process of blowing our minds; that things right now were already in motion to produce unfathomable scenarios. What if we lived as if joy was just up ahead, around the next corner? How would that trust and hopefulness impact our day today?

I read once about a helpful exercise. Take some quiet time and journal a scene from your life, a future date when everything that worries you now is resolved. Write everything down; don't skip any details. Include every relationship you struggle with, every fear you have, every area of bondage, every lie you believe, every failure that defines you. Describe your life with these areas totally restored, and how it feels to live it. Write across the top, "With God, all things are possible." Date the paper, fold the paper, and put it in your Bible. I did this exercise five years ago, when I never believed that I could feel better than numb. Almost everything in my dream entry has come true, so it must be time for me to write another one.

On him we have set our hope that
he will continue to deliver us.

2 CORINTHIANS 1:10

∂

I have a friend whose family life in the past ten years has read like a long soap opera. Plot twists have included breast cancer, bankruptcy, infertility, parents moving in, a new baby, depression, insomnia, colon cancer, job loss, a suicide note, hospice, cancer death, ADD diagnosis, drowning death, starting a company, and homeschooling. Through most of these times, I have been at her house for dinners with friends and family, drank wine or margaritas, prayed, laughed, cried, watched the kids play, and done Bible study.

The point is, my friend and her family have continued to live despite their circumstances. They have praised God for as long as I've known them, and for many years before that.

It's no mistake that I met them when I was finding my own stride in my walk with the Lord. I will never forget a conversation I had with my friend's father before he died. We were at a soccer game, and I was complaining about God knows what, to the man who was suffering from depression and cancer. He listened patiently to me, compassionate to the core, even with my nonsense. He said something that imprinted on my brain: "Remember Psalm 37:4. You just delight yourself in the Lord. That's all. And He will give you the desires of your heart. Wait and see." I have said it over and over again. I can't help but think that his confidence in God's deliverance was founded in delight.

God did not give us a spirit of timidity,
but a spirit of power, of love and of self-discipline.

2 TIMOTHY 1:7

Fear traps us and cajoles us into playing small. It whispers to us that we can't, we aren't enough, and it's not possible. It's the voice of the enemy, wanting to ensure that God's people are held back. What does fear say to you? What does it say you cannot do? When does it tell you that you can't handle it? Do you know that the voice of fear is never from God? He speaks words of power and healing and love over us. When you hear a resounding *Yes!* and you respond with a shrug and a maybe, the yes is from God and the shrug is from us. Not only does God know we can do it, He will also supply the power for it. He will teach us the discipline we need to get it done, to persist, to endure, to be victorious.

When I am about to do something that freaks me out, I claim this verse, out loud if possible. I want to be a positive, brave, strong, and motivated woman. Even more than I want that for myself, I want that for my children. And they won't absorb these traits by virtue of my nagging at them over the years to "do their best" and "be all they can be." Conquering fear is not a lesson to be learned from a sideline cheer. Our children are going to learn about courage only by watching people they love and respect get in there and try. That means us. What are we afraid of? Where are we holding back? Halftime is over, ladies. Let's get in the game.

There is no fear in love. But perfect love drives out fear.

1 JOHN 4:18

An Eleanor Roosevelt quote hangs on my kitchen pantry door. I am a snacker, so I see it often. It says, "Do one thing every day that scares you." I try to take it to heart. So I said yes to a trail-running group and learned how to run trails in the dark, with a headlamp on. Talk about facing my fears of the dark! I agreed to speak to a high school AP English class. I said yes to a conversation I had been avoiding even though I dislike conflict. If perfect love casts out fear, then any time I refuse to hide from my fear, I welcome more perfect love into my life.

I want my kids to see me try new things, whether I fail miserably or sail through victoriously. Everything from giving a speech at the starting line of a race, to running that race, to bonking terribly and barely finishing that race. If they don't see me try, fail, holler for God, get dusted off, and try again, how will they know that they can face fear and survive?

Luke hates to try new things right now. He doesn't want to be the fool who messes up, the one who doesn't know what he's doing. I can help him with that by not minding being the fool, not caring if I mess up, and trying things when I don't know exactly what I'm doing.

I am attracted to and repelled by my comfort zone, often in equal measure. The thirst for adventure might actually quench the desire for perfect love.

God is our refuge and strength,
an ever-present help in trouble.

PSALM 46:1

❧

As parents, specifically mothers, part of our gift to our children is creating sacred spaces for them. Maybe it's a child's home in its entirety, the warmth and safety of it, the way it smells, the way it feels to enter, the food eaten there. Maybe it's their room, cozy and personal, reflecting their passions and hobbies, the way their bed feels when they fall into it, exhausted or sad. Maybe it's a grandparent's house, a total refuge from the world. Maybe it's our family room, the sofa filled with family, board games, books, dogs on the floor, fire in the fireplace, movie night with piles of pillows and blankets. Maybe it's the kitchen table, the heart of the home, a family meal, favorite dishes, a reliable ritual, a conversation zone without judgment.

Looking back on moving thirteen times as a child, I have to marvel at my mother. She was a teacher, so her work life was continuously uprooted as we followed my father's career. She had to have been exhausted, but in my memory she was always positive, always up for adventure. She worked long into the night, city after city, to set up our home. My brother and I always got our rooms set up first, so we could feel at home right away. The kitchen and family room were next, then everything else as it fell into place. She made a refuge for us again and again, and in doing so she taught me how to make a refuge for my children.

When we make a home for our children, we illustrate the refuge of God. He is our hiding place, our help, our peace, and our strength.

*My intercessor is my friend as my eyes
pour out tears to God.*

JOB 16:20

The ordinary and extraordinary moments of motherhood are better when shared.

Whether we are cheering at a game, praying beside a hospital bed, struggling with a learning disorder, buckling under the weight of an imbalanced marriage, or celebrating a hard-earned milestone, our victories and our trials are better experienced as part of a community. As a single mother in particular, my friends are my family, too. I call them to share a great report card or a discipline problem, a touchdown at a game or struggles with playground friendships. I expect I will be calling these same friends to compare notes on teenage dating, appropriate consequences for deception, issues with technology, driver's ed, and college applications. These women are my sounding board, my prayer team, my cheerleaders, my protectors, and my heart.

I have been racked with sobs and rendered speechless with grief, and they have prayed on my behalf. I have been ecstatic with joy and they have praised God beside me and toasted my good fortune. I have been muddled with indecision and they have prayed for clarity and wisdom. I have been trapped by sin and they have reflected God's light into my darkness. They are my intercessors, and I am theirs.

When you lie down, you will not be afraid;
when you lie down, your sleep will be sweet.

PROVERBS 3:24

Restful, restorative sleep is a gift from God. We've all had young children; we know how it feels to go without sleep! We feel sloppy, grumpy, scattered, distracted, hopeless, vulnerable, and emotionally raw. Anyone acquainted with insomnia knows how brutal it is to lie awake and long for sleep. Our to-do lists float and grow in our heads; the conversations of the day are replayed with growing doubt and escalating criticism. Our fears grow and mutate, taking up more space than they would be afforded in daylight hours. Glances at the clock turn into a mind game of how many hours are left before the alarm will ring, before we enter the day exhausted and ill-prepared.

Our children have the same struggles, though often their sleep disruptions have horns, wings, and breathe fire. Ours do, too, actually. A lack of good sleep is a sign of spiritual attack. I pray this verse over my kids when they wake up at night to set them at ease and restore their confidence in God's protection. I ask for rest, which is just as important as readiness.

Just as we can't stomp on the gas pedal as we approach a red light, we can't hurtle through time at top speed all day, fall into bed without transition, and expect immediate rest. We need to wind down, and so do our children. We are more purpose-ful about this when our children are babies, but we need to be mindful of it as they grow. A bath, a book, some readings from Psalms, some snuggles. We all need to remember to slow down so we can accept the sweet sleep that God wants to give us.

I remind you to fan into flame the gift of God,
which is in you through the laying on of my hands.

2 TIMOTHY 1:6

From the moment our children are born, we use our hands to care for them. We hold them, stroke them, clean them, feed them, and comfort them. We pray for their faith as they continue to make it their own.

A precious notation written in the front of my Bible says that on December 14, 2004, when Luke was five, he invited Jesus into his heart. We were driving on a road in Austin, and Luke was asking me about car accidents. He asked what would happen if a car hit ours. I explained how the air bags would protect us from the impact of another car. Then he asked me if air bags always kept people from getting hurt and I said no they didn't always; there is only one true kind of protection.

"What kind of protection is that?" he asked. "It's the protection that comes from God." I said. "How do you get that kind?" he wanted to know. "You invite Jesus into your heart so His Spirit lives in you, and that's how you are saved," I said, unsure how to make something so huge into a child-sized portion of understanding. But he understood perfectly.

"I want to do that right now. Show me how to do that," he said. So I led him in a prayer and drove home with tears in my eyes, knowing that moment was ordained by God.

On July 26, 2006, Luke prayed the same prayer with his sisters as they came to faith. Never underestimate the power of your hands as you lay them on your children and offer your prayers to God.

Before they call I will answer;
while they are still speaking I will hear.

ISAIAH 65:24

As a mother, I feel every nuance of my children. When they have the flu, I ache. When they are sad, I am often brought to tears. When they are hurt or betrayed, so am I. When they are goofy, I laugh with them. When they are quiet or pensive, I turn inward as well. When they have a bad dream, I often wake up before they make a sound. When they try something new, I'm nervous. When they fall in love, I probably will, too. If their hearts are broken, mine will shatter into a million pieces.

I know what's behind that whine, if they need food, a hug, a listener, an early bedtime, some time alone, or some alone time with me. Before the sentence is out of their mouth, my heart already understands. The same connection exists with my mother. Many times I have picked up my phone to call her, only to see that she has called me moments before, or our lines are busy because we are calling each other at exactly the same time. Mothers just know.

Imagine what God knows. He knows our days before we've lived them. Our arrival before we are there. Our departure before we've gone. Our thoughts before we acknowledge them. Our feelings before we feel them. Our actions before we move. Our words before they pass our lips. Even though He already knows everything, He wants the relationship that grows from the conversation. Tell Him everything.

The more the words, the less the meaning,
and how does that profit anyone?

ECCLESIASTES 6:11

✥

Have you ever watched a *Peanuts* cartoon on television? You know how the adults sound?

There are no clear words at all, just a repetitive nasal sound: "*Wah wah wah, wah wah wah wah WAHH.*" The kids glaze over and say, "Yes, ma'am," a lot.

I know I am at risk for overusing words, particularly with my children. I can explain something many different ways, often long-winded. I can see the beginnings of an eye-roll revolution in my rearview mirror when I'm driving and instructing them about something I think is important. Whether making an important point or taking disciplinary action, the fewer the words, the greater the impact. Saying something once, in a quiet voice, followed by an action or consequence speaks volumes more than nagging or yelling. Otherwise, the meaning and importance of the message get lost in the delivery. *Mom's nagging me again, time to check out.*

My mom was a pro at this. She would quiet my fuming father by saying, "Is this life-threatening? If not, save it for later." Somehow she was able to keep him from throwing a fit about my purple eye shadow and my blue mascara. She had a good point; if we throw a fit about everything, what will make an impact when something is really serious? If our kids build up a tolerance to our words, what happens when we need to say something really, really important?

Encourage one another and build each other up,
just as in fact you are doing.

1 THESSALONIANS 5:11

❧

Our families have to be our place of refuge. The world will give us enough messages that tear us down and chip away at our hearts; our homes have to be sanctuaries. My friend Saskia describes home life as an island. She explains that on your island you aren't totally disconnected from the world; there is ferry service when you need it, but don't build a bridge. You don't want traffic flowing freely on and off the island. You want to guard your private place where the inhabitants (your family) can be totally free and comfortable being themselves.

This verse from 1 Thessalonians gives insight into the kind of language that should be spoken on the island. Words of encouragement and healing are meant for family dialogue. Even if a rebuke or reprimand is needed, there is a way to deliver it without damaging someone's heart. Our job as family members is to build one another up, not tear one another down, and to protect what has been built up.

As mothers we have to be mindful of our own word choices and nonverbal language, as well as the way our children speak to one another. Many adults today are haunted by the way their parents defined them, or the teasing inflicted by a sibling. We cannot tolerate a lack of respect or kindness without correction. Kids learn how to treat people by the way they have been treated at home. It's a big responsibility. But island life is worth it.

My dear brothers, take note of this: Everyone should be quick to listen, slow to speak, and slow to become angry.

JAMES 1:19

≥

I notice sometimes, especially in a heated conversation, that I am more focused on what I'm going to say next than I am on listening. This is an ugly manifestation of pride, thinking my choice of words is more important than hearing someone else's point of view. This verse helps me keep things in order: listen first, then speak; keep anger at bay. Like anything else worth cultivating, it is a daily practice.

If we want to become better listeners, we have to follow the advice of Mrs. Ross (Bella's first-grade teacher): "Mouth closed, ears open." We aren't listening if we're talking. It sounds so simple, but it's just as difficult at age thirty-seven as it is at seven. When my child or my friend has something important to share, I remind myself to show my love and support by being quiet. A child shouting, "Mommy! I'm talking to you!" has reminded me more than once to stop what I'm doing, make eye contact, close my mouth, and open my ears (and my heart).

There have been countless studies done on being a good listener, how people perceive good listeners as wise and prefer their company over others. Of course listeners are wise; they can learn a lot by listening more than they talk. Being a good listener is a worthwhile trait to model for our children. If they feel heard, they are more apt to hear other people out. If they feel understood, they are more likely to grow up into the kind of people who seek understanding. If they feel respected, they will respond by being respectful.

He seldom reflects on the days of his life, because
God keeps him occupied with gladness of heart.

ECCLESIASTES 5:20

❧

This verse reminds me so much of the clichéd lament of mothers everywhere: *Where does the time go?* This is expressed in a variety of ways. *Can you believe the school year is almost over? Summer passed by in a blink! How is my baby already graduating?* Or with little babies, a wistful remark from an older woman in the grocery store: "Enjoy it now; it will be gone before you know it."

My own mother warned me that the years pick up speed as they roll along, and already I see that she was right. Every time I look up it seems another yearly mile marker is upon us: holidays, birthdays, summer vacation. It's all so fleeting. I remember when my mom was thirty-seven and I thought she was such a grown-up. Now I'm thirty-eight and I still feel like a kid in many ways, just trying to figure things out. I am not sure how my life is speeding by so fast. I guess this verse is the godly equivalent of the quip "*Time flies when you're having fun.*" If we mothers are living well, we are completely occupied with gladness of heart.

I want to be the person in the grocery store who responds thoughtfully to the wise older lady, "Yes, I know, it is flying by. I hear you. I'm soaking in everything I can. Thank you for reminding me." I don't want to reflect on these precious years as a blur; I want to purposefully mark moments of clarity for me and for each of my children so that when we look back later we will have memories of purposeful pauses.

After three days they found him in
the temple courts, sitting among the teachers,
listening to them and asking them questions.

LUKE 2:46

❧

Can you imagine how scared Mary and Joseph were when they could not find Jesus for three days as they were caravanning back from Jerusalem after a Passover celebration? I lost sight of Grace when she was a toddler for about forty-five seconds, and I nearly threw up. I can't imagine hunting for my child for three days, only to find out that he had remained behind on purpose. They found Jesus in the temple, amazing everyone with His understanding, but Mary was justifiably peeved. *"How could you do this to us? We have been so anxious!"* Jesus didn't take the guilt bait; instead He said, "Why were you searching for me? Didn't you know I had to be in my Father's house?" (Luke 2:49).

There comes a time for all mothers when we have to let our children grow and follow their passions. They have to respond to the call of their purposes just as we do. I have read stories about a mother who let her young prodigy child go live at Juilliard to pursue music, and another mother who let her young teen take off and sail solo around the world. These mothers could not stand in the way of their children's lives unfolding.

I can relate in smaller ways, trusting God's timing to change from flag football to tackle, going to camp, or learning to surf or sail. It's such an intimate, incremental tug-of-war—loving and letting go. Every child and every situation is unique, requiring prayer, discernment, and trust.

*He said to them, "Go into all the world and
preach the good news to all creation."*

MARK 16:15

I spoke at a book club recently and a woman asked me a question that had an overtone of skepticism or annoyance. Or perhaps I misunderstood her tone; I can't be sure. She said, "Your book has wisdom, but it's so clearly Christian. What do you say to people who don't believe in God?" I wasn't sure if she was asking the question generally, or because she herself did not believe. I knew I was on slippery terrain, so I paused to collect my thoughts and say a quick prayer. I never want to be the one who turns someone off to God.

I took a deep breath and made eye contact, saying, "I don't say anything at all."

"What do you mean?" she responded.

"I mean just that, I don't say anything. I just hope to live my life in a way that creates an invitation, forms a question, or fosters conversation. That's all."

I guess the answer was okay, because she didn't press on. But it made me think long after the book club was over. Then I found this verse, and it helped me because Jesus didn't say that we are supposed to go and convert people. He said we are supposed to go and share the good news. Thankfully what happens after that is God's domain. If we can live an invitation, and teach our children to do likewise, we can preach the gospel always, with words or without.

Jesus said to them, "Come and have breakfast."

JOHN 21:12

This is such a tender example of the Lord's patience with us. His own disciples kept having trouble recognizing Him and believing Him after the Resurrection. He let them touch His wounds and He ate with them so they would realize He was not a mere vision or ghost. This verse is such a sweet invitation, and it's one that I believe is extended to us as well. A little extra time in the morning to commune with God is a blessing that lasts throughout the day. Everyone knows that breakfast is the most important meal of the day, so perhaps we should consciously consider sharing it with the Lord.

My usual schoolday ritual consists of hurrying, frantic lunchbox stuffing and sandwich making, and serving breakfast at the counter like I am a short-order cook. I have a feeling that this verse is calling me to something higher than ziplock sandwich bags and Pillsbury cinnamon rolls with microwave bacon. I think it has something to do with time and intent. I wonder what would happen if I set the alarm fifteen minutes earlier on a weekday, eliminated the scattered rush with a few advance preparations, and had a family breakfast at the table. I wonder if we would start the day on firmer footing, if we would be more prompt, if we would be nourished by both food and love, if a pause to bless our food would ultimately bless our day. If you already do this, I commend you. I want to grow in this way, so I'm going to try it tomorrow.

*The woman, knowing what had happened
to her, came and fell at his feet and, trembling
with fear, told him the whole truth.*

MARK 5:33

This poor woman had been physically ill for twelve years, bleeding continuously in a way that no doctor could cure. She sensed the possibility for healing was upon her and she took her moment, touching the Lord's cloak. He felt His power drain into her weakness, and He stopped, asking who touched Him. Can you imagine the courage, the audacity, it would take to reach out and touch even the robe of the Son of God? She decided to come clean and just tell Him everything. His next words to her sear my heart: "Daughter, your faith has healed you. Go in peace and be freed from your suffering" (Mark 5:34).

Imagine with me the power of this moment. Jesus did not say she was healed because she touched His cloak, as if the fabric were magic. He said she was healed *because of her faith*. Her courage to reach out to Jesus and seek healing, believing that He alone could save her, was what healed her.

In what areas do we need healing? Where do we need peace? Where do we need freedom from suffering? Let's push through the crowded world and reach out to Him. Let's be brave enough to have faith in His healing. Let's be bold enough to ask, to fall at His feet with the whole truth.

Again Jesus said, "Simon son of John,
do you truly love me?"

JOHN 21:16

Jesus repeated this question to Simon Peter three times, so his answer must have been very important to Him. Peter finally cracked after the third round of questioning and said with exasperation, "Lord, you know all things; you know that I love you" (John 21:17). So Jesus said, "Feed my sheep" (v. 17).

The meaning is clear to Peter and to us: If you love Me, feed My sheep.

As mothers, we are blessed to have an immediate, clear vision of little sheep—our children. If we love Jesus, He wants us to feed (but also love and nurture) His sheep. If we think of the caretaking tasks associated with raising children, building a family and a home, and we look at them in the context of loving Jesus, each seemingly ordinary task takes on deeper context and meaning.

The way we feed our children spiritually is extremely important. Along these lines, when we illustrate to our children the importance of caring for the poor and needy, we teach them how to feed God's sheep. Once, we drove past a homeless man with a sign and Luke said, "Why is he there with that sign?" I thought before I spoke. "He wants money, help, food, drink, clothing, attention, love." So Luke asked, "Then why don't we give it to him?" Why don't we, indeed?

I try not to pass up clear opportunities to feed sheep. Jesus had to ask Peter three times. He has had to ask me three thousand times.

You will grieve, but your grief will turn to joy.
A woman giving birth to a child has pain because
her time has come; but when her baby is born she
forgets the anguish because of her joy that a child
is born into the world. So with you: Now is your time
of grief, but I will see you again and you will rejoice,
and no one will take away your joy.

JOHN 16:20–22

The pain of childbirth and the recovery afterward become no big deal whatsoever compared to the bliss of holding your baby. Put into proper perspective, the pain of that experience disappears. What if the same principle applied to other situations like the painful period before the birth of a new passion, new job, new identity, new talent, new perspective, or new era? We put so much emphasis on the pain involved in change and loss that we rarely look at the gifts we hold afterward.

God promises us that our grief will turn into joy. If you are in the midst of a difficult time right now, or if you love someone who is, these verses are for you to own or share. A period of trial always results in the birth of something wonderful; our laboring seasons are never without fruit. We have to trust that God will redeem everything. We have to believe that He will take every bit of our pain and repurpose it for His glory and for our growth. Just like the charred remains of a burned forest become the fertilizer for the new growth that eventually sprouts through the ash, our scorched areas are never permanently barren. He is never early and He is never late; He is always right on time.

Now, compelled by the Spirit, I am going to Jerusalem,
not knowing what will happen to me there.

ACTS 20:22

Paul traveled all over with this spirit of trust, never understanding the details of his missions as they were assigned, but
allowing them to be revealed as he went along. He trusted
God to go before him and make his path straight. Our life
journeys are somewhat like that. We don't know when we
graduate from college how our careers will develop. We don't
know on our wedding days how our marriages will unfold. We
don't know when we give birth to a child what the journey of
motherhood will hold. We don't know when we come to faith
where or how far our spiritual walks will take us.

How is the Spirit compelling you right now?

Is something weighing on your heart that feels uncomfortable or impossible, yet you are unable to shake it off? Are
you drawn to certain things without a full understanding of
why? Have you met people in situations recently that seem to
fit together, only you aren't sure what picture the puzzle pieces
represent? That pull is unmistakable when it comes from God.
We can run from it as far as we like, or try to hide, but we
can't escape our calling. We were born for times such as this;
it's our destiny. We don't know what will happen when we get
there, but we are somehow certain that we have to go.

He determined the times set for them and the exact places where they should live. God did this so that men would seek him and perhaps reach out for him and find him, though he is not far from each one of us.

ACTS 17:26–27

When we walk on eggshells, keep our thoughts and ideas to ourselves, hold back or play small, we are not fully playing the role that God intended for us when He created us. Reading these verses makes me think about how absolutely awesome it is to consider that God made each of us to be a certain person, in a certain place, at a certain time. He orchestrated all of it, and all of us, so that we would bring everyone during our time closer to Him. It hurts my brain to think about the wisdom and the planning going on behind the curtains of eternity.

If the stage is set for each of our lives at the appointed time, what happens when we shrink back when we are meant to step forward? What if we are too afraid to play our roles with great aplomb? When one person holds back, we all suffer, every single one of us. We each have gifts that were intended to be shared at this particular time and in this particular place where we happen to find ourselves. When we minimize our parts, or prepare as understudies for others' roles, the casting is thrown off. Be yourself.

Teach me in your way, O LORD, and
I will walk in your truth; give me an
undivided heart, that I may fear your name.

PSALM 86:11

What a sublime request to God, to ask for the gift of an undivided heart! Imagine how an undivided heart might serve me well as a mother:

- To love God with a whole heart.
- To follow Jesus with a whole heart.
- To trust the Spirit with a whole heart.
- To be present with my family with a whole heart.
- To listen to my children with a whole heart.
- To grow my faith with a whole heart.
- To follow my passions with a whole heart.
- To do my work with a whole heart.
- To minister and love with a whole heart.
- To love each child uniquely, with a whole heart, without favoritism.
- To love to learn with a whole heart.
- To seek growth, understanding, and wisdom with a whole heart.
- To repent with a whole heart.
- To heal and have a whole heart.

This is how we know that we love the children of God:
by loving God and carrying out his commands.

1 JOHN 5:2

My faith has known seasons of neglect. There have been times in my life when I made idols of other things...my social life, my job, my appearance, money, my husband, even my children. Looking back from my vantage point today, I can see that those times were marked by striving, futility, and lack of contentment. I feel regret today, knowing I missed out on so many things God had prepared especially for me at that time, and now they are lost forever. But it does motivate me to keep from straying into another season of departure or distance.

I am thirty-eight years old, and only in recent years have I understood to the core of my heart that loving anyone well means loving God first. Even as much as I love my children, I have to be able to put them second when it comes to the immediacy of following God. Loving God is not a draining kind of love, it is restorative. When I am in proper alignment to the King, my cup is filled to overflowing and I can do more and love more than ever. I have yet to have a gut-wrenching conflict, a showdown between a God assignment and my mothering. If I made an idol out of my work, or pretended that things were His assignments when they were really based in pride, I can imagine that things would not flow quite so nicely for me.

I want my children to understand that it is because I love God most and first that I am able to love them at all. I want them to see me struggle to be meticulous with His commands. I want to love them with the lavish outpouring of an obedient heart.

Dear children, do not let anyone lead you astray.

1 JOHN 3:7

This is a great verse to stick in the face of peer pressure. Instead of building up our own authority as parents, and enforcing the expectation that our children should be pleasing to us, what if we built up the authority of God? What if we stressed the importance of pleasing Him? When our children's friends want to take them off track, or cause them to stray from what they know is good and right, it becomes clear that this is not true friendship.

We must fill our children with light so that they are able to discern immediately and easily what is dark. We must help them cultivate a life of peace, so they can recognize discord. We must educate them on what is right, so what is wrong has glaring contrast. We must love them so fully that they are not trying to stave off emptiness. We must offer the sweet scent of truth so they can smell a lie. We must build their confidence in a Christ-centered way so that they are not easily dismantled by the opinions of others. We must build their foundation on a rock, so they will know the difference when walking on unstable ground.

We must nurture incredible friendships in our own lives so they will know the difference between real friends and counterfeit relationships in their lives. We must build them up, so that it is very difficult for others to bring them down. We must teach them to pray for wisdom so they realize that being smart isn't enough.

My dear friends, as you have always obeyed—not only in my presence, but now much more in my absence—continue to work out your salvation with fear and trembling, for it is God who works in you to will and to act according to his good purpose.

PHILIPPIANS 2:12–13

We can't always be with our children to monitor their choices, words, and behavior. They go on playdates and sleepovers, they go to camp, they go to college, they study abroad; they work and grow up and live their own lives. The kind of obedience Paul was talking about with the Philippians is exactly the kind of obedience we want to cultivate with our children. We want them to make good choices in our presence, but even more so in our absence. This is precisely why we cannot own the spiritual growth of our children. Their individual walks with God are not ours; they have their own journeys. Their relationships with God are not extensions of our relationship with Him, but are unique. They need to work out their own salvation with fear and trembling, whether they are in our company and under our roofs or out in the world.

It is the presence of God in our children that works in them to will and act according to God's purpose. This might come as a shock, or a major relief! It is not the image of us, hovering over their shoulders or nagging at them to do what is right. It is ultimately their relationships with God that will keep them on track—those are the relationships we need to pray for. Obedience is founded and fostered in love, or it is nothing.

*The end of all things is near. Therefore be clear minded
and self-controlled so that you can pray.*

1 PETER 4:7

Before I can get to work on a writing assignment or any other project, I have to have order. Before I settle in to write, my desk cannot be a disaster zone of unpaid bills, unsorted mail, and haphazard stacks of books. Before I start on a recipe, my kitchen sink cannot be full of dirty dishes and the countertops covered with half-eaten snacks and half-completed homework. I cannot begin a road trip with a dirty car. I can't pack for a trip without doing laundry first.

Maybe the symbolism behind clearing my work area is the idea of clearing my mind.

It is no different with our prayer lives. Before we enter the throne room of God, we have to clear our hearts of sin and our minds of distraction. We need to be able to focus so that we can present our praise and petitions to God, and, more important, so that we are able to listen. We all know that the most important thing to remember in any emergency situation is *Do not panic.*

When we go to God in the morning, we have no idea what lies ahead in our day. It might be an ordinary, uneventful day. Or it might be a day when we are called to think fast and respond. Since we can't possibly know what we will need before we pray, we need to have our heads clear and our emotions in check so we can center our day on God. That way, no matter what comes at us, our default setting will be peace, not panic.

Search me, O God, and know my heart; test me and know my anxious thoughts. See if there is any offensive way in me, and lead me in the way everlasting.

PSALM 139:23–24

To really pray this verse back to God with our whole hearts takes some spiritual maturity. A combination of three major things makes this verse incredibly powerful: One, it takes humility to admit that there likely are some offensive areas within us. Two, it takes courage to desire growth over comfort. And three, it takes deep trust in God to ask Him to illuminate areas of weakness in our lives and take steps to correct them.

If we really understand how much God loves us, we should not be afraid to ask Him for pruning or refinement. He wants to heal us, not hurt us. But the lessons, even when we've boldly asked for them, are not always fun. I often pray this prayer, or a version of it, with my friends as we run together in the morning. Days later something happens in my life and I am struggling and frustrated, venting to my friend Paige. She laughs and reminds me that I asked to be examined and pruned accordingly, so I can't complain now that it's happening and my prayer is answered. Oh, yeah, that's right, I did ask for this.

I do want to be better, stronger, more refined in my faith. When my anxious thoughts are exposed for what they are (weakness in character, weakness in faith, or both) and placed in the light, I can examine them with God's guidance and see how to address them.

I praise you because I am fearfully and wonderfully made; your works are wonderful, I know that full well.

PSALM 139:14

I have a ceramic plaque that hangs in my closet above my full-length mirror with this verse on it. When I am not liking my clothing options, my body, or my attitude, this verse stops me mid-complaint. I should write it on sticky paper and stick it to dressing room mirrors everywhere, especially in bathing suit departments. We women are so hard on ourselves!

I read an article in *Family Circle* magazine about girls and body image. It said the best thing a mother can do for her daughter's body awareness and self-esteem is to compliment herself. Huh? How strange. But that idea combined with this verse amounts to a pretty interesting perspective.

Imagine the gift we could give our daughters, and our sons who will marry other people's daughters, if we helped ease them into a deeper comfort level with their physical selves, and with aging. If we talked about ourselves kindly, from a perspective of godliness and love rather than vanity, wouldn't we be teaching them by example how they should be treating themselves? Scripture teaches us that our bodies are the temples of the Holy Spirit. As such, we need to care for our bodies and clothe them appropriately. We also need to honor them as temples, speaking about them with respect.

If you are tempted to belittle yourself instead of celebrate yourself, change your tune today.

I am the true vine, and my Father is the gardener.
He cuts off every branch in me that bears no fruit,
while every branch that does bear fruit he prunes
so that it will be even more fruitful.... Remain in me,
and I will remain in you. No branch can bear fruit
by itself; it must remain in the vine. Neither can you
bear fruit unless you remain in me.

JOHN 15:1–2, 4

❧

There are two trees on either side of my front steps by the sidewalk. During the winter, they are totally without leaves; their branches look like spindly bones. At a certain point in early spring, the gardener comes and hacks the branches back so far that they look like embarrassed children with bad haircuts. They look so pathetic that it appears they will never have leaves again.

Without fail, at some point when I'm not looking, these trees spring back to life. New branches burst forth, leaves unfurl and multiply. Clearly the gardener knows what he's doing. Just like our Father, the Gardener, knows what He's doing with us. He knows precisely at what point we need to be pruned back. He knows what branches are deadweight, and they are chopped off and cast away. He knows what branches have potential, When the appointed amount of time passes, we begin to grow and blossom and bear fruit.

If you have endured a season of pruning, you know that at first the clippers do not feel like our friend. But they are! It hurts to be pruned. But it's also a great honor, because it means that God sees something worthwhile in us, something worth cultivating.

If you remain in me and my words remain in you,
ask whatever you wish, and it will be given you.
This is to my Father's glory, that you bear
much fruit, showing yourselves to be my disciples.

JOHN 15:7–8

For the uninitiated, this may sound like a blessing free-for-all. Ask God for anything and get it? Sounds good to me! But upon closer examination, there is a very clear caveat: "*If you remain in me and my words remain in you.*" This means that before you ask anything, the prerequisite is that you are already walking closely with God. This means an intimate relationship, as well as obedience to His Word.

God loves us and wants to bless us, but He ultimately wants us to bear fruit for His glory, not for our comfort or convenience. The funny thing is, the more closely we walk with Him, the more we, too, want our work to be for His glory and not our own. A life that bears much fruit is indicative of a life well-lived, a life connected to the Source, the Vine. When people look at your life, what do they see? Do they see the fruit of an intimate relationship with God? Do they see evidence of an obedient lifestyle? Do they see choices made that glorify God? Do they see blessings flowing from the Source, through you, to other people? When people look at your children, do they see the same thing?

If we can talk to our children about the correlation of remaining or abiding in God and bearing fruit, they will learn what is behind the decisions we make for our families. They will see the importance of seeking God first, and glorifying Him in everything.

This is my command: Love each other.

JOHN 15:17

Yes, we should love our children, well and always. They are easy to love, because they are our flesh and blood, they are often adorable, and because they are experts at making sure their needs are front and center.

My dad always says that one of the best ways for a man to love his children is by deeply loving their mother. The same is true for a woman, loving her children by deeply loving their father. But we women can get so caught up in the love and care of our children that we often have nothing left for our husbands. By the time they get home at the end of the day we are tired, having given the best of ourselves to everyone else already. We think they understand because they are adults, but they get tired of leftovers and hand-me-downs when it comes to love.

It's too easy to become so focused on the family that we forget ourselves as a couple. Without a regularly scheduled date night, regardless of what it entails, we run a serious risk of living parallel lives, sometimes diverting so far apart that the distance becomes insurmountable. Don't wait. Don't be blind. Your children like to know that your marriage is a priority. It comforts them and establishes a firm foundation and a healthy hierarchy.

What can you do today to love your husband? Make an effort to reach across and connect, to listen, to ask, to call him first with news, to be vulnerable with him, to seek intimacy with him on all levels, to take specific steps to remember why you loved your guy in the first place.

I have much more to say to you,
more than you can now bear.

JOHN 16:12

We are told to answer our children's tough questions by responding in only as much detail as they need to know. A question about how babies are made from a four-year-old, for example, may not warrant the whole birds-and-bees presentation. A simple, "They are a gift from God," may suffice. No, some things are best answered honestly, but succinctly. Children are not able to bear everything at once.

And clearly, neither are we. In John 16, Jesus told His disciples why He had to leave and why this was in fact good for them, since they would receive the Holy Spirit in His absence. He launched into an explanation and then stopped Himself, realizing that He was about to go too far.

This reminds me of the way my children press me to tell them things, and I promise them more details when they get older. I want to protect them, yes, but I also want to ensure their full understanding on important subjects. Jesus knows our limits just as we know our children's limits.

Is there something going on in your life that feels muddled or confused? Are you trying to understand *why* when you should maybe just be asking *how* or *what next*? Remember that the Lord will always enlighten us as we go along. He won't leave us vulnerable and in the dark. He also won't confuse and frighten us with things we can't understand yet. Pray for wisdom, and be grateful when it comes in pieces. The whole chunk of it would bury us alive.

A time is coming, and has come, when you will be scattered, each to his own home. You will leave me all alone. Yet I am not alone, for my Father is with me.

JOHN 16:32

My friend Paige's daughter, Layne, is warm and friendly; yet often wanders off or plays by herself. I see her sometimes on the playground and love to go and talk to her. "What are you doing, Layne? How's it going?" I ask her. "Oh, I'm good," she says. "Just thinking." I ask her if she is lonely. "No, never," she says and smiles. She often has her nose in a book, usually the Bible. She is one person who is always aware that God is with her.

These words from Jesus echo my heart for my children. Whether they are feeling left out on the playground, excluded from the in-crowd in high school or lonely on Sundays away at college, I want them to know one thing: They are never alone. We can't be with our children in all their moments to ease the sting of hurt feelings or to protect them from betrayal or loneliness. We can't always see them when they feel invisible or unimportant or hold them in the moment their hearts break. But God can. And He will.

How differently would we live our lives if we eliminated any and all fear of abandonment? What if our awareness of God's presence was so strong that the idea of being alone lost all its power? Imagine our clarity of thinking, our standards for loving, and our freedom in relationships! No one could ever dangle our fear of abandonment over us as an unspoken threat. We could calmly and confidently walk away from any unhealthy relationship or environment. We would live our lives always having the better deal, because we do.

God is just: He will pay back trouble to those who trouble you and give relief to you who are troubled.

2 THESSALONIANS 1:6–7

The desire for revenge is the result of anger run amok. I see it in my kids all the time. Someone wrecks something that belongs to someone else (like Luke's latest Lego creation), and retaliation is immediate and physical. A tease is met with a slap. An insult gets a shove. My girls are notorious for what they call "the claw." One of them won't play according to the rules, and the punishment is a puncture grip to the forearm. I try to keep their nails as short as possible to avoid bloodshed.

I suppose the technique of controlling anger and the immediate gratification of revenge is similar to potty training: there is a process of recognizing the urge before it's too late. I'm trying to help my children see *If I hit Bella, then I get in trouble, too. If I let Mom handle it, Bella gets in trouble and I'm free.* I just want them to recognize that they have power over their feelings, not the other way around.

Even as adults we are in a similar situation. When we get angry, especially if we let our anger run unchecked, we are at risk for sin. Our impulsive reactions could hurt someone else, which makes us equally guilty. Or we can take those emotions to God and get them all out. If we truly believe that He is just, then we can trust Him to have our backs. He will handle the situation on our behalf and we are free, from both the burden of that emotion and the sin we would have committed had we lashed out on our own.

He said to the paralytic, "Get up, take your mat and go home." And the man got up and went home.

MATTHEW 9:6–7

༄

Imagine if the paralytic had not believed Jesus. What if he had stayed on his mat, stretched out flat as he had been for many years, and said, "Yeah, right. Sure." He would never have known he was healed and could walk because he never tried to stand!

So much of our healing and our growth is a collaborative effort between God's power and plan and our getting up off our mats. I have loved to write since I was a child. Before 2003, aside from school assignments, I wrote mostly in my journal. I ran my first marathon during a difficult year and wrote a letter thanking my two friends for helping me train and for the gift of the experience that was instrumental in my healing and in reclaiming my confidence. They suggested I send it in someplace. Feeling shy, I e-mailed *Runner's World* magazine, not knowing how rare it is to get work published by random solicitation. But God was waiting for me to get up off my mat; He had plans for me. They published my first article. I later became a contributing editor for the magazine. I also write columns and freelance for other magazines, and you are reading my fifth book.

If my friends had never told me they saw a worthy talent, or if I had preferred to stay on my mat, I might still be there, missing out on living my passion and my purpose. We have to work together with God to achieve His best for us. We can't ever tell our children to get off their mats if we are still lounging on ours.

Be diligent in these matters; give yourself wholly to them, so that everyone may see your progress. Watch your life and doctrine closely. Persevere in them, because if you do, you will save both yourself and your hearers.

1 TIMOTHY 4:15–16

Diligence is the willingness to groom our characters with impeccable attention to detail. Diligence for the skin is hydration, sleep, and daily sunscreen. Diligence for the body means wise nutrition and sustained fitness efforts over time. Diligence for the mind is consciousness about how we are feeding our thought lives, whether through books, media, conversations, or study. Diligence for the soul is prayer and rest. Diligence for the heart is integrity and intimacy.

The most common barriers to diligence are laziness and busyness.

We start to slip up in one area, but it's small and we rationalize it, so we let it go. This takes us a bit off track, and when it happens again (it gets easier) we are a bit further off track, and so on, and so on, until we are way off course from our intentions. Just as it's easier to lose five pounds than twenty-five pounds, or to pay off one painful credit card bill rather than rack up a pile of interest, being diligent requires more effort on the front end. It's easier to correct a minor slipup and come clean than it is to dig our way out of a pit.

Are there any areas in your life right now where you have let things go a bit? If it isn't obvious to you, ask a trusted friend or your spouse, and pray to God to illuminate areas that need to be addressed.

They will lay up treasure for themselves as
a firm foundation for the coming age, so that
they may take hold of the life that is truly life.

1 TIMOTHY 6:19

Our culture defines life in so many ways, but mostly in terms of "the good life." This is comfort, financial gain, public approval, perceived status, and material accumulation. Times are rapidly changing in our country. We were living large and riding high for so long that our hedonistic, opportunistic lifestyles became the standard for normal. Our country has now been proven vulnerable, both in terms of security and in terms of financial power. We are no longer immune to the problems of the rest of the world. The bubble has burst, and reality has flooded in.

This is sad in some ways; the end of an egotistical era is always a bit painful (like exiting our twenties!). Our untouchable status gave us a sense of comfort. We are now in a new era, one where we are going to have to define life in a more personal and purposeful way. We are going to be called to make some uncomfortable choices about morality, about finances, about values, about freedom, about what it really means to live the good life.

Babylon is falling. But for believers, this may actually be encouraging news. We want to take hold of the life that is truly life. We want to understand what is counterfeit and what is real. We want to store up treasures where they cannot be raided and cannot rust. We want to hope in what endures. We want to believe in what prevails. We want our foundation to be firm. We want our love to be eternal.

*[Jesus Christ] gave himself for us to redeem us
from all wickedness and to purify for himself a people
that are his very own, eager to do what is good.*

TITUS 2:14

We are constantly being reformed and transformed. The
further we go along in our spiritual journeys, the more God
molds and purifies our characters. God uses everything for
good, even our rough patches and our mistakes.

Several months after my friend Paige and I went through
a tough spot in our friendship, our daughters got into an argument at school. I happened to be in class that afternoon; the
final bell rang and they started to exchange some sharp words.
I explained that Paige and I went through something similar
recently and it was really hard and it really hurt. They were
incredulous. Paige's daughter Riley asked, "Really?! You and
Mom got in a fight?"

"Yes," I said, "we did. When you are really close to someone, it's going to happen sometimes. We aren't perfect."

"So what happened?"

"Well," I explained, "I think when you love someone so
much you can take them for granted sometimes and forget
how lucky you are. Maybe I took your mom for granted and it
hurt us both. Now our friendship is even stronger than before.
Maybe you guys need to have a talk like that?"

They threw their arms around each other, and said, "I
love you!" "I love you, too!" I wrapped my arms around them
both, thanking God for the wisdom to use something painful
from my life to bless and heal theirs.

*I pray that you may be active in sharing your faith,
so that you will have a full understanding
of every good thing we have in Christ.*

∾

I come from a background of faith. My father's family is Catholic, and my mother's family is blended Catholic and Lutheran. So much of what I learned in weekly CCD classes involved the memorization of prayer and a sense of reverence for what is holy. My family prayed formal Catholic prayers, not extemporaneous or intimate. As I grew older I had seasons of both closeness and waywardness in my walk with God.

Then, in 2003, a time of brokenness and desolation in my life, everything was stripped down and my faith was tested. The roads diverged and I had to choose. My faith was actualized at that time. It went beyond ritual and became relational.

All of it began to unfold and make sense, and the rites and rituals of my childhood faith took on adult-sized appreciation. The combined smells of candles, incense, and old hymnals make me swoon with delight. The quietness and mysticism of time spent kneeling in adoration fills me. The Eucharist heals me. The confessional cleanses me. And yet I can go to informal, nondenominational Christian services with my friends and be filled in other ways, worshipping with praise music and hands held high.

Our faith must be active and growing, challenged and honed. I want my children to experience God in many ways, to personalize their faith, activate it and actualize it, and have their own, unique relationships with our Lord.

*Keep watch, because you do not know on
what day your Lord will come.*

MATTHEW 24:42

❧

Doesn't it always seem like company drops in unexpectedly if your house is a mess? Or you run into someone significant at the grocery store when you look like a slob? Or you are arguing with your husband and wearing a bad outfit when you walk into a room and a crowd of friends and family shouts, "SURPRISE!"?

Yep. It's always when we least expect it. We need to be ready precisely when we are not. That is the point of this verse: to be ready, to live in a state of readiness. Be watchful. Be mindful. What if your conversation with your children was being recorded? Speak as if it were.

Keep your house and yourself presentable, just in case. Live as though your final moment might be the next one. Tell people you love them; apologize for your mistakes; speak the truth; walk in the light; invite people over; go on adventures; make the tough choices; take time for hugs, notes, and phone calls; remember birthdays; visit new babies in the hospital; go to funerals; keep your affairs in order; pay your bills; give to those in need; make amends and rebuild burned bridges.

Time is short, ask anyone who loves someone who has died. Our day is coming, possibly soon, when God calls us to something higher or He calls us home. We should make every effort to live the way we want to be remembered.

*"Why this waste?" they asked. "This perfume
could have been sold at a high price and
the money given to the poor."*

MATTHEW 26:8–9

❧

I have known my friend Peggy my entire life. Her mother, Nancy, was my mother's best friend until she died of cancer in 2001. Nancy helped my mother with the ins and outs of breast-feeding, mothering, and being a corporate wife. She always had the perfect recipe and the right thing to say. Both Peggy and Nancy are the kind of women represented by this woman in Bethany who poured the expensive perfume on Jesus' head and anointed Him.

The disciples were outraged at what they perceived to be a wasteful move. She poured out what could have been sold and given to the poor. But this woman knew better; she knew that no gesture was too lavish when you had a singular moment to honor the Son of God.

When I go to Peggy's house I am a guest of honor. When we go, she cooks the foods we like, she buys treats for my kids, she puts fresh flowers, Junior Mints (my favorite candy), new books, and magazines I like next to the guest bed. She is the only friend who keeps a framed photo of me and my ex-husband on her shelf.

"Your past is safe and honored here. Your kids need to know I love their dad, too," she says. She loves extravagantly. She isn't a wealthy woman, but if she loves you, she loves you large. Whatever she has, she pours over you, just like the woman in Bethany. We could all take a lesson.

> *"If you can?" said Jesus. "Everything is possible for him who believes."*
>
> MARK 9:23

I am sometimes puny when I come before God. I don't mean that I am humbled, I mean wimpy and small-minded. In this chapter from Mark, a father brings his boy to Jesus for healing, and says in a sniveling way, "But if you can do anything, take pity on us and help us" (Mark 9:22).

If you can do anything? If? Can you imagine the audacity of minimizing the power of the Son of God? We come before God with slumping spiritual posture and mumble our requests, feeling hopeless and dejected, possibly even considering our prayers to be questionable last-ditch efforts.

We are children of God, not beggars in the kingdom! We need to come before God with humility, of course, but also with the boldness of knowing we are loved. With clean hearts and obedient wills, we can come before our Father and pour out our hearts. We can tell Him everything and ask Him to fix it. But we have to ask Him faithfully, believing that nothing is impossible for Him. Without belief, our prayers sound like mumbling.

I love the response of this desperate father in verse 24: "Immediately the boy's father exclaimed, 'I do believe; help me overcome my unbelief!'" Isn't this honesty refreshing? I often incorporate his response into my own prayer life, stating the intent of my heart before God and simultaneously confessing that my faith wavers but I want to make it strong.

Many who are first will be last, and the last first.

MARK 10:31

From picking teams to forming lines, we are conditioned from childhood to vie for first place. Adults continue to do this, too; watch people next time you are waiting at the airport to board a flight. It is in our nature to push and shove on our own behalf to the point that planes have to be boarded by announcing seat assignments and cattle shoots have to be created to contain lines for rides at amusement parks. Left to our own devices, we are ill-mannered and self-promoting.

Our Bible study had a family retreat at a nearby camp. On the wall in the dining hall was written in big letters, "I am third." I inquired about it because I hadn't heard that before. One of the counselors explained that it meant "God first, others second, self third." What a beautiful and easy way to remember how Jesus wants us to live. Anytime I see one of my children take this third place, I try to acknowledge it in some way, whether I let them go first the next time or I hug them and compliment them. It inspires me to monitor how often I am third in my own life, or whether I am missing opportunities to love God and others with greater intention.

How can we take an opportunity today to illustrate this concept for our children? How can we make it real for them? How can we show them that God always takes care of those who let others go first? It is a different discipline to attempt to live this way, but the younger we start, the sooner it becomes part of our character. It is a mindful and missionary way to live.

We work with you for your joy,
because it is by faith you stand firm.

2 CORINTHIANS 1:24

❧

You have to stand for something or you'll fall for anything. In our culture today there are so many mixed messages and rationalizations that allow us to deviate from our values. It is more important than ever that we be consistent and clear with our children when we are talking about family values. This is the only thing that will give them firm footing when peer pressure starts to rock their worlds.

I think it's important to define our values together, so that we all have a part in setting the standards for our family. One day, I got out some large pieces of white tagboard and some color markers. I called a meeting of the minds in my kitchen with my kids. "Guys, who are we?" I asked. "What does it mean to be an Armstrong? What does that look like to people outside our family?" The children were five and seven, and you would not believe the responses I got. Things like, "The Armstrongs are kind, faithful, compassionate, and strong; we help others, we don't give up...."

It was incredible! We brainstormed and made a list of the Armstrong family values which we call our Code. When one of us (myself included) deviates from who we are, we ask one another, "Are you being the person you want to be right now? Are your choices in line with our family code?" We keep one another accountable.

*Praise be to the God and Father of our
Lord Jesus Christ, the Father of compassion and
the God of all comfort, who comforts us in all our
troubles, so that we can comfort those in any trouble
with the comfort we ourselves have received from God.*

2 CORINTHIANS 1:3–4

I have crumpled into a pile of tears on the floor of my kitchen and found myself wrapped completely by three sets of arms and legs. I have had a miserable cold and had orange juice and chicken soup delivered on a wobbling tray. I have smacked my head on the corner of a cabinet, cried and felt a little hand reach up and hold ice against my bruise. I have been edgy and nervous before a speech or a race, rushing to get ready when I hear, "Don't worry, Mommy, you are going to do awesome."

Compassion is a chain reaction. God comforts and fills me, because that's just who He is. Since I am whole and healed, I am able to love my children abundantly. I comfort them always and everywhere. They grow up feeling full, first filled by God, then by me, and they go on to comfort others. When we give thanks to God for His comfort, and respond by lavishing love on our children, they learn how to be thoughtful, kind, generous, and compassionate people.

It is only by learning how to receive that we are truly able to give. Are you allowing God to comfort you to the point of healing?

No matter how many promises God has made,
they are "Yes" in Christ.

2 CORINTHIANS 1:20

No matter where you find yourself when you read this page today, know that God has plans in place for your healing and your good, regardless of any circumstances. Nothing is impossible for Him; nothing is too much or too hard for our almighty God. He is triumph, He is victory, He is patience, and He is power. Every promise in Scripture applies to you and your family. Every word spoken of redemption and mercy, forgiveness and grace is penned in timeless ink and has your name on it. When we believe in Christ, we are held firm by God's "Yes." So pray to Him this morning with the full confidence of one who is deeply understood and unconditionally loved.

I have a quote from Emily Dickinson posted in my office that says, "Dwell in possibility..." Are you dwelling in what is possible today? Or are you stuck in what you think is impossible? The difference is where we decide to hold our gaze. Are we going to keep staring at the circumstances or are we going to lift our eyes up to the one who can help us? Shifting our perspectives changes the way we see everything, especially when faith is our lens. God gets bigger and our problems get smaller as things move into proper focus. Belief is the catalyst for the fulfillment of all God's promises.

*The Lord is the Spirit, and where
the Spirit of the Lord is, there is freedom.*

2 CORINTHIANS 3:17

~

Bella got in the car one day after school with a sad, confused look on her face. "What's wrong?" I asked her. "Did you have a bad day?"

"One of the kids in my class said I was weird," she said with a sniffle.

"Why?" I asked.

"Because of what I'm wearing today." Her eyes were downcast. She was, admittedly, dressed a bit odd; she has her own ideas about fashion, she always has. She was the one who wore her princess costume for weeks on end, months probably, as regular attire back in her preschool days. On this particular day she was wearing an adult man's size large University of Texas football jersey, which looked like a shapeless dress, with ARMSTRONG emblazoned across the back and a huge number one. She paired this with white lace-trimmed socks and sneakers.

"Well," I ventured, "how do you think you look?"

"I think I look cool," she said matter-of-factly.

"Then you look cool," I said. "People who are free to be themselves are often called weird. It can be a very big compliment."

"Really?" She got a big smile on her face and went on with her day, unscathed. I love her freedom; in fact, I envy it sometimes, to be perfectly honest. Both she and her sister are free spirits, relatively unconcerned with other people's opinions. I pray every day that this will last as long as possible, long enough to build a solid foundation of confidence built in Christ.

Such confidence as this is ours through Christ before God.
Not that we are competent in ourselves to claim anything
for ourselves, but our competence comes from God.

2 CORINTHIANS 3:4–5

❧

Confidence that is not founded in Christ is faulty. It is a structure with a cracked foundation, walls infested with termites, and covered by a roof that leaks. I should know; I used to have confidence based in myself, and every time a storm hit, the wind blew, the ground shook, or it started to drizzle, I was vulnerable. I would work hard to make things right or try hard to pretend they were right, but my efforts were insufficient. I finally hit a point in my life where I could no longer function like that. I needed something bigger than me to get me through. My breaking point became my release.

After this, I could rebuild my confidence with Christ at the center. If I trusted Him to see me through, it didn't matter as much whether I could handle it or not. The God of the universe had my back. It soon became clear that He would either equip me or rescue me. Meanwhile I worked, not on solving my problems, but on building my faith.

This lesson stays with me. I don't want my children to have to repeat my journey on those roads. I'd rather help them today to build their confidence with a firm foundation in God, solid walls, and an impermeable roof. Cultivating a relationship with God might take a little longer, or require a bit more effort than simply believing in yourself, but you have only to build it once, and it will last forever. A life built upon your own abilities and your own strength has to be rebuilt after every storm.

You ought to forgive and comfort him, so that
he will not be overwhelmed by excessive sorrow.
I urge you, therefore, to reaffirm your love for him.

2 CORINTHIANS 2:7–8

For a period of time in the beginning of his year in third grade, I spent too long holding court in the kitchen and monitoring Luke's homework progress. We were both frustrated. He wanted to relax or get out of it, and I wanted it done quickly and correctly. Cracking the whip was not working. I talked to Luke's wise teacher and she told me to simply stop what I was doing and trust him.

A new scenario followed that meeting. "Luke, are you going to get started on your homework?" I asked. "Yeah, sure. But I want to have a snack and watch TV, then I'll do it," he said. I trusted him as Ms. Underwood suggested.

One day he forgot a math assignment, and in Ms. Underwood's class, if you forget your homework, you have to sign "the Book" and you automatically miss recess. Luke got into the car after school and said he'd had a bad day, that he forgot to do his math, had to sign the Book, and missed recess. He stopped and waited for me to start berating him. I thought for a minute, and I hugged him instead.

"I'm sorry you had a rough day, it's no fun to miss recess." He knew without a doubt that I was on his side. But he really felt it when I finally got out of the way, let him be responsible, and reaffirmed my love for him.

If anyone is in Christ, he is a new creation;
the old has gone, the new has come!

2 CORINTHIANS 5:17

I love the idea of a fresh start. I love the before and after photos in magazines, I love the news stories of personal triumph over adversity. I love second chances, late-in-life love affairs, do-overs, I'm sorrys, and photo retakes. I love the confessional booth, and I think forgiveness smells like candles. I love New Year's Eve, even though I rarely go out. I love a new journal with fresh, blank pages. I love power-washing mildew off the patio. I love a new calendar—yes, I still use paper calendars. I love renewed wedding vows, meeting newborn babies in the hospital, housewarming and retirement parties, and that new car smell.

So it's no wonder, then, that I love this verse and you can find it scrawled in my calendar, notebooks, and stuck on sticky notes in random drawers and cabinets at my house. I am someone who can get stuck replaying my mistakes and holding out on my own forgiveness while I "punish" myself. It's ridiculous, I know, and I wouldn't allow a friend or my child to treat themselves like that, but I do it sometimes. I need to be reminded that God's forgiveness, if requested from a truly repentant heart, is immediate and complete. We are instantaneously made new.

Come, let us go up to the mountain of the LORD.

MICAH 4:2

In late winter or early spring of each year, I try to steal my kids away for a night in Fredericksburg, a tiny German town in the Texas hill country. We stay in a rented cabin or cottage. It usually has no television. We have dinner together at a casual spot and come back and read before we fall asleep. After breakfast the next morning we head to Enchanted Rock, about fifteen miles away.

Enchanted Rock is a state park, with a huge rock hill in the middle of it. We pack hats, hiking shoes, water bottles, and sunscreen and make our pilgrimage. The hike begins at the base of the hill, and winds around for a bit before the steep ascent to the top. There is no trail here, just rock, and I always worry one of us is going to slip. When you get to the top of Enchanted Rock, the view is long, unencumbered, and beautiful. The people at the bottom look like ants, and we always congratulate ourselves on our teamwork and on completing the climb. Then we flop down on the summit, drinking our water and stretching out flat to look at the sky.

The last time we were up there, a breeze passed over us as we sprawled out, and I knew it was the Holy Spirit. I thanked God for our little family unit, His protection over us, and the beauty and majesty of His creation. Going on an adventure together is a very good thing. It takes us out of our normal routine and gives us fresh eyes to see God and one another.

To the roots of the mountains I sank down; the
earth beneath barred me in forever. But you brought
my life up from the pit, O LORD my God. When my
life was ebbing away, I remembered you, LORD, and
my prayer rose to you, to your holy temple.

JONAH 2:6–7

I can relate to this Scripture, taken from Jonah's prayer, because I, too, have at times veered from the path of faith and been restored. For me it wasn't so much defiance as it was laziness, more like a fade than an abrupt turning of my back. I made small choices and sacrifices that led me further from God until I got far enough away that I forgot how to get back. When we get off track spiritually, we often falter and fall into the nearest pit.

When I fell into a pit in my early thirties, it took me a while to realize where I was. But then realization dawned on me like a missing puzzle piece fitting into place; I knew what I needed, or, better said, *whom* I needed. And I cried out in prayer. God was where He always is, nearby, and He heard my plea for help and responded with might and mercy.

This is the gift I want buried deep in the core of each of my children. I want them to have the base knowledge that they belong to God, no matter what they've done or where they are. If the twists and turns of life lead to a situation where they are in a pit and I cannot be nearby to assist or remind them, I want them to have that one thing. It is what remains standing when everything else has fallen away, and I want them to recognize that.

*Let us run with perseverance the race
marked out for us.*

HEBREWS 12:1

❧

Today I got to watch Luke run the fifty-yard dash at Track-and-Field Day at school. When you are running in a race, your focus has to be within yourself. It is your race, your ability, your endurance, your strategy and your results. When you run, you run alone. Even if you can feel someone behind you in hot pursuit, breathing down your neck, you can't turn around to see how close they are. You can't try too hard to out-run them for risk of wearing out too soon. You must continue to run your own race and hold your own pace, even when you are surrounded by distractions.

Our spiritual journeys are just like this. We each have to maintain focus on our own relationship with God. There are all kinds of distractions around us. When we start to pay more attention to what other people are doing, we lose our concentration and get off pace. We adjust to other people's strides instead of maintaining our own. Endurance is built by sustained effort over time. It is the unshakable willingness to persevere. This ability transcends any one category of life and applies to them all.

We need endurance in our faith, in our relationships, in our careers, in our fitness, and in our learning. We need endurance to retain balance and humility when times are good. And we need it to survive and help others in hard times. It is worthwhile on many levels to learn how to run a good race.

My dear children, for whom I am again in the pains of childbirth until Christ is formed in you, how I wish I could be with you now and change my tone, because I am perplexed about you!

GALATIANS 4:19–20

❧

Children go through confusing periods, trying to transition and adjust to internal and external changes as they grow, leaving one stage and entering the next. I read a great series of parenting books that call these various stages "periods of harmony or dissonance," referring to the state within the child and consequently the family unit. Children are constantly being reborn in a sense as they evolve, so it stands to reason that the pains of childbirth ebb and flow over a mother's lifetime.

Sometimes my children are fully engaged with me and enjoy my company. Other times, without warning, one can become sullen or angry, provoked by the slightest shift of a breeze. When I ask them about it later, they often have no idea how or why that happened. I suppose that until Christ is fully formed in all of us (which isn't going to happen anytime soon; we each have so much work to do), we are subject to tumultuous waves as the Spirit and our nature fight over custody of our hearts.

I am often confused by my children, especially when they make choices that I know they know better than to make. But this helps me to remember that I am also oftentimes a mystery to myself. I do or say something and later wonder what on earth I was thinking. Birth is painful, unpredictable, and ongoing.

If you keep on biting and devouring each other,
watch out or you will be destroyed by each other.

GALATIANS 5:15

Sometimes the scene in my car looks like a wrestling ring. Words and fists are flying, hair is pulled, and skin is clawed. Sometimes I get so frustrated that I don't know whether to turn up the radio or pull over and become a dictator until order is restored. I try to explain to my children in times of peace how it feels to me when they fight, and while they seem to understand, all awareness and good intentions fly out the window when one of them is outraged by a sibling.

I know some of this is natural and normal, a microcosm of learning how to be an advocate for yourself in this big world.

If our homes and families are our primary sources for discovering who we are and how we are received by the world, we have to be very careful that our children do not harm one another. Of course this a safety issue, but injury can also occur spiritually and emotionally. Some adults today are haunted by the teasing of their siblings, and they still hear the words in their heads that cut them down as children.

If our primary job is to make sure our children know God, then they have to feel God's love at home. It is worth it, no matter how tired we are or how immune we think we have become, to be diligent about monitoring levels and enforcing limits with sibling rivalry and infighting. We learn how to treat others by the way we love and are loved at home.

> *Carry each other's burdens and in this way*
> *you will fulfill the law of Christ.*
>
> GALATIANS 6:2

When the kids and I go hiking, we usually start off strong, each of us carrying our own backpacks and water bottles. As time passes, my hikers heat up and start stripping off long-sleeve t-shirts, passing them to me to tie around my waist so they can move unencumbered. Then water bottles start to get heavy or they want to hike hands-free, and the bottles go in my backpack. Little by little, I am weighted down, carrying burdens that weren't mine to begin with.

But there is something to be said for the weight of burdens; they make us stronger. And within the context of family, when we divide burdens between us, they are more easily carried.

Just as burdens are divided when shared, miraculously joy is multiplied when shared. At the end of a journey, or in the reaching of a goal, when our family has traveled the road together the celebration is many times as sweet.

As children grow, they need to assume more responsibility for themselves so less of the overall burden falls on Mom.

When children realize how important their parts are, they begin to take pride in their own efforts and their own contributions. Just as a teenager who worked to buy a car is more apt to be careful with it, we all are more conscientious when we have a sense of ownership. We all are strengthened when we bear the weight of our own loads.

Are you so foolish? After beginning with the Spirit, are you now trying to attain your goal by human effort?

GALATIANS 3:3

I have been this kind of fool many times. I know better. I know the difference between being directed and empowered by God and going off on my own. When I take off on my own without staying connected to my Source, I lose steam. I feel overwhelmed, overly emotional, and easily exhausted. I doubt myself—both my capabilities and my motives. For the important things in my life, human effort simply isn't enough.

When I am conscious of living a Spirit-led life, I can do everything I normally do and more without stress or fatigue. My thinking is clear and focused. I don't worry about being or having enough because it isn't about my effort; I know God will equip me through its completion. I don't worry about what's next or if I'm ready.

If you have felt the weight of the world on your shoulders lately, remember that you aren't supposed to. Realign yourself with God and His purposes for you. Ask to be sure that what you are working on is truly an assignment from Him, and center yourself so you can better receive His guidance and direction. If you feel frustrated or low on energy, remember your power Source and check your connection. If you aren't plugged in, that will explain why your own battery keeps fading. For the biggest assignments in life, like marriage and motherhood, only a Spirit-supplied effort will suffice. Let's not be so foolish as to think we can do it all on our own.

I have not stopped giving thanks for you, remembering you in my prayers. I keep asking that the God of our Lord Jesus Christ, the glorious Father, may give you the Spirit of wisdom and revelation, so that you may know him better. I pray also that the eyes of your heart may be enlightened in order that you may know the hope to which he has called you, the riches of his glorious inheritance in the saints, and his incomparably great power for us who believe.

EPHESIANS 1:16–19

Whether a child is toddling off to preschool, walking down the aisle at their wedding, or starting a family of their own, this verse powerfully speaks of the commitment and love of a faithful parent.

I believe that if my children understand the hope they have been given, the promise of salvation that has been sealed, and the power that comes from faith—they will be able to face anything in this lifetime.

I need to put these verses on three-by-five cards in my car, in my purse, in my kitchen, and by my bedside so I can start committing them to memory. I want to know this passage by heart and pray it over my children, anointing them with these words like sacred oil.

God has a special place for mothers. I like to think that He has a red phone, a separate line, just for our prayers. I think if we truly understood how much power we have, we would hone it and use it more expertly. It isn't enough to fight for our children in this world; we have to fight for them in the spiritual realm with equal or greater tenacity. The Word of God is our spear.

Do everything without complaining or arguing,
so that you may become blameless and pure, children
of God without fault in a crooked and depraved
generation, in which you shine like stars in the
universe as you hold out the word of life.

PHILIPPIANS 2:14–16

When I pray for my children before school, I often pray that their faith would shine through them, that they would be a light to others. I love the idea of their little souls twinkling in the relative darkness of this world.

I think reflecting God's light is a finer invitation to faith than any specific words or teaching. There is a big difference between being directed or informed and being invited. Something shiny always catches your eye, whether it's a glint on the sidewalk or the horizon, or a person you can't help but notice, even in a crowded room. To me, that special something that shines is a love of God. It radiates from a faithful heart and attracts people, even when they aren't aware of what they are attracted to at first.

Certain people just sparkle; they make other people perk up and want to ask questions. They hold allure, mystery, hopefulness, promise, and joy. A person is better able to reflect God's light when they are less concerned with maintaining the spotlight for themselves. They become porous, transparent, translucent to the glory of God, until they themselves are one with the light. This is what I want for my children, to reflect God's light no matter where they are, whom they are with, or what they are doing.

> *Do not be misled: "Bad company corrupts good character."*

1 CORINTHIANS 15:33

For as much effort as we put into raising our children to have good character, our efforts can be thwarted at precisely the most critical time. At certain phases, children are particularly vulnerable to being lured into the wrong crowd. We all have to be very discerning about the company we keep.

When our children are young we can organize playdates with families we like and who share our values. We can do our best to cultivate these relationships and hope they become lasting ones. We can foster good and godly friendships in our own lives to be an ongoing example of what healthy relationships look and feel like. We can find camps and extracurricular activities that draw people of integrity and faith. But ultimately we can't control whom our children socialize with at school, whom they gravitate to at functions and activities, or exactly who is around them once they start driving and having more freedom. At this point we have to rely on the foundation that has already been laid, either that they will not depart from it at all, or that they will return to it if they get off track.

We have to pray protection over our children constantly, and ask the Lord to keep watch over the company they keep.

*When I said, "My foot is slipping," your love,
O LORD, supported me. When anxiety was
great within me, your consolation brought
joy to my soul.*

PSALM 94:18–19

One of the greatest faith builders is to remember God's faithfulness in the past. I like to journal all the times He has comforted me, calmed me, or answered my prayers. When I am struggling again later, I love to reflect on how far God has carried me, all the things He has already done to help me. Returning to these intimate memories, I am encouraged and filled with praise. And praise unlocks power.

When we praise God by proclaiming His faithfulness, His power, His righteousness, and His love, we bring God glory and delight. When our prayer language thanks God in advance for His solution or protection, His deliverance or healing, we are boldly stepping out in faith. Expressing gratitude *before a single thing has transpired* shows that we trust and believe that He is going to move on our behalf. We are proclaiming our way into a deeper level of reliance.

Our faith is built on relationship behind these experiences, one solid brick at a time.

Don't you know that when you offer yourselves to someone to obey him as slaves, you are slaves to the one whom you obey—whether you are slaves to sin, which leads to death, or to obedience, which leads to righteousness?

ROMANS 6:16

Of course I want my children to be obedient to me, but more than that I want them to be obedient to God. Pleasing your mother is not motivation enough to withstand the waves of childhood, adolescent, and adult temptation. There is no way to sufficiently motivate or ensure that our children will be obedient in our absence. Discipline that is rooted in pleasing a parent can waver depending on emotion or whether or not the parent is present or aware of the misbehavior. Discipline that is rooted in pleasing God does not waver, because God is omnipresent and omniscient.

God works on a heart level, giving us the desire to do what is right and good, and empowering us to carry through on those positive intentions. Integrity is born here, and it is born of the Spirit of God.

Human discipline can be easily delayed or derailed. Our children have to understand the significance of working out their own salvation through their own personal relationships with Christ. I try to take myself out of the "pleasing equation" by asking my kids how they feel about a certain choice, action, or decision rather than blasting them with my disapproval. "And how did you feel after you decided to do that?" More often than not, they will be honest about how a bad choice made them feel bad. I don't want to be the catalyst for good choices; I want their faith to be the catalyst for good choices. I am unreliable; faith is not.

Do not lie to each other, since you have taken off your old self with its practices and have put on the new self, which is being renewed in knowledge in the image of its Creator.

COLOSSIANS 3:9–10

Certain things require careful application: lip liner, sunscreen, hair coloring, and nail polish, to name a few. But nothing requires such diligent application as the application of truth. Just as our human default is set to pride and we have to cultivate humility, our human default also easily leans toward deception if we aren't purposefully and passionately pursuing truth. Rather than deal with things that are uncomfortable or risky, we are typically content to let things slide, gloss over infractions, and say what is pleasing rather than what is real.

Our homes and our families have to have a zero tolerance policy for lying. We can't march our integrity out into the world if we haven't worked on it at home. To lay the groundwork for clean living, we have to solicit and accept the truth from our children, even if it's something we don't particularly want to hear. The consequences for speaking truth always have to be milder than the ramifications of deception. Speaking truth is like learning a foreign language or becoming fit—if you don't use it, you lose it. We have to work on being impeccable with our own word before we can require it of our children. It's okay for them to see us struggle and come clean. They will learn alongside us, just as we learn from them.

We must constantly recommit to the practice and the promise of living in truth. To do this we must be renewed constantly in knowledge in the image of God.

Be wise in the way you act toward outsiders; make the most of every opportunity. Let your conversation be always full of grace, seasoned with salt, so that you may know how to answer everyone.

COLOSSIANS 4:5–6

As Christians we are called to be lights to nonbelievers. A light illuminates, adds warmth, offers direction, and provides clarity. People who are outsiders to a life of faith can be easily turned off by believers who come on too strong, act too preachy, or use churchy language that sounds more like judgment than love.

Think of the differences between Jesus and the Pharisees. The Pharisees possessed great knowledge of Scripture and ritual, but they used it to condemn and belittle. Jesus was God Himself, and yet He shared His knowledge with the intent to teach, include, and invite.

At some point we need to be clear whether we are following Jesus or our religion. Hopefully they are one and the same, but the difference at heart-level is often made clear in our interactions with nonbelievers. Jesus used different angles, tactics, and vocabulary depending on the situation, but He was always about love. If our words and actions are not based in love and truth, they will never represent Jesus. And that is our job as believers. We show people how it feels to be loved by Christ, and that is what invites people to faith.

Our children are just as capable, or more so, than we are to accomplish this. We have to learn together how to make the most of every opportunity to share faith, sometimes wisely using words, most often by saying nothing at all.

*I am not ashamed, because I know whom
I have believed, and am convinced that he is able
to guard what I have entrusted to him for that day.*

2 TIMOTHY 1:12

The single most important word in this verse is *whom*.

Our faith does not reside in what we believe, but in whom we believe. Taking it even further, it isn't even sufficient to *believe in Christ*, we have to *believe Him*. We have to know about what God and Jesus have said and are still saying, but even more, we have to know the Source behind the Word. What good is a promise if we don't trust the person speaking the promise? What good does it do to read if we aren't certain about the author? This is why no amount of knowledge is more powerful than abiding faith.

We can know God's promises in Scripture backward and forward, but if we don't know who Jesus is and how deeply He loves us, we will never be able to accept that those promises belong to us. There will be no way we can truly understand that God has been taking care of His people for centuries, and we are included in His legacy. If we don't trust in Him and His promises for us, how can we live a life with our hearts set on eternity? If we don't believe Him, why should we care?

It is imperative that we illustrate this difference for our children and make it real. We must help them to cultivate the caliber of faith that comes from believing Jesus, not just believing in Him or about Him. We have to help them live their way into the conclusion that God is actually talking to them, personally. After all, we don't abide about Jesus, *we abide in Him.*

May the Lord direct your hearts into
God's love and Christ's perseverance.

2 THESSALONIANS 3:5

❧

The image of Christ carrying the cross is the ultimate picture of perseverance. There is nothing we can ever endure that would measure up to bearing the suffering for the sum of all the sin of mankind.

But as followers of Christ, our own versions of a cross to carry are real and also unavoidable. We cannot commit our hearts to following Christ and not expect some difficulty, interference, and flat-out pain. This world of ours is a broken place, for now, and we want to hoist our burdens bravely as we trek on through this lifetime and into the promised land.

My friend Darby is leaving soon on a mission trip to Africa. She called me one morning after a night filled with insomnia and fear. She wisely went to Scripture, seeking to center herself and remember who she is as a daughter of the King.

I listened to her and marveled at her presence of mind in the face of fear. "Darby!" I said, suddenly certain that what was on my heart was from God. "Of course you are being tested right now. He's not just going to send you on a mission unprepared! If He's stripping some stuff away, it's only because you need to be able to pack light to go where you're going, girl." She knows a spirit of fear is never from Him, and that perseverance will be required.

We are each being honed for our next adventure, and if we can see our testing from that perspective, it's downright exciting.

*After that, he poured water into a basin and
began to wash his disciples' feet, drying them with
the towel that was wrapped around him.*

JOHN 13:5

As part of the preparation process for our children making
their First Holy Communion at our church, we have several
gatherings and rituals. One afternoon we meet with our children and string the rosary beads that they will carry on their
special day, and hopefully keep forever. Another afternoon
our children have their first reconciliation, confessing their
sins to the priest. At one meeting, our Director of Religious
Education talks to the kids and parents about the significance
of the Eucharist and the sacrifice behind the ritual.

To further illustrate the concept of sacrifice, the story of Jesus
washing the disciples' feet before the Last Supper is read aloud.
Then in succession, each child and their parent or parents comes
forward to several chairs at the front of the room. The child sits in
the chair while the parent pours water over their feet into a basin
to wash them, then dries them with a towel. I remember looking
up at Luke with tears in my eyes as I rubbed my hands over his
feet, feeling the tenderness and humility of the gesture so deeply
and seeing understanding mirrored in his eyes.

Just as Jesus had a servant's heart toward his disciples, we
have a servant's heart toward our children. As they see us bend
to perform a historically lowly task, they have a better idea
of what it meant (and what it means) to be a disciple and be
cleansed by the Son of God. Love transforms the most banal
tasks into profound intimacy.

> *God did not call us to be impure, but to live a holy life.*
>
> 1 THESSALONIANS 4:7

I have struggled with purity since I hit puberty. With my body, my thoughts, my words, my actions, my intentions, and my motives; I want to be pure. But I would be lying to you if I said that it was not a constant war within me, sometimes one side prevailing, sometimes the other. It isn't any easier now at thirty-eight either. So as I have varying degrees of conversation with my young children about purity as they grow, I want to be honest about the tug-of-war that ensues. I don't want to gloss over temptation with a blanket statement about avoiding sin and think that it will suffice. I already know it won't.

I have no idea how to navigate the crosscurrents of open communication, judgment, discipline, awareness, moral standards, forgiveness, emotion, integrity, the messages of the world, and the Spirit of God. I do know that it won't be easy, and I know that I have to be real. I want to model my parenting after Jesus, in His brilliant, loving school of thought that if we can maintain a relationship, then understanding is always possible. I may be naive (based on my own past, I don't think so), but I believe that if I can just keep them talking, keep them open and asking questions, keep them sharing with me, then we might have a chance to at least navigate these storms in the same boat.

I want them to understand something I had to learn the hard way, that obedience is the path to freedom. I want them to see that a life in Christ is not boring or confining, but liberating and full of joy and surprises. Feeling pure is the lightest way to travel.

*He guards the course of the just and
protects the way of his faithful ones.*

PROVERBS 2:8

I pray constantly for God's protection over my children. I say the same things over and over to the point that I worry it is rote: "Lord, thank You for Your protection and provision. Please guard Luke, Grace, and Bella against all harm."

It occurred to me as I sat down today with this verse that in the past two weeks I have been in a car accident with Luke, Grace was nearly drowned by a dog climbing on her in a pool, and Bella crashed on her bike and cut her hand open. Luke and I got out of the car unharmed, despite the fact that the other car was totaled. Grace was able to push the dog away and swim to the side, and I was right there to haul her out of the pool. Bella crashed on the side of the road, there were no cars near her, and we tied Luke's shirt around her hand to stop the bleeding and got her home safely. Her hand is healing.

Instead of labeling these occurrences a string of bad luck, I would be wiser to see God's hand in all of them and get on my knees in praise. Clearly He is hearing my daily pleas for protection, and He is responding by saving us over and over again.

This world is such a dangerous place; our children cannot roam around in it without a shield of protection, applied daily in prayer by a diligent mother. Do not take this assignment lightly. There is no day when it is safe to let your guard down.

My son, do not despise the LORD's discipline and do not resent his rebuke, because the LORD disciplines those he loves, as a father the son he delights in.

PROVERBS 3:11–12

It isn't enough to understand God's truth; we have to be able to apply it…consistently. He won't let go of it, or us, until He is sure the point has been made, the sin has been purged, the wound has been healed, the lie has been uprooted, and the truth of His love has soaked through to the core.

The Lord's discipline is not fun; in fact, He makes sure it is memorable. I always remind myself to be glad He is bothering. It's when He lets you slide without reprimand that you should be worried. Even if it hurts, I want God to bother with me. I want Him to find me worthy of refinement and instruction. I want Him to keep uncovering potential in me.

I used this lesson the other day with my children. They were annoyed that I was harping at them about their table manners. *Please put your napkin on your lap. Please stay seated until everyone is finished.* "You know, kids, I try to help you because I love you and I want you to always be welcome and comfortable wherever you go." They looked at me, surprised. I don't think it had occurred to them that there was more to it than nagging, just like us when we forget that God's discipline isn't merely about punishment. He wants us to be the best versions of ourselves we can be.

Choose my instruction instead of silver,
knowledge rather than choice gold, for wisdom
is more precious than rubies, and nothing
you desire can compare with her.

PROVERBS 8:10–11

The materialism of our culture is as addictive and intoxicating as any drug. We have a bad day and comfort ourselves with a little retail therapy. We go to Target for one thing and come out with a cartful of others. We collect, consume, and covet. Just like a drug, our tolerance builds and builds until the former spending levels are no longer giving us the buzz we enjoy, so we up the ante on our purchases. Soon we are living cluttered, burdened lives beyond our financial means and wondering why, considering how often we fill up, we still come away feeling empty.

Without knowing it, we are raising our children to think this is okay.

To make a shift toward a more spiritual and simplified existence takes focus and effort. It becomes a series of choices, and a path of purging. I am not talking about denial so much as I am discernment. I am talking about fewer things of higher quality. I am talking about filling up and finding comfort in things that have spiritual significance. I am talking about turning from gluttony to gratitude, from consumption to contentment. I am talking about getting rid of what we don't need so we are more clearly able to see what we do need.

The blessing of the LORD brings wealth,
and he adds no trouble to it.

PROVERBS 10:22

I keep a quote in my calendar from Bonnie Friedman that says, "An unhurried sense of time is in itself a form of wealth." How fine is that? To me, one of the finest luxuries around is not having to scramble and hurry. I love to be intentional, unhurried, relaxed, responsive, and aware. This isn't easy when you have three young children.

On Thursdays my children are usually with their dad. My favorite gift to myself on Thursdays is to try to leave white space in my calendar. My tendency is to pack that day with one thing after another, the things I don't want to schedule when I have my children. But that is precisely what leads me to becoming poor in spirit. I am spent and exhausted instead of restored and reenergized. When the Lord blesses me with the wealth of time, I want to use it wisely. I want to get done what needs to get done, but I also want to leave breathing room, time for rest, a pause to welcome spontaneity and freedom in the moment.

What is wealth to you? What constitutes a luxury? It's important to know these things about ourselves so we can position ourselves to welcome them, and to recognize them in gratitude when God blesses us with them. God's blessings and His outpourings of "wealth" do not come with trouble (like stress or striving). If we are working so hard to have the lifestyle we want, only to find ourselves with no life at all, we might be chasing the wrong thing. Make some calendar white space so you have room to think.

*You open your hand and satisfy
the desires of every living thing.*

PSALM 145:16

❧

As mothers we can get so caught up in caring for everyone else that we forget some of the things we care about. We can be so focused on feeding our family's needs that we forget what feeds our souls. We can get so lost in loving that we forget what we love.

Regardless of our level of contentment with our family lives, we all will have seasons of restlessness, times when our unfed desires growl and grumble like a hungry tummy. No matter how we like to perceive our devotion, our desires were never meant to be shelved or stunted forever. We have certain desires and passions because God made us this way. When we ignore them, we prevent ourselves from fully becoming the women God intended us to be when He created us. Not only do we miss out, but everyone we love misses out when we play small.

What do you absolutely love to do? What makes you lose track of time or forget your fears or inhibitions? Where and how do you really shine? When do you feel most beautiful? Most capable? Most authentic? Most free? Take some time today to reflect or journal on these questions. If you honestly cannot remember what you love, don't panic, call your mom or your longtime friend.

God wants you to follow your passion. He wants to open His hand and satisfy your desires. He put all these things within you to make you undeniably you.

Accept one another, then, just as Christ accepted you, in order to bring praise to God.

ROMANS 15:7

What good is a family, or a friendship for that matter, if it does not offer respite from the world? Within the loving confines of our primary relationships, we need to know that we are accepted and loved unconditionally.

Of course there are things about some people that are hard to accept because they are so different from us. A morning person cannot understand the mind-set of a night owl. A vegan cannot stomach the idea of a steak dinner. A homebody is not excited to travel. An extrovert would much prefer a night on the town to a quiet evening with a book. A sedentary person does not see the joy in a nice, sweaty run. A reader cringes at the droning sound of the television. An animal lover does not seem to notice dog hair or drool. A messy person thinks a neat freak is annoying; a neat freak thinks a mess is unacceptable. A music lover may not enjoy silence. A nausea-prone person isn't up for fishing or a road trip. A nerd loves homework as much as an athlete loves a game. A type A invigorates a type B, and a type B chills out a type A.

A family is a beautiful mess, a mix of all kinds of quirks and eccentricities, edges and curves. If we are lucky, we even one another out. If we are even luckier, we delight in the differences, seeing the humor and joy in one another, maybe even growing from experiences and angles we wouldn't choose or notice on our own. God created us all uniquely, and Christ accepts us all unequivocally. We should follow Their lead.

May the God who gives endurance and encouragement give you a spirit of unity among yourselves as you follow Christ Jesus, so that with one heart and mouth you may glorify the God and Father of our Lord Jesus Christ.

ROMANS 15:5–6

I went running with a friend this morning and had to laugh out loud as she recounted the experience of pulling her two children in the wagon yesterday, sweating and exhausted, and then panicking—it is only the second day of summer! God bless an honest woman. Summer can be daunting, especially when long, hot days stretch before you and hours formerly occupied by school and extracurricular activities are now slated to Camp Mom 24/7. It isn't easy to remain calm, cool, collected, creative, and fun while running your life, household, and making ends meet. It helps to have girlfriends to share and laugh with.

We need to pray for endurance and encouragement, for ourselves and our friends, as we try to be all the things we need to be to all the people who count on us. We need a spirit of unity, on the home front and between friends. It is imperative that we stick together.

Where do you go to get refreshed and renewed? How do you reenergize? Who helps you keep your sense of perspective and sense of humor? What things do you have planned in the upcoming days that you are looking forward to, for you? What activities foster a sense of unity in your family? Are you doing those things often enough to keep the good juju flowing? What fuels your endurance—keeping your patience, creativity, energy, and smile alive? Are you taking good care of yourself?

Do not be overcome by evil, but overcome evil with good.

ROMANS 12:21

On a hike with my friend Christi through the redwoods of northern California, we followed lush trails—literally and conversationally. Our discussion flowed from children, to relationships, to friendship, to spiritual growth, and we began to speak about the pitfalls of anger and unforgiveness. Dwarfed by the enormous canopy of trees, it was almost easier to talk about such huge subjects as we walked in the constant awareness of our small stature.

We talked about how easy it is to get stuck in many areas when we are snagged in just one. One person we struggle with becomes an impasse for many other things. Until we can get a handle on that situation, others are at a standstill. Christi practices meditation, and because of this her outlook is constantly refreshed and centered. When you master the art of casting extraneous thoughts aside, the important ones can come into clearer focus. Both of us have loosened clogs in our spiritual lives by practicing a simple but powerful form of release. Pray for the person who causes you to stumble.

It sounds easy enough, but the level we are talking about is far from easy. We are not referring to a sneeze-like "Bless you." No, this dedication in prayer involves a daily commitment to offer this person to God for healing, blessing, and a deep and deliberate application of goodness. When someone rubs you the wrong way, it is a major endeavor to focus this much love in their direction. But I encourage you to try it for three weeks. See what happens.

Share with God's people who are in need.
Practice hospitality.

ROMANS 12:13

My mom is the best hostess I know. She is thoughtful, generous, well-prepared, fun, spontaneous, a great cook, and keeps
a warm, welcoming home. She is never put out or tired; she
can stay up late with one guest and get up for coffee the
next morning with an early riser. She can host events at her
house without fuss or fanfare, opening her home to alumni
or community groups, teacher parties, or church events that
are meaningful to her and my dad. I, on the other hand, am
slower to open my doors. I am hesitant to host friends for
extended stays, often feeling overwhelmed by meal planning,
sightseeing jaunts, and general responsibilities. I get tired and
my style gets cramped. I selfishly like to do my own thing.

I want to grow in this area and be more like my mom. I
want to be more spontaneous and more welcoming. I want
to be more thoughtful and generous. I do love to cook and
spend time with friends, I just need to work on letting go and
loosening up a little bit. Blessings are useless gifts when they
go unshared. And time is short, best spent with people we love
or helping causes we care about. When we are connected to
God as our Source, we don't get overwhelmed or overwrought.
We are constantly refilled so we can pour our love and energy
out to others. We can practice hospitality with our homes and
with our hearts. I want my children to grow up and remember
me that way, with arms and doors open.

You did not receive a spirit that makes you a slave again to fear, but you received the Spirit of sonship.

ROMANS 8:15

In some ways I used to be a lot braver before I had kids. I would try most anything. I would try to ski down runs that were beyond my skill level. I would bodysurf in the ocean, the bigger the waves the better, and I never gave much thought to sharks. I even went bungee-jumping!

Today I am wimpier about these things. I wouldn't get near anything with a bungee cord. I ski modestly and carefully, and I think helmets are a great idea. When my kids play in the waves I am on constant surveillance for the telltale gray triangle. But in other ways I am braver. I would lay my life on the line in an instant to save any one of theirs.

In fact, I want to wisely feed their spirits of adventure. Teri Hatcher was once interviewed on a television program and she told about swimming with her daughter next to a whale. Her daughter really wanted to do it, the guide said it was perfectly fine, and although she was petrified, she jumped in with her daughter. She didn't want her own fear to prevent her daughter from having a once-in-a-lifetime experience. She said it was amazing, and it forged a huge and very cool bond between them. She wanted her daughter to know she was brave and open to new things. Now I am not sure about swimming next to a whale, but I am sure about being brave with my children. I want them to live boldly and freely, trusting God at all times.

*It is with your heart that you believe and are justified,
and with your mouth that you confess and are saved.*

ROMANS 10:10

Our children will never grow into boldness about sharing their faith if we are wimpy about ours. My kids are constantly watching me. They scream at me if I pass by a homeless person on a corner without offering a dollar or some water or a snack. They watch the way I treat people and the words I use to talk to them. They see if I am in a hurry or if I make time for someone who is hurting. They listen when I pray with friends over the phone. They understand when I tell someone that I will pray for them, and they often remind me of it when we are saying prayers before bed.

My faith has to be active, real, living, and breathing. I have to make choices that reflect a heart for God, and I have to choose words that speak faith, and light, and love. I have to not only know who Jesus is, but also know Him well enough to introduce other people to Him. I understand that faith can be private and intimate, but this verse illustrates that it isn't enough to keep it all on the inside. If our faith is all on the inside, how will our children know its depth and range? How will they understand the way we process things and the words we use to pray if we are silent believers?

It is with our mouths that we confess and are saved. Lord, help us to choose our words wisely.

Judge nothing before the appointed time; wait till the Lord comes. He will bring to light what is hidden in darkness and will expose the motives of men's hearts.

1 CORINTHIANS 4:5

It can be compelling to judge a person or a situation according to our own standards. It's very easy to assign meaning when we think we have all the facts, but we never do. We have to have a strong enough faith that we can be patient in difficult or testing situations and wait on the Lord to make things clear.

If you are struggling right now with a person or a situation, before you act or speak, get quiet with God. Ask Him if He wants you to speak or step forward, and do not move a muscle or open your mouth before you have total confirmation.

On the other side of the coin, are you living your life right now in a way that you are clean and confident that you can survive an inspection in the light? If your motives were all exposed right now, would you be free or would you be ashamed? Is your heart pure enough, and aligned enough, that you could withstand the judgment seat and emerge unscathed?

Probably not—we all have work to do. More than enough work, in fact, to keep us completely occupied in our own affairs. We walk the line when we walk in faith; sometimes we have to be strong enough to step out or speak out in faith, and sometimes we have to be strong enough to remain quiet. Wisdom lies in being able to discern the difference. Ask God.

"Everything is permissible for me—but not everything is beneficial. Everything is permissible for me—but I will not be mastered by anything."

1 CORINTHIANS 6:12

Think about it: If we tell our children, "You may not drink Coke. You may not eat sugar cereals. You may not watch cartoons," what do you think will be the first thing they do when they go to a friend's house where there are soft drinks, Fruity Pebbles, and Nickelodeon? We can't just give a blanket "no" to our kids without helping them learn when, why, and how much. When we issue a blanket "no" we effectively shut down all future lines of communication because we have made our point absolutely clear, thank you very much.

The same thing goes for topics with higher stakes, things like drugs, alcohol, and sexuality. Saying that beer is bad or sex is sinful are not learning statements; they do not help young people reach understanding. When we say things like this, we state our rules and make the assumption that they are simply going to obey. I believe that we need to be clear about our values and our positions on issues, but just not in a blowhard way that shuts down dialogue. It's good to acknowledge with our children that they will have many choices and many temptations in front of them, but that is not where their power lies. Their power lies in being able to evaluate and make sound choices, and this is an ongoing process that requires constant conversation and mentorship. That is the relationship we want.

Do you not know that your body is a temple of the Holy Spirit, who is in you, whom you have received from God? You are not your own; you were bought at a price. Therefore honor God with your body.

1 CORINTHIANS 6:19–20

I for one could stand to eat better, sleep more, and do more yoga. I want to live cleanly, be healthy, balanced, strong, and fit. I want my body, my shell, to reflect a healthy spirit on the inside. The choices I make on all levels contribute to an overall lifestyle of honoring God.

I think of my young children, and all the things ahead of them that can dishonor their bodies—things like an obsession with weight or appearance that can potentially develop into an eating disorder, anxiety, or depression. Things that could lead to abusing their bodies with toxic substances like drugs and alcohol, or degrading their bodies sexually. There are so many ways to disrespect the temple of the Holy Spirit. Our children are watching us, and they see the choices we make with our own temples as they grow up to choose how they are going to take care of theirs. We must live wisely ourselves, and help them to do likewise.

Are there areas of weakness in the way you care for your own temple? Are you honoring your body with the choices you make? How could you make the message of this verse more evident in your own life? Are there things you could do as a family that would reinforce this mind-set of reverence for what is holy?

If I speak in tongues of men and of angels, but have not love, I am only a resounding gong or a clanging cymbal.

1 CORINTHIANS 13:1

Without intimacy and relationship as forerunners, our words fall flat on the doorstep of humanity. The listener is always asking "why should I care?" I have to consider this from a professional standpoint. I can write about my personal experiences or insights, but if my words do not come from a loving heart that seeks connection, it is meaningless to other people. I could choose the most beautiful words and string them together in way that sounds so pretty, but they are just words, empty without some soul behind them.

We are helping our children write their life stories every day. We are helping with character development, even impacting the plot as we make decisions that affect their futures. When we teach, discipline, or nurture our children, our words have to come from love, or they are just like that resounding gong or clanging cymbal. No matter how much sense we might make from the perspective of logic, if we have no appeal to the heart, it is all lost.

The relationship is where everything begins, when we hold our little angel for the first time. And the relationship is where we want to end up, continuing to share time and life together far into the future. So relationship is where we must remain mindful; our priority must always actively reside here. I will choose my words more carefully because of this relationship, and I will both speak up and quiet down on its behalf.

Show me your ways, O LORD, teach me your paths;
guide me in your truth and teach me, for you are God
my Savior, and my hope is in you all day long.

PSALM 25:4–5

I love the start of school. New backpacks; fresh lunchboxes; reams of clean, white, lined paper waiting to be filled; crisp haircuts; brand-new, unbroken, sharpened crayons and pencils. I love the metaphor of the new year, the fresh start, the clean slate. And yet a new beginning always manages to include elements of an ending as well.

When small children head off to kindergarten, or young adults leave for college, there is an undeniable sense of letting go. This year my kids turned down my offer to walk them in on the first day, preferring a wave and a loud, "Love you, Mom!" as they bounded solo up the steps to school. Phases pass, and though it's important to acknowledge them fondly and grieve them a bit if necessary, we have to look forward with promise and joy to what lies ahead.

These precious children of ours are borrowed. They are God's children, loaned to us for a time, to raise and nurture and love. But ultimately, they are His, and He holds claim over them. We have to love them enough to be able to let them go and entrust them to heavenly hands. When we see them with spiritual eyes, we want to let them go, we want them to be safely in God's care, knowing that we can never do enough, never be there every minute, never protect them the way He can. One of the greatest steps of faith is trusting God with our beloved treasures, our babies.

He has them in the palm of His hand.

*I have said before that you have such a place
in our hearts that we would live or die with you.
I have great confidence in you; I take great pride
in you. I am greatly encouraged; in all our
troubles my joy knows no bounds.*

2 CORINTHIANS 7:3–4

I love Paul's passion when he wrote. He was writing to the Corinthians, and yet I can imagine penning these words to my child. I feel this way about my kids.

Just this weekend I watched my children participate in a kids' triathlon. They formed relay teams with their friends and each did one section of the event, which included swimming, biking, and running. The start area was so chaotic, getting their race numbers written on their arms and legs and heat numbers on their hands, getting numbers for the bikes, and making sure everyone was in their appointed transition areas. It was too much for one mom. I had to let them be responsible for themselves, trusting them to be in the right place at the right time without my instruction or interference.

I loved watching them. They were exactly where they needed to be, and they gave their best efforts for their friends and for themselves. I felt like I was going to explode with confidence and pride in them. They navigated a new experience and loved it. They are exactly the kind of people I would want for my team, if I were choosing. I could face anything with them by my side.

*... If you do not stand firm in your faith,
you will not stand at all.*

ISAIAH 7:9

It isn't easy as a single mom to become more open-minded about dating. It seems so unfathomably huge, the idea of starting all over again with someone new. As a thirty-eight-year-old mother of three—not on my own in my twenties—I am uncovering some interesting things about myself. If you have the opportunity for a total do-over, it makes you stop and think about what you really want, what really matters. I am discovering some nonnegotiable items, and in the process I am likely learning more about who I am than about the man I'm waiting for.

The guy for us has to be a man of faith, a man who loves children, loves animals, loves life, has passion for things bigger than himself, is generous but knows his boundaries. He has to be smart and funny. The list goes on, but these are the top.

Without my faith, I could not stand firm on these things. Knowing that God backs up the good intentions of my heart, I know He loves us and wants the best for my family. It's important for each of us to know our nonnegotiable items. Where do you stand firm? What are the things on which you simply cannot and will not budge? Where does your faith equip you to hold your ground and toe the line?

Give, and it will be given to you. A good measure,
pressed down, shaken together and running over,
will be poured into your lap.

LUKE 6:38

In terms of family, grandchildren must be the fulfillment of this verse.

Whether I am talking to my parents or to any of my older friends, they say that having grandchildren is the best thing that ever happened to them. My friend Ann says that having grandchildren is the only thing so far in her life that has completely exceeded every single expectation she ever held, without a trace of disappointment or difficulty, just joy.

I am not at that place in life, but I can imagine. As parents we pour so much into our children, all the work of taking care of them when they're small, all the worry, disciplining, praying, and energy required to raise a family. We give physically, emotionally, financially, and spiritually. We go through seasons of lopsidedness, giving and receiving in different proportions. We offer our hearts as a sacrifice in the building of our family.

If we do our best, if we seek God to make up for where our best always falls short, we reap a harvest of a relationship with our children that grows as they grow. And then they become adults, marry, and start families of their own. And we get to be a part of that experience, loving our grandchildren abundantly without carrying the primary responsibility of caretaking or disciplining. We already did that; we gave when it was our turn. And grandchildren are the harvest...they are a gift, a good measure, pressed down, shaken together, running over, poured into our laps.

Whether you turn to the right or to the left,
your ears will hear a voice behind you, saying,
"This is the way; walk in it."

ISAIAH 30:21

I ran with my friend Leticia this morning, and she was sharing a story about her niece having some tough decisions to make regarding college selection. Leticia's advice was to solicit and take wise counsel under advisement, but to be sure to get quiet and consult the Lord first.

This reminded her of her own college experience, when she left Emory University to return home to attend the University of Texas. She prayed hard over this decision, after angst about financial and family concerns, finally releasing it to God and agreeing to come home. This impacted every decision that followed, leading her to her life here, her career, her husband, her son, and also many beautiful years of living close to her parents. Her father died last year.

Recalling this string of events brought Leticia to grateful tears in my car on the way home from our run. "The Lord knew I needed to be here," she whispered. "I regret nothing and would not trade one minute of life with my father. God knew our time was limited. Always ask Him because He sees what we cannot. You can trust Him."

Do you have some tough decisions ahead of you? Or does your child? Are you diligent about asking God first? He knows the portions of the story that have not yet been revealed. Be sure to ask. Be sure to trust.

"Woe to the obstinate children," declares the LORD, "to those who carry out plans that are not mine, forming an alliance, but not by my Spirit, heaping sin upon sin."

ISAIAH 30:1

I have been an obstinate child of God before, a willful proponent of my own agenda. I have stupidly taken treks off road that I thought were shortcuts, only to find myself way off course and dangerously lost. I have formed alliances with people I thought were "good" or exciting or interesting. I did not bother to consult God to see if these relationships were of Him. I heaped sin upon sin like a glutton filling a huge waffle cone with ice cream. I feel ill when I think about it.

I no longer feel pulled or compelled to be an obstinate child; on the contrary, I desire to be obedient. And yet I am still at risk, despite my best intentions, of forging ahead and making plans without consulting God first. I don't always realize that I have started off without Him, until I get that sinking feeling that something is missing, and I have to hurry back and start over. Without constant monitoring, I am always at risk of forming improper or unhealthy alliances. I have to pray for constant protection for me and my children, knowing that deception always starts off as something innocuous.

The way to avoid heaping sin upon sin is to become more sensitive to it, so sensitive that a small taste is enough to spoil our appetites. Then we get up, excuse ourselves from the table, and hightail it out of there. Our alliances are extremely important, because they have access to our hearts.

The Lord longs to be gracious to you;
he rises to show you compassion.

ISAIAH 30:18

On the last day of first grade, Bella's teacher, Mrs. Ross, had a final class meeting. The children were seated in a circle around her, and one by one she called each child to come up and stand in front of her. She held their hands and looked into their eyes and poured words from her heart over their heads like an anointing of oil. She said things like, "You have gotten so brave this year; I want you to keep standing up for what you believe in and the people you love. You are so creative; keep being exactly who you are and never be afraid to be different. You let me challenge you so much this year, really push you in your reading, and when I see how you can read, I'm so proud of you." She finishes each anointing with a hug as a send-off into second grade. It is the final, overflowing splash into the cup she has filled each day, all year long.

I think the Lord is often gracious and compassionate to us through the loving people He places in our lives on earth. I will never forget watching Mrs. Ross compliment each child and tell them exactly how she saw them, knowing that most of these kids will bury her words in their hearts and use it as they build their individual definitions of themselves. It occurred to me how much adults still need this kind of affirmation and encouragement. We can be this kind of provision for others when we take the time to compliment and acknowledge people, to truly see them the way Mrs. Ross sees her first graders.

Be the voice of Christ and speak words of love.

He looked around at them all, and
then said to the man, "Stretch out your hand."

LUKE 6:10

Jesus asked the leper to stretch out his hand in order to receive healing. Healing of any kind requires that we make the first, bold move to reach out for God. Perhaps He wants to know that we know the depth of our need, or that we understand the impossibility of true healing apart from Him.

Reaching for God often means a stretch on our part. Maybe we have to extend beyond our comfort zones, toward relationship with God, or relationally in terms of fellowship with other believers. Maybe we have to stretch in our prayer lives or in our pursuit of understanding Scripture. Maybe we need to move beyond our past, finally seeking peace, forgiveness, or resolution. Like the verse that tells us to seek God first and all other things will be added to us (Luke 12:31), healing is one of those additions. It never comes before God is sought, earnestly and wholeheartedly.

What areas of your heart, your life, or your family could benefit from God's healing right now?

Do you sense Jesus is asking you to reach out to Him? In what ways do you think you could stretch beyond your usual comfort zone and extend yourself toward God's love?

Let the little children come to me, and do not hinder them, for the kingdom of God belongs to such as these. I tell you the truth, anyone who will not receive the kingdom of God like a little child will never enter it.

LUKE 18:16–17

Although we have so many things to teach our children and a huge responsibility to raise them well, they have much to teach us as well.

My children have taught me enough things to fill all the pages of this book, things about unconditional love, devotion, and gratitude. They have reminded me how to live fully present. They have rekindled my sense of joy and spontaneity. They help me to play, relax, and let go. They bring my priorities to life in brilliant color. When I see evidence of their abiding trust, their bold questions, their hopeful expectancy, and the ease with which they offer and accept love, I am in awe of their faith.

We can learn a lot by watching our children's faith and asking them questions about what and how they believe. The most amazing and profound messages can come from the simplest statements. Luke once said to me, "Mom, you either believe God, or you don't; that's all you need to know." God often speaks to me directly through my children; clearly they don't filter or tune Him out the way my accumulated years manage to create spiritual clogs. Little people have big impact, especially where God is concerned.

Pay attention.

Give careful thought to your ways. You have planted much, but have harvested little. You eat, but never have enough. You drink, but never have your fill. You put on clothes, but are not warm. You earn wages, only to put them in a purse with holes in it.

※

I believe with total conviction that each of God's children is created with an innate, God-shaped hole. Without an awareness of this hole or any idea of the only way to fill it, we are doomed to a life of constant striving without satisfaction.

If we can live lives that honor our spiritual needs first, our children will grow up understanding that their own need for God should be met first and honored above all else. When that hole is filled, other things we add to our lives don't fall directly out the bottom. We can harvest a full crop, eat and be satisfied, drink and be quenched, dress and be warm, and earn wages that support our families without making an idol of money.

It becomes a rich life when we focus less on having what we want and more on wanting what we have. When we seek God first, this transformation happens naturally.

This is my body, which is for you;
do this in remembrance of me.

1 CORINTHIANS 11:24

Receiving the Eucharist at church is a highlight of my week. I love the idea of becoming clean in mind and spirit and the symbolism of receiving the body of Christ. My absolute favorite part of Mass is when we say, "Lord, I am not worthy to receive You, but only say the word and I shall be healed." When I receive the body of Christ, I feel like I am being nourished in hard-to-reach places.

When my son, Luke, made his First Communion in second grade, I was surprised by how overcome with emotion I was. To watch him, in his navy blue sport coat, too-long khaki pants, and poorly knotted tie, walk up to the altar with his hands outstretched to receive; I could not breathe. In that moment I saw my son growing up in his faith, receiving the Lord in his own unique, intimate experience.

It is essential that we pass down the traditions and rituals of our families and our faith. In this way our family legacies are built and our faith is handed down with love and reverence. It is important that we isolate and name our undeniable hunger for God. None of us are worthy to receive Him, but when He says the word, we are always healed.

This is what the Sovereign LORD,
the Holy One of Israel, says: "In repentance and rest is
your salvation, in quietness and trust is your strength."

ISAIAH 30:15

My pet peeve is the word *busy.*

People say it too much, too flippantly, too breathlessly, and too often as an excuse. I hate to point out that every single breathing person on this planet has twenty-four hours in a day. I know some people who are brilliantly swinging bright careers, raising great kids, and loving amazing men. They rarely talk about being busy. They are too excited about what's going on, and too interested in what and how other people are doing. I also know plenty of people who don't work outside the home, whose husbands handle most things, and who use "but I have two kids, three kids, four kids" as an excuse for why their loose ends are flying about in a tangle, and then they complain that they are sorry, but they are just so busy. Huh? I am convinced that there are two sets of people: those who are making it happen, and those who are making excuses.

Forget busy. I decided to ban that word, and I don't use it anymore in the context of my life. I prefer to think that my life is full, wonderfully so. I will find time for repentance and rest, and I will cultivate quietness in my life. Watch what happens to your life if you eliminate busyness—both the word itself and the spinning, striving pursuit of it. Just because the culture hypes it as the norm does not mean that we have to subscribe to it. Even if we have to come to a screeching, skidding halt to reclaim our sense of time and ownership of it, it's worth it. Put the brakes on.

Come to me, all you who are weary and
burdened, and I will give you rest. Take my yoke
upon you and learn from me, for I am gentle and
humble in heart, and you will find rest for your souls.
For my yoke is easy and my burden is light.

MATTHEW 11:28–30

In the strangest moments, you can literally feel God's might. Right when you expect to be utterly crushed, exhausted, or miserable, you surprise yourself by feeling refreshed. You get a miraculous "second wind." Did you ever wonder where a second wind comes from? A second wind describes the phenomenon of Jesus' exchanging yokes with us. Suddenly we can go on.

I have felt this at the end of a marathon, when everything about me was saying *no* but suddenly I was transported toward the finish line. Or during an all-night gig of caring for sick kids with stomach flu . . . changing sheets, answering cries and pleas for water. I felt like I could collapse, but I didn't, I kept on, and on again the next day as we moved forward. It isn't coffee; it's an almighty God.

Inversely, there are moments when I am moving along nicely and I am suddenly dropped to my knees, overcome with the staggering weight of my burdens. For a moment I feel the weight of what God is carrying on my behalf, and I praise Him for the reminder that there is no way I could carry on without Him. He switches the yokes again, and I move on unencumbered. I need the Lord to swap yokes with me, and He does.

Thank God.

*If I must boast, I will boast of the things
that show my weakness.*

2 CORINTHIANS 11:30

When I was a younger woman, I never wanted anyone to know my weak spots, my secret hurts, my fears. I was afraid that to show these areas would expose my vulnerabilities and weaken me further, at least in the eyes of others. I preferred to be the strong one, the tough one, the capable one.

This week has been a hard one for me, a series of tests that have left me fatigued and emotionally raw. Instead of acting like everything was fine, I was honest. When a friend or family member asked me how I was doing, I admitted I was struggling and shared my raw spots. The most amazing things began to happen. I got phone messages, text messages, and e-mails from people saying they were praying for me...everyone from my grandmother to my child's teacher to some girls in my running group. When I heard their words of comfort and confidence I let them soak into me like a marinade for my soul. I did not feel ashamed or needy; I felt cared for and empowered. I am learning to allow other people to minister to me the way I love to minister to them. It takes more strength to admit to weakness than it does to bear up under weaknesses alone.

Maybe that was the lesson behind the tests this week, and not the individual tests themselves. Maybe God wanted me to learn the valuable lesson of humility and healing that comes from sharing weaknesses.

I will not be a burden to you, because what
I want is not your possessions but you.
After all, children should not have to save up
for their parents, but parents for their children.
So I will very gladly spend for you everything
I have and expend myself as well.

2 CORINTHIANS 12:14–15

The costs of raising a family and keeping a household running are daunting, especially on my own, and while I could likely make more money if I were willing to spend more hours away, or travel more often, there are associated costs to my family that I am not willing to pay. I figure when the kids are grown I can always go back and make more money. I can always go back and work in an office again. I can always scale back and live in a smaller house or drive a different car. I can easily live with less stuff. I can always pursue this or that, or pick up the thread of a dream or an idea and follow it. I can always figure it out and make ends meet.

I can see myself as an old woman, and I know I won't want possessions; I'll want relationships with my children and grandchildren. I need to live today with that future in mind.

The one thing I cannot do is go back and have a do-over on Luke's, Grace's, and Bella's childhoods. No, this time will be impossible to get back if I miss it or mess it up. And so I'm giving all of myself now; I am living in the moment, soaking them in, ladling out love and time and watching it spill over them. This is one choice that I made the instant I became a mom, and I wake up and make it again every day.

Set your minds on things above, not on earthly things.

COLOSSIANS 3:2

At any moment, in anyone's company, in any situation, in the midst of any emotion, we can rise above everything. From this vantage point, and with the added closeness to God, we can see solutions we might not see otherwise. We can notice how transitory something is when we aren't standing in the thick of it. We see how much smaller it looks when we have the perspective of looking at it from a distance. We can feel God's comfort and know that this, too, shall pass.

To the untrained eye it appears a subtle thing, as simple as adjusting one's stance or shifting one's gaze, but to those who are trained in the art of transcending, it is far from subtle. To be able to transcend is to always have an option, always a way out, a way around, a way through. To be able to transcend is to have the ability to vacate even your own body, should the need arise, and keep your soul safe from harm. This is what it means when people say, "No one can touch you."

Practice transcending in ordinary situations, ones that pose no extreme threat or emotional angst. Notice how it feels to grow light and shift your heart and mind toward God's perspective. If we practice this art in everyday living, when we are tested by something far more serious we will know exactly what to do, where to go, and how to get there. Transcending will become a reflex response in an extraordinary moment if practiced in ordinary times.

Do not be surprised, my brothers, if the world hates you.

1 JOHN 3:13

As part of my job as a contributing editor for *Runner's World* magazine, I keep a blog on their website, which I update each week. For me, running is a constant theme and an unlimited source of everything metaphorical in my life, so keeping this blog is easy and fun for me. I am blessed to truly love my work. But not everybody loves my work.

Like most blogs, there is a comments section, and to be perfectly honest I rarely look at it. I have friends who review it for me and alert me to anything I need to see. Sometimes other friends or acquaintances say, "Whoa, have you checked out the comments from so-and-so on your blog? Man, she hates you." Sometimes I am curious and I look, most times I do not.

The thing is, when we are being our authentic selves, we are going to be met with resistance. It's that simple. When we step up and step out, we are opening ourselves up to being judged. I have concluded that it's much easier to be the anonymous one who posts a catty comment than it is to have the courage to put your heart out where people can pick at it. When we are bold about who we are, where we stand, and what (or shall I say, in whom) we believe, we can expect and prepare for opposition. Just as John told us in this verse, we should not be surprised by this.

I need to be able to work through these things, and so do you, so that we can help our children when the same thing inevitably happens to them. There will be people who do not like them simply because they are children of light.

*This then is how we know that we belong to
the truth, and how we set our hearts at rest in his
presence whenever our hearts condemn us. For God is
greater than our hearts, and he knows everything.*

1 JOHN 3:19–20

Do you ever go to bed at night and replay situations and conversations that you feel you "messed up"? I lay there and think about things I could have said, or things I said that I wish I hadn't. I reenact in my head how I could have handled something more gracefully or wisely. I call to mind the teachable moments with my kids that I missed because I was too caught up in being frustrated. It's hard to sleep when that junk is your bedtime story.

By this point, I am usually mad at myself, so I switch on the light, open my Bible, and keep reading until I remember who I am and whose I am. I am a child of the King. I am enough. I am forgiven.

When our hearts get into a pattern of self-condemnation, we have to break the pattern with the Word of God. Once we are realigned, we can find our way back to His presence and then peace floods in.

We have to be on the lookout for our children when they get stuck in self-condemnation. We can permit them to dwell there briefly, but we cannot allow them to remain where seeds of unworthiness and futility are planted; these are not acceptable shoots in the gardens of their hearts.

God is greater than our hearts. He knows our intentions even in moments of failure—and He can heal us there and set us free to go on and try again.

Splendor and majesty are before him;
strength and joy in his dwelling place.

1 CHRONICLES 16:27

Joy is an underdog in today's vocabulary, underused and undervalued. Joy is bigger than happy and lasts longer than fun; it is a gift of faith, and as such it does not depend on circumstances. Children have the leading edge on us grown-ups when it comes to joy. We take ourselves too seriously most of the time and think we are too important to play.

I like to remember joy and try to look for it.

Bella and Grace notice when I pursue joy. They call it "the kid inside of Mom," and they love it when she makes herself known. Like when I ride a Razor scooter, zipping far ahead of them and acting like I can't hear them as they try to chase me down and stop me. Or when I jump on the trampoline with them in their dad's backyard, screaming and laughing, my long hair flying in all directions. Or when I mandate a pajama adventure and we all go to a park or get ice cream when we should be going to bed. "Your inside kid is coming out to play!" They laugh at me, loving every second of it.

If I have to leave this life too soon, and stories are told at my funeral (and there will be some doozies, I can assure you), I don't want my kids to wonder who is this woman that was my mother? I want them to have some crazy stories of their own to share. I want them to know, love, and be loved by, a mom who was filled with joy. *Have fun with your children.*

Come with me by yourselves to a
quiet place and get some rest.

MARK 6:31

In exactly eleven days, I have a very special getaway planned. I have been dreaming about it, planning what to pack, trying to get everything done so that I can really let my hair down and have some fun.

If you think I have a vacation planned with a very special man, you are exactly right. But it isn't just any man, it's our heavenly Father.

He invited me to spend some time with Him. He sought me out in countless small ways, trying to get my attention, whispering to me that I was moving too fast and trying to do too much. He issued an invitation, an opportunity to escape with Him and go to a quiet place and rest. I didn't even have to think about it. And so, eleven days from today I am going to spend some time alone with God.

I imagine it will be like a spiritual spa—with soul spa treatments like yoga, and quiet time to read and pray. He wants to walk on the beach with me. He wants to run on the mountain trails beside me. He wants to have coffee at sunrise on the patio outside my office. He knows exactly what I like, what I need, and what is good for me. He knows I need rest and recreation, with lots of room in between.

When was the last time you let God take you away?

*Stop judging by mere appearances, and
make a right judgment.*

JOHN 7:24

Recently I showed my children the performance of Susan
Boyle on *Britain's Got Talent*. I think likely everyone has seen
it, but if you haven't, check it out. It's a great lesson for all
of us. A frumpy, small-town, middle-aged woman takes the
stage. Her hair is graying and frizzy and she's wearing a lumpy
housedress with bad shoes. They pan the judges and the audience and you can sense the major eye-roll going on; *yeah, right,
get this over with.* Then she opens her mouth to sing.

It's as if an angel overtakes her, and the heavens spill out
of her mouth. Her voice is sublime, rich and resonant and
perfect. You could have heard a pin drop; the judges and the
audience were spellbound. It is impossible to see this video and
not be covered in chills. She gets a well-deserved standing ova-
tion, wins the show, and garners instant worldwide fame.

But the lesson was for all of us. Amazing talents lurk in
the most unlikely packaging. We need to be open and aware.
My kids stared at my computer screen for the entire performance and the judges' comments afterward. It ended and they
sat silent. "Well, what did you think about that? Did you see
a lesson for us?"

"Don't judge a book by the cover," Grace said matter-
of-factly, nodding somberly. She was exactly right.

There is a time for everything, and
a season for every activity under heaven.

ECCLESIASTES 3:1

We cannot be and do all things for everyone, all the time—there are indeed seasons. For me, it has been challenging to learn how to alternate between loving and letting go ("a time to scatter stones and a time to gather them, a time to embrace and a time to refrain" [v. 5]) as the kids go back and forth between my house and their dad's house. When we first divorced, Luke was three and the girls were one, and it would cause me physical pain to part from them. I felt like I had an unending ache, an emptiness, a lack of equilibrium. The only way to get over it was prayer and the passage of time. I had to learn to make a life, a good life, apart from my children—or I would never survive.

Today I don't feel the anguish I felt back then, and I do enjoy my solo time, but I am not sure that I will ever be an expert in loving and letting go. It is the timeless challenge for all mothers.

The only possible way to love and let go gracefully is to first have enough faith to remember that God is ultimately in charge of our children and only He can really keep them safe. Second, we need to know that love is not limited to time and space, and our love does not start or stop; it flows continuously whether we are with our children or not. And finally, we need to trust God that He has ordained our separations as well as our togetherness.

There is... a time to keep and a time to throw away,
a time to tear and a time to mend,
a time to be silent and a time to speak.

ECCLESIASTES 3:1, 6–7

We know what to do when we clean the refrigerator. We can see the wilted produce and check the expiration dates on containers and toss the things that are past their prime. We know at the end of the school year when the kids amass giant piles of art and schoolwork that we cannot keep it all, so we go through it and keep our favorite things (usually when the kids aren't looking). When we clean out the kids' closets we can read the sizes on the tags and know what no longer fits (I wish my closet were so simple; don't even get me started...).

It's easier to purge when it comes to things, harder when it comes to people.

But there are times when we have to decide if we are going to maintain certain friendships, cut them abruptly loose, or quietly let them slip away. We have to discern if a difficult or broken relationship warrants mending or tearing, if we need to speak up and reach clarity or closure, or if it's best to let things go unspoken and allow the relationship to die of natural causes. I don't know any of these answers, for you or for me. But I do know that when we pray and bring these situations before God, He will direct us in how and when to resolve them.

There are seasons for everything, even relationships. Some special ones are forever, but most serve a certain purpose at a prescribed time. The forever ones sparkle even more when we realize how rare they really are.

There is . . . a time to weep and a time to laugh,
a time to mourn and a time to dance.

ECCLESIASTES 3:1, 4

If I am annoyed or frustrated or have gotten my feelings hurt, I often explode and the dust settles quickly afterward. But there are times when I simmer for a while, when I am irritated or if I happen to be in a sour mood. I don't want to ignore those feelings or stuff them, but I also don't want to allow them to run rampant all over my day. So I give myself an allotment of time to indulge my feelings and often that is enough to validate them and bid them adieu.

I want my kids to see me working on this so they better understand when I try to help them do the same thing. "I can see you are really angry right now. How about if I give you ten minutes to be as angry as you need to be and then we'll move on. Sound good?" It works most of the time.

It works with bigger things, too, the whoppers, the doozies, the things that take longer to heal or recover from. We have to have a limit on even the biggies—things like loss and grief. We have to experience these things and run the gamut of emotions to work our way back, *but we have to come back*.

Ancient times required a grieving widow to wear ashes on her forehead for a prescribed time (or fast, or wear black), and then she had to clean up and rejoin the living. We have to do the same thing. We have to make room for joy to come back into our lives. There is a season for weeping and mourning—but laughing and dancing come next.

There is…a time to search and a time to give up.

ECCLESIASTES 3:1, 6

Sometimes this is easy to discern—when to keep looking for car keys and when to call AAA, when to keep dialing the lost cell phone and when to pony up and get a new one, when to admit your suitcases are gone and just go buy new bathing suits and get on with your vacation.

Other situations are more complicated. Only God can tell a woman when to stop looking for a man and get on with living her own (single) life. Only God can tell a questioning heart to stop asking and start living out the answers. Only God can tell a dreamer when to stop seeking and get to work. Only God can tell an unsettled woman when to stop trying to find herself and allow Him to define her.

My grandma Millie always said to pray to Saint Anthony, patron saint of lost things and missing people, when you can't find something. Prayer is the key idea here. I think we all have to do our own part in any given situation, but we also have to know when to stop, have faith, and wait for God to move. He will always do His part after we have done ours; and He alone is the Maker of miracles.

What are you looking for now? Is something lost in your life or missing from your heart? Are you striving to fill some void only to keep coming up empty? Have you already done your part? Do you struggle with giving the rest over to God?

*I know, my God, that you test the heart and
are pleased with integrity. All these things have
I given willingly and with honest intent.*

1 CHRONICLES 29:17

❧

I love going to yoga. I used to hate it, but now I've done it long enough that I care less how goofy I look doing it than how good it makes me feel. I love that doing yoga is called a practice, or *your practice*, to be specific. It's your time, your effort, and your experience to own. I like how even the word *practice* signifies a certain level of acceptance for the unskilled.

With other things, like my work or my running, I measure myself—my productivity by my ability to pay the bills; my running skills by how fast I can run or how long I can go. In yoga I never feel compelled to measure myself, and I am totally accepting of a different result in each class.

At the start of each yoga practice, we set our own private intention for the class. It can be anything as long as it is positive and personal. You can set an intention for yourself or you can devote your practice to someone else. At the end of class the teacher asks you to check back in with the intention you made, to make sure you have a sense of closure. It's a beautiful ritual, one that has impacted my life in other areas.

I have begun to set intentions at the beginning of each day before I do anything else. It's a way of checking in with God, with my heart, with my integrity and with my purpose. It keeps my intent honest. If God is going to be testing my heart, I may as well test it regularly, too.

...an unloved woman who is married...

PROVERBS 30:23

I cannot write a book about mothering without talking about marriage. It is not helpful to spend 365 days honing our mothering if our marriages are crumbling. Husbands need attention, too. It's easy to get so caught up in the needs of our children that the needs of our husbands slide down the priority scale into oblivion. Our personal needs can fall somewhere even lower if we aren't careful.

No relationship can survive on autopilot. Sure, there are stretches of time when it is nearly impossible to give a husband what he needs, like when you have a brand-new baby. Between nursing and exhaustion, there is barely anything left for a shower, let alone a man. This mentality cannot continue, but, sadly, it often does. The children get the firstfruits and the husband starves. In situations like this, the primary intimate relationship (with God) is starving, too, because if that relationship were healthy, all others would be in proper order and perspective.

If your marriage is starving but still hanging on, you need to wake up today and make a real effort to pour some of yourself into your husband's cup. Even if he does not react or reciprocate right away, pour anyway. We love our children when we nurture and protect the marriage that formed them. Children look to their parents for their first picture of what real, committed love looks like.

Show them something beautiful.

If we are thrown into the blazing furnace,
the God we serve is able to save us from it, and
he will rescue us from your hand, O king. But
even if he does not, we want you to know, O king,
that we will not serve your gods or worship
the image of gold you have set up.

DANIEL 3:17–18

The story of Shadrach, Meshach, and Abednego in the fiery furnace is one of my favorite stories to teach my children. It is a lesson for all ages in conviction, strength of character, and belief. King Nebuchadnezzar made a ninety-foot-statue of gold and commanded everyone to worship it. He caught wind that these three guys were not following orders so he threatened to toss them into the furnace. Their reply was captured in the verses above. These men would stick to their principles even in the face of death by fire.

The king was so mad that he had the furnace heated to seven times its usual setting; it was so hot that even the guards burned to death when they opened it to toss in the prisoners. But when he looked into the furnace, the king was astonished to see "the fire had not harmed their bodies, nor was a hair of their heads singed; their robes were not scorched, and there was no smell of fire on them" (v. 27). I can't even walk past a campfire without my hair smelling like a fireplace, and yet they emerged without even a whiff. That's what faith in an almighty God looks like, and smells like. We need to teach our children to stand tall and stand firm.

We want each of you to show this same diligence
to the very end, in order to make your hope sure.
We do not want you to become lazy, but to
imitate those who through faith and patience
inherit what has been promised.

HEBREWS 6:11–12

We have a long haul ahead, ladies.

I look at my grandparents: Mille G. is almost ninety-one, and my maternal grandma is ninety-five and my grandpa is ninety. Despite growing older, they have not grown lazy. They faithfully and patiently love God and their family and friends. They remember birthdays, holidays, and are always up for a visit. They are living the beautiful legacies they have built over the years, and carrying on with dignity and diligence all the way through.

They have never abandoned hope or their faith, in turbulent times or in ordinary ones. They give generously, from their pocketbooks, their refrigerators, and their hearts. I delight to take my children to visit them, knowing how lucky they are to have any great-grandparents at all, let alone ones that still live at home and are fun to talk to and play games with.

Thank God for the history and the legacy that is your family tree, both the roots of the past and the branches growing into the future.

Strengthen your feeble arms and weak knees.
"Make level paths for your feet," so that
the lame may not be disabled, but rather healed.

HEBREWS 12:12–13

I became a runner after the birth of my children. It seemed an easy and efficient way to reclaim my figure and retain my sanity. If I had a spare thirty minutes and someone to watch my baby or babies, I could duck out for a run. This worked well for me for a while. My weight got back on track, but I was often still tired and achy.

My friend KT suggested I might want to spend a bit of time in the weight room. She could see, but I could not, that my upper body was puny and my posture showed that I carried babies around. I started to work out with weights and it changed my body and my attitude. Over time I grew stronger and was able to haul around my kids and their stuff. My aches stopped bothering me at night. I began to learn that it was not enough to build only endurance and aerobic fitness; I needed to build my strength as well.

This lesson applies to the the mind and spirit. We need variety and we need specific training goals in order to prepare, grow, and heal. Our spiritual muscles, just like our physical muscles, will become stronger only as they are used. Left idle, they will atrophy.

Are you challenging yourself equally in all areas of your being? Are you growing stronger, especially in your areas of weakness? How can you be more purposeful about your spiritual training program?

...so that what cannot be shaken may remain.

HEBREWS 12:27

All of us go through a time or times in life when the walls quake around us and the earth seems to move under our feet, when things we thought were solid and reliable are suddenly untethered and sliding away. Our lives get shaken up now and then, like a thumb-covered shaken bottle of soda before it explodes.

Knowing that God is sovereign and nothing can happen to us that does not pass His approval, I sometimes wonder why He allows such rigorous and often painful upheavals? Why does He allow our worlds to be rocked? When the shaking stops and we try to put back misplaced and broken items, we realize that not everything has survived the quake.

Some relationships can't handle difficult circumstances, and they disappear at the first sign of trouble. Some material items are not hardy enough to withstand the shocks of life, and they, too, must go. Sometimes jobs or activities lose their meaning when juxtaposed beside a significant set of circumstances, and new and more meaningful avenues must be discovered.

Sometimes God takes us through a turbulent season to jostle everything loose, and to remind us of one crucial piece of evidence, something that once we realize it for ourselves, we are no longer the same people. It is this: When all else is shaken, He remains. If you don't yet know this fact intimately and profoundly, your time of turbulence has not yet come. Be watchful and prepare.

*Do not forget to do good and to share with others,
for with such sacrifices God is pleased.*

From the time they are toddlers, we nag our children to share. Share your toy. Share your snack. Share your ball. Let so-and-so have a turn. We become the Sharing Police at beaches, playgrounds, play groups, and parks everywhere. Before they even have a chance to fully appreciate the fleeting *"Mine"* stage, we are already on them to share and take turns. I've always wondered about the validity of this; it's kind of like making our children clean their plates at mealtime and then later wondering why they have food issues. Bossing our kids about sharing is different from helping them cultivate a generous heart.

Just like love, forgiveness, and a sense of humor—you have to know you have it for yourself before you can freely give it away. I think it's fair for kids to have certain things that belong to them, and to learn to negotiate boundaries about these things. Acting out the lesson of sharing as a mother is far better than nagging. Our kids need to see us sharing things not only with them but with our friends, our spouses, and our extended families.

The concept of doing good and sharing with others is a lesson better learned through kindness than deprivation. We typically grow up to treat others the way we have been treated. Let's be mindful today of our treatment of others.

*Give my son Solomon the wholehearted devotion to keep
your commands, requirements and decrees.*

1 CHRONICLES 29:19

I need to pay greater attention and place higher emphasis on the desire for my children to be obedient to God than the desire for them to be obedient to me. It's one thing for a child or teenager to make a good choice because they fear getting grounded, and it's another thing to make a good decision because they genuinely want to please God. The former has a shorter shelf life, with the deterioration of good behavior coinciding with departure from home. The latter, the desire to please God, is a lifetime pursuit, a joy. One line of reasoning produces an adult whose actions depend on who's watching, the other will eventually become a part of an adult's good character that reveals itself regardless if anyone is around to observe or not.

And so it is to this end that we need to be praying for our children. This verse is an excellent one to reword into prayer, inserting the names of each of our children as we pray for them specifically. It is a deeper way to pray, for the formation of a heart that follows and longs for God rather than for a mind that makes good choices.

Solomon was able to finish the temple that his father only dreamed about. King David was a good man, in spite of his many flaws, but Solomon was a man of impeccable character. The Lord highly exalted Solomon in the sight of all Israel and bestowed upon him royal splendor such as no king over Israel ever had before (1 Chron. 29:25). The prayers of a faithful parent have incredible power.

Rejoice in the Lord always. I will say it again: Rejoice!
Let your gentleness be evident to all. The Lord is near.
Do not be anxious about anything, but in everything,
by prayer and petition, with thanksgiving,
present your requests to God. And the peace of God,
which transcends all understanding, will guard
your hearts and your minds in Christ Jesus.

PHILIPPIANS 4:4–7

My running partners and I have a certain hilly course that we have lovingly named Mount Burden. It is a winding route up steep, breathless hills that leads to a rock wall with a ledge. When we make it there, after we've caught our breath, we select a few stones from the gravel on the ground. We hold them in our palms, noticing the shape and weight of each, and we quietly assign them the burdens du jour. We say a short prayer and each place our burdens on the ledge before we turn and head downhill toward home.

This symbolizes exactly what we are supposed to do with every worry and burden in our lives: leave them at the foot of the cross. My problem isn't so much in depositing my burdens as it is to not return and pick them back up. I have a tendency to trust God initially, but then run back and reclaim my troubles in the vain hope that I can rectify them on my own. That's why the physical act of leaving the stone there is so meaningful to me. If I catch myself mulling over an anxious thought later in the day, I remind myself that I left that stone on the ledge and it's not mine to worry about anymore.

How good and pleasant it is
when brothers live together in unity!

PSALM 133:1

My friend Dawn had an excellent reflection for Lent this year. She decided that every single time she felt herself getting irritated with anything or anyone, she was going to turn the mirror back on herself. Instead of allowing her frustration with someone else to dominate her emotional landscape, she was forcing herself to have a perspective change.

She had one revelation after another as she noticed the things that typically spurred a reaction. She, being a highly intelligent and insightful woman, had the keen sense to deduce that the common denominator in every one of those equations was, yep, you guessed it—herself. She began to see that the thing that had her so bothered in each case was something about herself that was unhealed or undesirable. She prayed to God and asked Him to reveal Himself and He did, every time. It was a great lesson to me, and one I have carried far beyond Lent and Easter.

Why am I so annoyed by this? What is it about me that is reacting so strongly? What is my part here? Certain irritating or frustrating people and situations in our lives, particularly the ones we cannot escape, are put there on purpose by God to refine us. Once we get over being bugged, we can get on with being healed.

In all these things we are more than
conquerors through him who loved us.

ROMANS 8:37

This verse is one to memorize and file someplace handy on the shelves of your mind. Every day we face challenges of varying degree, but even seemingly small challenges can have larger implications later. We must determine from the outset, like at the beginning of the day, that we are going to adopt a victorious outlook. If we know already how the story ends, that we overwhelmingly conquer through Him who loves us, then we can begin with gratitude, no matter where we find ourselves from moment to moment.

A dieter has to be able to see herself thin. An athlete has to be able to see herself making the play or winning the race. An alcoholic needs to be able to see herself sober. Just as in order to be successful you have to visualize your success; in order to be faithful you have to visualize God triumphing over your challenges. Making a "faith picture" with our future helps us both to clarify our direction and desires, as well as open ourselves up to the power and possibility of God. Try this next time you are up against the clock, a wall, a challenge, a mystery, or a force to be reckoned with.

*I consider everything a loss compared to the surpassing
greatness of knowing Christ Jesus my Lord.*

PHILIPPIANS 3:8

❧

The longer we live and the more amazing, faithful people we meet,
the more we see the constant theme evidenced by this verse. I have
friends who have experienced the following tragedies: a devastating
car wreck with burns and injuries, the loss of a child, a stillborn
baby, the inability to conceive, a broken marriage, the death of
a husband, bankruptcy, alcoholism, depression, bipolar disorder,
thyroid disorder, eating disorder, a brain injury, a CP diagnosis, the
birth of a Down syndrome baby, the death of a parent. But even as
excruciating as these circumstances were, they would not trade the
gift of knowing Christ because of them. It is in the midst of a trial
that we gain intimate knowledge of our Savior.

We don't always get to know Jesus in the easy or ordinary
times because it often takes extraordinary circumstances to get
our attention and open our hearts to bigger things. My friend
Paige would not trade her car wreck in high school; she would
not go back and revise her history even if she could, because her
faith was founded in that hospital room. Her perfect face was
cut, burned, and bandaged up; her ear was stitched back on;
and her jaw was wired shut. But she recalls total peace, having
felt God whispering to her that everything was going to be just
fine, to just trust Him. And she did, and she's never looked
back. No matter what is happening in your world today, as
time goes on and it is reabsorbed into the tapestry of your life,
you, too, will consider even this a loss compared to whom and
what you know because of having gone through it.

*I press on to take hold of that for which
Christ Jesus took hold of me. Brothers, I do not consider
myself yet to have taken hold of it. But one thing
I do: Forgetting what is behind and straining toward
what is ahead, I press on toward the goal.*

PHILIPPIANS 3:12–14

If you are a self-flogger like I am, this is a great verse to keep in mind. I punish myself by dwelling on mistakes and missteps.

Yet, I cannot tolerate it when anyone else is too hard on themselves, particularly the people I love. If one of my children is down about a mistake they made, I ache twice as much as they do. I go to great lengths to remind my loved ones how much God loves them, how if we don't forgive ourselves, we are denying ourselves the liberation that is already ours. It's like sitting on a wafer-thin, dingy mattress, in a grimy prison cell marking days spent in captivity with etched tally marks on the wall *when the door is wide open and we are free to leave.*

Paul was telling us to cut this out. His message was, "Look, guys, I know none of us are perfect, but keep trying. Press on and don't look back."

What mistakes are you holding on to in your life right now? What grudges are you holding against someone else? Wherever you are struggling to let go, ask God to help you find release. It is for a life of freedom that we have been set free, so let's start living it.

Their destiny is destruction, their god is their stomach,
and their glory is in their shame. Their mind is on
earthly things. But our citizenship is in heaven.

PHILIPPIANS 3:19–20

I don't want to be someone with my mind on earthly things, but if I don't constantly reset my default to heaven, I am apt to get off track. I wonder if I make a god of my stomach, especially when it comes to Mexican food, PMS snacking binges, or eating dough when I'm supposed to be baking cookies. My glory can quickly become my shame when I am following pride instead of God.

Knowing my citizenship is in heaven, I carry the passport of my belief as proof of my identity in Christ wherever I go. As I travel, as a citizen of heaven, I have to keep my mind focused on heavenly things. It's easy to get delayed by earthly concerns. An untrained mind is a wandering mind, so how can we train ourselves (or reset our default) to things above? Paul went on to say in Philippians 3:20–21 that "we eagerly await a Savior from there [heaven], the Lord Jesus Christ, who, by the power that enables him to bring everything under his control, will transform our lowly bodies so that they will be like his glorious body." In other words, as we travel through life as believers, we are being remade in the image of Jesus. It is through His power, not ours, that we can be mindful of things above instead of getting stuck in various pits down here.

As we constantly look up, turning our thoughts and our hearts over to God, our perspectives remain heavenly and our children will be blessed.

May the Lord make your love increase and
overflow for each other and for everyone else.

1 THESSALONIANS 3:12

There is an old adage that says, "Absence makes the heart grow fonder." My mom used to console me with this when I was a teenager on a family vacation, pining for my boyfriend back at home.

Today, when my kids are gone (at school, camp, a friend's house, or spending time with their dad), I tell myself the same thing. It's not a bad thing to have some purposeful times of separation in our loving relationships. We all need time to rejuvenate and regroup. Moms need it, and kids need it. It's good to spend time away from Mom and have the space and the chance to recall all the things you love about her, how she is a comfort to you, you know—miss her a little bit. As moms it seems we are always there, and this is a gift of course, but it also creates something equivalent to a tolerance level. If it gets too high, it can veer off into the territory of being taken for granted, and though this is never intentional, it admittedly isn't a good feeling.

As Kahlil Gibran said in his famous book *The Prophet*, "let there be spaces in your togetherness." Into these spaces flow fresh air, new perspectives, a heightened sense of appreciation, and new things to talk about and share. If you are overdue for some time apart, even an hour, make some plans to have space in your togetherness. Pray this verse over your time apart as well as your time together, and watch how love can grow with a bit more light and room to bloom.

What is our hope, our joy, or the crown in which
we will glory in the presence of our Lord Jesus when he
comes? Is it not you? Indeed, you are our glory and joy.

1 THESSALONIANS 2:19–20

This verse sums up my heart for my children. I want us all to love and honor God together, because the icing on my joy in heaven will be spending eternity with my beloved. It isn't enough for one of us to cross that finish line and receive the crown of salvation; we all need to make it home.

That is the essence, after all, of family. To ensure that if one of us stumbles or gets lost, the others will be there to catch them or search for them. If one of us is weak in faith, the others have to be strong. If one of us goes too far into the ways of the world, there have to be people on the other end of the rope to pull back. If one of us grows weary, we wait to rest, or we redistribute a burden so that we can all move along together. If one of us becomes lukewarm, the rest have to guard the flame. If one of us is broken, the others are called to mend. If one of us is paying the price for a bad decision, we can still stand together in solidarity until righteousness is restored.

If my children know anything about my heart, I want them to know how I love God and know without question that they are the glory and joy of my life. My hope, my joy, and my crown do not sparkle without the jewels of my children…Luke, Grace, and Isabelle. I love you, my angels.

*You then, my son, be strong in the
grace that is in Christ Jesus.*

2 TIMOTHY 2:1

This is Paul talking to his beloved Timothy, but this is also me speaking to Luke and anyone else speaking from their heart to a beloved son—by blood or by love. In the hurry of our modern times, we have lost the art of writing love letters. It is a worthwhile endeavor, an elegant expression, a gift that transcends time. Put your heart on paper and pen some words for your child today. Here's one of my love letters to Luke:

Luke,

I have loved you from the minute I laid eyes on you, understanding my legacy as it unfolded when I held you for the first time. I was awestruck by the honor of raising you, forever altered by the desire to be a better woman on your behalf. I want to be stronger so that I might protect you, smarter so that I might be wise enough to challenge and guide you, bolder so that I can fight mightily for you until you are bold enough to fight for yourself, wiser so that I might know how to better intercede for you in prayer, more faithful so that I can teach you in the way you should go, more humble so that I can admit when I fail you and recommit to trying harder and again.

I want so much for you, my dear. I pray for you to have a deep and abiding faith that sustains you long after I am gone. I pray for friends who are loyal, understanding, funny, and godly—friendships that will challenge you and lift you beyond yourself, in the direction of God. I pray for a wife who loves you for who you are and who you are becoming, a woman whose faith has a depth and power that match or exceed yours. I pray for children for you to cherish, lucky little people to blossom and thrive in the love that pours from your huge heart. I pray for a career that blesses you, with passion, purpose, and provision for your family. I pray for you to glorify God with your talents, work hard, make a difference, and be free of financial slavery. I pray for you to have good health and take good care of the body God gave you. I pray for you to have a joyful spirit, one that sees humor and travels light. I pray for you to be strong in the grace that is in Christ, and to be a man of intent, a man of character, a man of integrity, a man of passion, a man of God. And to match all your strength, I pray for a heart that is soft in all the right places— compassionate, kind, forgiving, and vulnerable.

Know that my heart is for you, always, in this life and forever in the next. May our glorious God hear my prayers for you and bless you with every good and perfect gift from above. In the name of the Father, Son, and Holy Spirit, amen.

Mom

*[Keep] with the prophecies once made about you,
so that by following them you may fight the good fight,
holding on to faith and a good conscience. Some have
rejected these and so have shipwrecked their faith.*

1 TIMOTHY 1:18–19

Relativism and rationalization have shipwrecked the faith of many well-intended sailors.

We set off into the world on a journey of faith, and find ourselves lost or distracted by the voices of the world, unable to hear God for all the noise and commotion. The voices of the world tell us things like:

- *C'mon, it's not so bad.*
- *Look at so-and-so; they do whatever they please and their life looks pretty good.*
- *You deserve better/more.*
- *Just this once.*
- *He'll/She'll never know.*
- *Those standards/commands were meant for ancient times; the world is a different place today.*

If we are aware of the lies and the ways we can get hooked, it's easier to stay true to our course. As parents we are not alone in our boat, so if we get shipwrecked the whole family is stranded. We must navigate carefully.

I thank Christ Jesus our Lord,
who has given me strength, that he considered
me faithful, appointing me to his service.

1 TIMOTHY: 1:12

Do you understand what God sees in you for Him to have given you the enormous honor of mothering a child, one of His beloved children? When He appointed you to this service, He knew that you have a heart that is capable of loving beyond yourself. He knew you have the strength to live in a constant state of vulnerability and watchfulness. He knew you have the fortitude to teach and guide, even when you are tired or feeling unworthy. He knew you are able to forgive and move on, that you can look beyond the current moment and see the value of pressing on toward what lies ahead, that there is a much bigger picture.

He knew that you can keep your cool, that even when a dangerous or challenging situation presents itself, you can think on your feet. He knew that you will protect what you love, at any cost. He knew that you don't and won't give up, not on your faith, not on the people you love, not on your dreams. He knew all of this in advance and instilled in your heart everything you would need to be a success in this appointment.

Have you stopped to consider these things? Have you thanked God not just for the gift of your children, but for the gift of His commendation? Your role as a mother is part of the legacy and lineage of Christ. When you wake up in the morning and wonder about the meaning of your life, meditate on these things and be filled.

Godliness with contentment is great gain.
For we brought nothing into the world, and
we can take nothing out of it.

1 TIMOTHY 6:6–7

Ah, the beauty of living a life of openhandedness, free from the clenched fists of striving and clutching and struggling to hold on. Why do we work so hard to stash so much? It gets harder and harder to be clear about our priorities when they are buried under so much stuff.

Our true gift is not things but time, and our time is depleted by our acquisition of stuff. Maybe this sounds familiar: Why are you traveling so much or working such long hours? *So I can make more money.* Why do you need to make more money? *So I can make a better life for my family/pay my bills/buy a bigger house/have more freedom.* Why do you want more freedom? *So I can spend more time with my family.* Why do you need more time with your family? *Because I'm working so hard that I am always gone; even when I'm home I'm distracted.*

You can see how this pattern runs in an endless, miserable circle. The only way to have more time is to have less things. Less things to pay for, less things on the calendar, less things to replace, less things to store, less things to want, less things to worry about. Contentment comes when we can clear the way to see and appreciate what is already there.

If we can take nothing out of this world, why on earth don't we prefer to travel light as we pass through?

Guard what has been entrusted to your care.
Turn away from godless chatter and the opposing
ideas of what is falsely called knowledge,
which some have professed and in so doing
have wandered from the faith. Grace be with you.

1 TIMOTHY 6:20–21

There is so much godless chatter around us that it can become a constant drone, white noise.

It's everywhere. I was getting a pedicure the other day in one of those crazy, bustling places that smell like acrylic nails and hum with busyness and the sound of concurrent girl talk in English and Vietnamese. I completely zone out when I go there, so I barely notice my surroundings.

Between the television tuned to some Hollywood entertainment channel, the stacks of tabloid magazines, and the gossip flying between customers, it's a wonder I hadn't noticed the godless chatter overload before. This is really how women relax? With gossip and tabloid news updates?

It seems more valuable to me to spend our time making our own lives and our own relationships more interesting, rather than looking to other people to do that for us.

Guard what has been entrusted to your care...meaning your children, your relationships, your responsibilities and your talents, sure—but also your heart.

Don't have anything to do with foolish and stupid arguments, because you know they produce quarrels. And the Lord's servant must not quarrel; instead, he must be kind to everyone, able to teach, not resentful.

2 TIMOTHY 2:23–24

I had dinner with a couple I dearly love who have raised five beautiful daughters. They are happily heading toward the empty-nest years with a strong marriage and a great sense of purpose, adventure, and humor. I asked them for some parenting pointers.

They said that it is a waste of time to parent or discipline a child for the sake of looking righteous in the eyes of other parents. They encouraged me to be confident in my own mothering letting the perceptions of others fall to the wayside. They said open communication is ultimately far more important than strictness. They said not to sweat the small stuff; save the no's for the things that really matter.

"Pick your battles" is a statement I often hear. Or, as this verse says so well, don't argue over the foolish things; we can't teach if we are resentful or busy quarreling. I noticed that I had gotten into the habit of saying no too often. But my "no" will have no impact if I say it all the time. I told my kids I was going to get in a "yes mood," and they thought it was hilarious as I went to great lengths to find a way to say yes.

The humor, positive energy, and change of perspective did wonders to lighten the mood of our entire household. Try surprising your kids with yes when you can and saving your no's for when you need them!

When you and your children return to
the LORD your God and obey him with all your heart
and with all your soul according to everything I
command you today, then the LORD your God will
restore your fortunes and have compassion on you.

DEUTERONOMY 30:2–3

Fortunes come and fortunes go; the same could possibly be said for beauty, love, jobs, and luck. This is a problem, of course, but the degree of devastation is directly proportional to the degree to which we have turned any of those things into an idol.

If we have idolized money, and we lose our jobs or our savings, we are devastated. If we have made an idol out of our spouses, our marriages, or the picture of "the perfect life" and our husbands die or leave, we are devastated. Loss and pain are unavoidable; we are living in broken times. But God does not let idolatry go unnoticed. It may be that the one thing you think you cannot do without is taken from you specifically so you are restored to the awareness that the one thing you cannot live without is God.

If you are currently in a place of brokenness, my heart aches for you, I know it's hard. But look to these beautiful verses in Deuteronomy to remember the only place to return when everything else is falling about around you is home. Return to the Lord, and bring your family with you. Seek Him first and dwell in His Word. Find out what He wants from you, what needs to be restored, where you need to demonstrate obedience, and He will always have compassion on you.

Do not be afraid; do not be discouraged.

DEUTERONOMY 31:8

I was talking to a friend who helps prison inmates on death row. He was explaining to me how terrifying it was to walk into a meeting that would affect the fate of another human being, how nervous and inadequate he felt before he entered the room. For someone so educated and esteemed, I was amazed at his humility. He went on to say that being afraid is actually an encouraging and useful thing. He made the illustration that if we were a vine, fear would be the wall. We need something for resistance, something to scale, something to work against in order to grow.

We are conditioned to think that fear is a bad thing, something to avoid, an enemy to conquer. What if we changed our school of thought about fear? I cannot stand the thought of becoming complacent. For as much as I love the ease of my comfort zones, I force myself to bust out of them as often as possible so I don't get stuck. Remember the quote on my pantry door by Eleanor Roosevelt: "Do something every day that scares you." It may be trying a new thing, or meeting a new group of people, speaking in front of a group, going on an adventure, or having that conversation I have been avoiding. I try to incorporate that idea into my daily life, even if the degree of fear is always different. I want to practice welcoming fear instead of hiding or running from it. I would rather grow in trust, courage, and confidence than in complacency.

Do you remember what casts out fear? Perfect Love does, and we know Him.

I will give you every place where
you set your foot, as I promised Moses.

JOSHUA 1:3

❧

At the beginning of every large task, assignment, or identity shift, it is easy to feel utterly daunted, afraid, and ill-equipped. Starting a new job, getting married, having a baby, pursuing a passion, all of these things are huge. When we step out and stake a new claim in our lives, we often have second thoughts, driven by fear.

Dear God, maybe I'm not cut out for this marriage thing; what if I mess it up? Maybe I wasn't ready to have this baby; I have no idea what I'm doing! I don't know why the boss picked me for this promotion; he should have known better. I don't know why I signed up to teach or take this class; what if I'm a total fraud?

I sometimes hear these voices at the start of a running race, walking up to a podium to give a speech, smiling into a camera and doing an interview, signing up for a French conversation group, or staring at a blank page and trying to begin a new chapter or an article. I feel overwhelmed with how to start and how to feel comfortable with my discomfort.

God so badly wants to take this away from us. He sweetly tells us, just as He told Moses and Joshua, not to worry about it; He's got it all figured out. He will direct us, not just with an overhead GPS kind of map, but even more specific than that. He will tell us where to plant each foot as we walk forward into the calling He has on each of our lives. The key is to ask, be ready, and be quiet to listen.

Joshua set up the twelve stones that
had been in the middle of the Jordan at the spot
where the priests who carried the Ark of
the Covenant had stood. And they are there to this day.

JOSHUA 4:9

The Lord parted the Jordan River so that the Israelites could pass through with the Ark of the Covenant into the promised land. The water literally stacked up on either side as if it was dammed, and they walked through on dry land.

I love that when God wants to make something happen for us, He stops at nothing. He will find a way to make it happen. When the path seems totally blocked, He will take us across.

Even in the midst of such a mind-bending experience, Jacob remembered to mark the moment. I can barely remember to take pictures on a holiday! Jacob had each of the tribes of Israel pick up a stone at the dry bottom of the Jordan and carry them across. When everyone had safely crossed over, Jacob arranged the stones on the other side so that future generations would know what happened and who made it happen.

I have started keeping artifacts from my life—stones, feathers, shells, books, photographs, whatever marks a moment in time and brings it immediately to mind. I want to have a history like this, richly marked and remembered, to pass these stories down to my children. I want them to know how God has moved in my life.

*They brought out her entire family and put
them in a place outside the camp of Israel.*

JOSHUA 6:23

Rahab's decision to be faithful saved her entire family.

Rahab was a prostitute living in Jericho who hid Joshua's spies in her house because she believed that their God was almighty. When the king demanded that she turn them in, she said they had already headed for the hills. As soon as the king's search party left, the spies left freely and Rahab asked that they spare her family in exchange for her kindness. When Joshua's army returned later to destroy Jericho, Rahab's family was freed while the rest of the town burned.

When we make the decision to honor God by honoring or protecting His people, we never know what the consequences will be. But the story of Rahab is a major lesson to women everywhere that our decisions about the way we treat people can have enormous implications. When the road diverges and we have a decision to make, that is the time to go with God. There is no earthly king who will ever be able to save us, no army, no police, no government, nothing.

Only the Lord is mighty enough to save in this way. The lives of our family members might have to depend on our faithfulness. We have to see to our diligence in all decisions, even those that seem inconsequential in the moment. They may become the difference between life and death.

I will make every effort to see that after my departure you will always be able to remember these things.

2 PETER 1:15

There are a lot of things I want for my children. I want them to be healthy and happy. I want them to ask for and accept forgiveness. I want them to know how to give and receive love. I want them to know and pursue their passions. I want them to have nice manners and a keen sense of integrity. I want them to have a sense of clarity, adventure, purpose, and humor. I want them to love learning and be able to escape into a good book. I want them to speak their minds without fear or inhibition. I want them to have both confidence and humility. I want them to be hard workers but always remember how to play. I want them to be comfortable with silence, their bodies, and differing opinions. I want them to be content with what they have without being complacent. I want them each to have lifelong friends, a forever lover, and a houseful of children. These things are wonderful, aren't they?

But none of these things have meaning without the basis and context of faith. These things are nothing more than the overflow of a heart that is rightly related to God. And so now is the time for me to teach my children about God, Jesus, the Holy Spirit, heaven, and Scripture.

Now is the time to share the teachings of Jesus and lay a foundation of love, obedience, tolerance, and discernment. Now is the time to build this foundation and bury these roots because long after I am gone, my children and grandchildren will still be forging a path in this world. I want them to stay on the path that leads them home.

What he opens no one can shut, and
what he shuts no one can open.

REVELATION 3:7

This verse is a powerful meditation for those of us who have a tendency to be control freaks. If you have ever tried to manipulate circumstances, adjust timing, or influence opinions in a feeble attempt to unveil your own plan, you know what happens when God shuts a door. That's right, it slams.

If we approach crossroads in our lives as opportunities to grow in faith, then our hearts and minds will be opened in direct proportion to our trust in and submission to God. No matter how long we knock or how hard we tug on the handle, if the Lord says no, it won't open. He has a path in mind for us, and the sooner we can come into agreement with Him on that, the sooner the right door will open. Forcing love, a career path, an opinion, or an ultimatum in this world all come to the same fruitless conclusion: It wasn't meant to be.

But humbly walk down a hallway ordained by God, and you will see that we could never approximate what He has in mind for us. It would blow all our dreams and ideas out of the water. He opens doors for us that make absolutely no sense. He has timing that we could never orchestrate, even on our most controlling days. He makes a way that is beyond our abilities, beyond our expectations, and beyond our control.

He withdrew by boat privately to a solitary place.

MATTHEW 14:13

Jesus knew the value of getting away. There are several examples in Scripture where Jesus withdrew from the crowd, even from His beloved disciples, and took a breather. We all need this; it's imperative that we create the time and space in our lives to restore and regroup. We need it alone, for ourselves. We need it together, for our marriages and friendships. We need it as a family with our children, and we need it individually with each child as well.

Do you heed the signs that indicate you are overdue for some alone time? Do you build alone time into your schedule when you plan your life? Do you know where to go when you need to get away? Do you have a place of respite for your family?

A few summers ago my family and I bought a small house in California. It's nothing fancy to anyone else, but to us it's the finest resort in the world. It's our hideaway from the rest of the world. I go there alone to rest, to work, to see friends. In fact, anytime I have a manuscript to finish, I like to finish it there. I go there with my friends when we need a girls' getaway. I go there with my children. And my entire family goes together.

The time we spend away creates a separate identity for us as a family, and builds relationship in ways that are hard to achieve in the regular settings of our lives. It doesn't have to be a literal vacation; it can be another special place, like a park, a picnic, a hike, whatever. The important thing is to go. The best part about being there is that we disconnect from life everywhere else and plug back into the abundant life that is right in front of us—one another.

Let your "Yes" be yes, and your "No," no.

JAMES 5:12

❧

Having clear and firm boundaries can save us from a world of hurt and frustration. The choices we make about where we will invest our hearts and how we will spend our time determine our characters and the plots of our life stories. Above all else, we want to honor God.

We all get asked to do a lot of things—at work, in the classroom, at church, with our friends. It is easy to become overcommitted and overwhelmed. We are not honoring God or our families when we are scattered, tired, and resentful. Being busy is not a good thing; but having a full life is beautiful. How do we navigate the difference?

We have to cultivate a prayerful and powerful "Yes" and "No." We have to put our options before God and ask Him for direction. He is happy to multiply our efforts, increase our impact, and expand our time—but He does this when we are doing His will, not following our own.

I want my choices to bless my family. I want to have enough of me left over so that I can go the extra mile for my children when they need me. I want to have enough padding in my schedule that I can be flexible when the Holy Spirit gives me a nudge. I don't want to be so busy and so distracted that I get passed over by God when He has assignments.

By choosing wisely, our "Yes" will have greater impact because we have more time and energy to invest our hearts. Our "No" will get easier as we walk in the freedom of our good boundaries. Our children will watch and learn to do the same.

*He asked them, "What are you discussing
together as you walk along?"*

LUKE 24:17

Has your cell phone ever dialed someone unintentionally and recorded an entire conversation from your home or car? Dawn's phone dialed me the other day and it took me a minute to recognize that she wasn't talking to me, that's how kindly she was speaking to her children. I had to wonder if I would want my tone with my children to be recorded at any time. It definitely makes one more mindful.

The Lord is always privy to every one of our conversations. Just like the disciples as they walked along the road to Emmaus. Jesus Himself came up and walked alongside them, even started a conversation with them, and they had no idea that it was Him. I wonder how often Jesus is in our midst, listening to our words, watching the choices we make, and trying to help us.

Throughout the day today, imagine Jesus walking behind you, sitting next to you, or getting an unintentional voice-mail recording of your conversations. Would Jesus be pleased by what He heard? Would He call you back and compliment you on your kind and respectful tone with your children or your husband?

Just being mindful of these things can help us to live more transparently. When we have nothing to hide, we are truly free.

The Spirit helps us in our weakness. We do not know what we ought to pray for, but the Spirit himself intercedes for us with groans that words cannot express.

ROMANS 8:26

There are some emotions that words simply cannot express; things we call love, anguish, elation, devastation, loneliness, terror, loss, liberation. We have words that approximate these emotions, but nothing truly sufficient.

When our experience defies explanation, we must turn to the Holy Spirit to unlock our emotions and translate our prayers. The Spirit is glad to give breath and life to our prayers, especially in moments when we are rendered speechless. When our hearts are so broken we cannot utter a word, when we are so terrified that no sound comes out, or when we are so full of joy that no words could possibly convey our gratitude—the Spirit speaks on our behalf. He aligns our requests with God's will so that our prayers are more readily heard and more rapidly responded to by our Father. This is a benefit of living a life attuned to the Spirit of God.

Never underestimate the power of intercession. When your child needs help, or a family member, friend, or stranger is troubled, never be intimidated to pray with them. Never worry that your words will come out feeble or wrong. It is impossible to offer your heart in prayer for someone else and "mess up."

If you have ever prayed for someone in need and later wondered where on earth those thoughts and words came from, now you know. You had a translator.

I pray that out of his glorious riches he may strengthen you with power through his Spirit in your inner being, so that Christ may dwell in your hearts through faith.

EPHESIANS 3:16–17

Yoga class is a humbling experience for me. I see women of all ages, shapes, and sizes around me doing things with their bodies that I can't do with mine. My body simply does not always want to obey the way theirs do. My teacher once said, "Be patient with yourselves; just because you are fit in one way does not mean you are fit for yoga. This happens with work over time." So much of what allows for the balance, flexibility, and strength necessary to do many yoga positions is having a very strong core. A strong core keeps your abdomen and back steady and solid and takes the pressure off other weaker body parts. If my core is weak, I am attempting certain positions using the wrong muscles and it is no wonder I shake and fall over; I cannot hold the pose. You cannot tell this by looking at people, because core strength is on the inside.

Our spiritual strength is a kind of core strength. You can't tell the condition of someone's faith by just looking at them. But when a time comes that requires balance, strength, or flexibility in life, who do you suppose are the people who can remain steady? Yes, the ones with core (soul) strength. Just because we know how to be emotionally, mentally, or physically strong does not mean that we know how to be spiritually strong. The training is completely different.

We want to be fit in all ways, in things seen and unseen. Let's be patient with ourselves and get to work.

I, Paul, write this greeting in my own hand.
Remember my chains. Grace be with you.

COLOSSIANS 4:18

Remember my chains.

We have all been in chains in some way or another, areas of limitation or bondage, held back by our own sin. Maybe you are living in chains in some area of your life right now, pining for freedom. Or maybe you are living in glorious liberation, well aware of how far you have come.

Regardless of how long ago we left our shackles, we would do well to remember them. For it is only by recalling our bondage that we appreciate the joy of living in freedom. Some places we have visited we don't ever want to return. Keeping the memory fresh helps us to stay on the well-lit path and also constantly refreshes our gratitude and reverence toward the God who freed us.

In the right way and at the right time in the lives of our children, our tales of chains can and should be shared. Our children need to understand our struggles, our victories, our Savior, and our histories. If we stuff our faith-building experiences (difficult though they may be) into a box in the attic of our souls, we are not using them to build the faith of those entrusted to us. God uses everything, even our mistakes and our weaknesses, for His ultimate good. Our trials and painful seasons can and will be redeemed as we use them to strengthen and guide others who are struggling or lost. We have knowledge, experience, or compassion in certain areas for a reason. We walked that path to get to the other side…and to help others cross over.

Whatever is true, whatever is noble,
whatever is right, whatever is pure, whatever is lovely,
whatever is admirable—if anything is excellent or
praiseworthy—think about such things.

PHILIPPIANS 4:8

So much of the battle for our souls is waged in our thought lives. Our thoughts are the gateway to our hearts, as our hearts are to our souls. As we mature in our walk as believers, the enemy finds it impossible, difficult, or cumbersome to access our souls, perhaps our hearts as well, but our thought lives can be vulnerable to his deception, so he keeps whispering lies. We may not even be aware that we have bought into his blathering until we have gone further along that path. When we start thinking about things that make us worry, or make us feel anxious, unworthy, ill-equipped, or unprepared, we can be certain we have granted access to the enemy somewhere. This kind of thought trail never comes from God.

Paul knew very well that if we weren't actively training our minds to meditate on good and holy things, we would be more apt to hear the whispers of the liar. The exciting thing is that we can change our train of thought, once we begin to clue in to the fact that we have gotten off track. At times I have to literally stop what I'm doing, pause for clarity, and go immediately to God.

*Keep this command without spot or blame
until the appearing of our Lord Jesus Christ,
which God will bring about in his own time—God,
the blessed and only Ruler, the King of kings and Lord
of lords, who alone is immortal and who lives
in unapproachable light, whom no one has seen or
can see. To him be honor and might forever. Amen.*

1 TIMOTHY 6:14–16

I wonder about love in my life, why it left when it did and when, if ever, it's coming back. I can talk to God until I'm blue in the face about exactly what kind of man would be great and when he should enter the scene. But God has other ideas. He knows what lies ahead and what will be required. He considers timelines other than my own. He knows the trajectories and the hearts of everyone involved. My attempts to dictate timing are nothing other than a sign of the sin of unbelief. Our God is the Master of the universe, the one who made heaven and earth, and I can't seem to trust Him to restore my love life.

Do you have areas where you try to dictate time or attempt to control outcomes? Where do you struggle when it comes to God's perfect timing? Are there things that you want but are tired of waiting for? Let's press our Reset buttons today and remember that He is in charge, He has our best interests in mind, and He is already at work behind the scenes. If we can just trust Him, He would love to make our wildest dreams a mere shadow of the blessings He has in mind.

In the sight of God, who gives life to everything…

1 TIMOTHY 6:13

What were your dreams when you were a little girl?

Did you want to be a veterinarian, a ballet dancer, a teacher, an oceanographer, a newscaster, a designer, a writer, a doctor, an actor, a chef, a singer, a soccer player, a musician, an astronaut? Did you doodle on the sides of your notebook and write about it in your journal? Did you make plans and read books and talk boldly about your future?

Do you sometimes look at your life and wonder where all that went and how you got where you are? The unfolding of a life is a grand mystery, with so many layers, characters, sidetracks, and switchbacks. I want you to think about your dreams today, remember them, and write them down someplace. Even if your life looks nothing like your childhood imaginings, it's crucial to remember what they were and who you were when you conceived them. Because when we remember our dreams, they always have something to tell us. They remind us of who we were, who we are, and who we are becoming. If the dream still resonates with you, if it still makes your heart beat faster and makes you wonder what if, then it's still alive for you.

You can take steps, even tiny ones, in that direction. You can begin to gather the materials needed for the construction of your dream. Even if the timing and the circumstances are not conducive to building right now, you can always begin to work on the foundation. Any movement in that direction creates two magical things—momentum and hope. Momentum and hope have changed the world. That means they can change your life, too.

Dear friends, now we are children of God, and
what we will be has not yet been made known.

1 JOHN 3:2

We all are amazing packages of potential—each one of us and each of our children. As children of God, our potential is limitless, because when He gives us our assignments and simultaneously equips us, we are unstoppable.

Raising a child is like the unfolding of a flower; a tiny tight bud becomes a blossom, then a blossom becomes a flower. Our job is not to determine what our children will be, even though it's tempting to assign meaning to their talents or point them in directions of what we think would yield a good life for them. It is not our job to select their friends and dates and spouses. We might be mistakenly choosing the career we think is interesting or the kind of friend or son or daughter-in-law we would want to spend time with. But none of these things are about us. It's easy to get confused and think our lives are somehow woven together. Our hearts are indeed connected, but we each have a life and a calling, unique and alone.

As parents our job is to go before our children and pave the way. As we walk forward in faith and in truth, we clear a path for those who are following behind us. As we teach them about God and provide opportunities for them to grow in faith and develop their own relationships with our Savior, we help them connect to the Source. God has all the answers about who and what we will be, and with whom.

Dear children, keep yourselves from idols.

1 JOHN 5:21

There are things I enjoy that could become vices; things like coffee, wine, and exercise. I love to wake up in the morning and brew a cup of joe, and plop on the sofa in my pajamas with some devotionals and my hot mug of coffee (with cream and sugar). It's a ritual that makes my morning. I like to wind down the day, pour a glass of wine, and prepare dinner for my family. I like to listen to music, chop vegetables, and answer questions about homework. It's a ritual that makes my evening. I like to wake up right before my alarm goes off, turn it off, and pull on some running shorts, shirt, and shoes, and head outside to meet my friends for an early morning run. It gets my day started on the right foot, so to speak.

Here's the deal: I like these things and they have become a part of my life. But I need to know that I own them and they do not own me. If I woke up in the morning and could not function without caffeine, then my cup of coffee would have become a crutch instead of a cozy ritual. If four o'clock rolled around and I started eyeing the clock and acting jumpy, then my glass of wine would be an addiction instead of an addition. If I stepped obsessively on the scale and wouldn't eat unless I ran, then my enjoyable morning run would enter into the realm of compulsion and obsession, both unhealthy manifestations of a healthy activity.

Even good things can become idols. We need to be on the lookout for pleasures that hold a danger of becoming idols—in our lives and the lives of our children.

The peoples around them set out to discourage the people of Judah and make them afraid to go on building.

EZRA 4:4

Trying to build anything of consequence always seems to provoke a spirit of fear, doubt, or intimidation in some people. Throughout history, naysayers have always arrived right when someone brave tries to take on something big. *You can't do that; are you kidding me? You've certainly bitten off more than you can chew, eh? Why bother? It's just going to be torn down. You'll never finish.*

The same thing happens to us today as happened to the Israelites when they began to rebuild the temple in Jerusalem. If we truly have a heart for God, we are trying to build our families in a different way from the rest of the world. It will look different, our plans and materials will be different, and people are going to gawk and wonder. *Why bother? It's just going to be torn down.* Well, my family was in fact torn down, but construction did not stop; it was just a setback. It is intimidating to go on building in the face of a setback, but we must. We need to tune out the voices of the naysayers and listen to the voice of God.

Where is the construction zone in your life right now? Your heart? Your faith? Your family? Your dreams? Are there people or circumstances that are trying to make you afraid to go on building? Don't listen to them. The temple of the Lord is in all those things: your heart, faith, family, and dreams. Build Him something magnificent.

*I proclaimed a fast, so that we might
humble ourselves before our God and ask him for
a safe journey for us and our children.*

EZRA 8:21

⁂

When a petition is significant enough to warrant constant prayer, a fast is a beautiful offering to God. Hunger is a constant reminder to turn to God and humble ourselves, and it also provides a sense of clarity and purpose in a world mired by overindulgence. A collective fast is also a way to pray in solidarity with your prayer group. Fasting on behalf of someone you love is a gift of devotion and selflessness. The theme of sacrifice is often lost on us today, and fasting is a good reminder to live leanly and cleanly. We have to be willing to give something up.

A fast doesn't always have to be about food. I have friends who have fasted from other things, such as television, gossip, cell phones, e-mail, wine, worry, complaining, negative thinking, nagging, raising their voice, shopping, sugar, magazines, and pride. A fast from anything removes its ownership over you and places it in the context of being owned by God. It is a way to gain mastery over the things we struggle with.

A mother fasting for her child or a wife fasting for her husband represents a willingness to do without so that someone else can thrive. It blesses the person we fast for, and it blesses us at the same time.

If I have found favor with you, O king, and if it pleases your majesty, grant me my life—this is my petition. And spare my people—this is my request. For I and my people have been sold for destruction and slaughter and annihilation.

ESTHER 7:3–4

This book of the Bible glorifies God as the Redeemer of the impossible, even though God's name is not mentioned one single time. The book of Esther is a beautiful story of how one woman changed the fate of her people by being brave enough to claim her heritage, even at the risk of death. King Xerxes had no idea that Queen Esther was Jewish! And the Jews were slated to be destroyed by a power-hungry man named Haman. By boldly claiming her identity as one of God's people, Esther saved the people of Israel.

There will be a moment, or moments perhaps, where each one of us will be at a crossroads in our faith. Either we will publicly align ourselves with our God, or we will hide and blend in with the masses. The decision made at the crossroads may reveal itself in different forms: stating a countering opinion, saying no when everyone is saying yes, saying yes when everyone is saying no, taking a stand against discrimination, taking up for the poor, making it clear that you are on a different path. You may be met with silence, cheers, anger, or quizzical looks—you won't know until the moment comes. The point is that you care more about pleasing God than pleasing humanity.

If we want our children to be bold enough to stand steady in the current, or strong enough to swim upstream, we have to be the person who first does those things.

From the LORD comes deliverance.
May your blessing be on your people.

PSALM 3:8

I will never forget one night when the kids were little and we were living in a small town outside Barcelona. It was late and we were driving home from dinner with the girls' godfather. My friend Melanie was driving, I was in the passenger seat, and the kids were strapped in the backseat. We stopped at a stoplight, the only car at the intersection. We were always diligent about locking the doors, but for some reason, this time we forgot. Out of the shadows, four or five men jumped out and started opening our car doors. My scream was so loud and so primal that I did not recognize my own voice. I slapped and clawed at the arms that reached into the backseat. Somehow as one man reached across her for the keys, Melanie had the strength, wits, and adrenaline to slam the door on his arm and step full throttle on the gas.

We flew through the intersection and the red light, leaving the men behind. We drove several blocks to a more crowded area with the doors banging open against the car before we had the nerve to get out and shut them. When I checked on my babies, crying from all the commotion, I totally lost it, realizing what might have happened if the men had taken off with my children.

I thank God that He delivered us from that danger. I know His power to save; I have seen it with my own eyes. No matter what we think, we are powerless at times to help them. Pray every day for protection over your children.

May my vindication come from you;
may your eyes see what is right.

PSALM 17:2

So often we want to make our case clear, our intentions known, our words or actions justified. Many times in the attempt to put ourselves in the clear, we actually make a bigger mess. It takes an enormous amount of faith to be able to step back and stop talking, trusting that God will make everything right. If we are living authentically and transparently, we do not have to be our own proponents, our own best defense. We do not need to justify ourselves because God will take up on our behalf.

It's not an easy thing to let go of the need to explain ourselves all the time. Particularly in our own parenting, if we are doing what is best for our children in a prayerful and purposeful way, then we don't have to worry about what other people are thinking about us and our mothering. God knows what is right and best for our families. It may look different to someone else...and that's okay. We don't need to please everyone, or have others in agreement with our position all the time—as long as we have sought God first; it will always work out in the end.

His eyes see everything, even beyond the mistakes and messes we can make of things, deep into the heart of every woman who is really trying to do her best. He blesses our efforts and our intent. He makes up for us and takes up for us. Everything is unfolding as it should; be patient.

The boundary lines have fallen for me in pleasant places; surely I have a delightful inheritance.

PSALM 16:6

We grow up so much when we learn to define ourselves through healthy boundaries. It's essential to know where you begin and end; what is your true responsibility and what is not. In the book *Boundaries* by Henry Cloud and John Townsend, the authors define good boundaries as a fence line that clearly marks the "yards" of our existence. The things that are contained in our property are the things we are responsible for tending to and protecting. Outside the fence line is somebody else's property. It's up to us to be diligent about walking our fence line from time to time, making sure that there aren't holes or broken fence posts.

It's an interesting thought that while our children are indeed in our yards, they also have to be working to develop their own set of boundaries, their own "yards." We can help them with this by teaching them and showing them what their boundaries are, and letting them practice managing them at home where they already feel safe. We can add to their responsibilities appropriately so they learn to carry their load as they grow. We can allow them to "suffer" the consequences of their decisions as part of a natural sowing-and-reaping process, which mimics their lives in the world beyond our homes. We can teach them how to prepare for and cultivate their delightful inheritance. We must model good boundaries in our own lives so we are able to instruct and encourage with credibility.

Keep me as the apple of your eye;
hide me in the shadow of your wings.

PSALM 17:8

If your child ever went through a phase of shyness, you know the feeling of a child hiding behind you, peeking around your legs to say hello. It's a precious time, when they feel so secure tucked behind you, meeting the world from the perspective of protection. Or how about watching your young child perform at anything, and seeing that huge and adorable grin they get when they spot you in the crowd and know you are watching them? When I catch my child's eye at a recital or school program, they light up in full bloom and try so hard to show me their stuff. Or when I watch my kids at a race or athletic event, their speed or effort increases in direct proportion to the volume of my yelling their name. That is sweet enough to make me cry, my child giving their all to cross the finish line where they know I'm waiting.

They want so deeply to know they are the apple of my eye. And they are. Every single human being has that desire, to be the apple of someone's eye, whether it was ever realized or not.

These same feelings are echoed throughout our spiritual walk with God. Regardless of our age or experience, we are the shy toddler many times, peeking out at new people or new situations from the shadow of His wings. We are the ones who long so desperately for His approval, for His eyes to be on us, for the awareness that He loves us like that—as the apple of His eye. And He does.

Show the wonder of your great love.

PSALM 17:7

☙

In a world of electronic screens, there is nothing more intimate or heartfelt than getting a real letter, especially a love letter. It doesn't necessarily have to be from a man (but that's really nice); it can be from a friend, a family member, or a child. Grace and I have a hiding place for a secret journal we pass back and forth, leaving each other love notes. I will have that journal for the rest of my life, mark my words. When my kids go away for Daddy time, I like to send with them some stamped envelopes self-addressed to me, so they can drop love notes in the mail when and if they feel inspired. I love to drop a card in the mail to a friend, who lives locally or far away, just to tell them how much I love them, or recall something they said or did that really touched my heart. It's a beautiful gift, to acknowledge someone by putting words on paper.

Did you know that God leaves us love notes all the time?

He does. You just have to know how to look for them. There are certain things you just love, right? Things like a certain smell, a certain song, a certain feeling. For me some of these things are: the scent of gardenias, the smell and sound of the beach, sunflowers, shells and sand dollars, fireworks, driving with the top down or windows open at night, finding pennies. When these things are in my midst, I know God has been there. He's giving me a shout-out from on high, reminding me that He knows and loves me best. Be on the lookout; He knows and loves you best, too.

You broaden the path beneath me,
so that my ankles do not turn.

PSALM 18:36

✻

I almost have to laugh out loud at this verse, thinking of my lack of coordination and foibles when I started trail running. I have no sense of direction and I am clumsy, so you can imagine how that unfolded. But it was an incredible experience for me. I signed up for a training program, and with that got a new coach and a group of strangers to run with. Some of these training runs were in the dark, so the combination of uncertain footing and wearing a headlamp in pitch darkness was highly unsettling.

Robert, my coach, kept telling me I needed to relax, lighten up, trust my footing as well as my ability to roll with the rocks if I had to. He told me to look straight ahead and not at my feet; to choose a path and go for it.

I knew the metaphor was for me, to pick my line by keeping my eyes on God. With Him, I can trust my footing. He will keep me safe and upright; He will prevent me from getting lost; He will light my path; He will keep my ankles from turning. I needed to practice these things in a physical sense to begin to better understand them in a spiritual sense. I must learn better that way, because God wanted to show me, not just tell me.

If you have an opportunity to learn something new outside your comfort zone, I want to encourage you to give it a try. See what God has in store for you; there is so much to learn.

He brought me out into a spacious place;
he rescued me because he delighted in me.

PSALM 18:19

If you are living in cramped spiritual quarters right now, I feel for you. I know the feeling of going about your daily existence and feeling as though the world is starting to close in on you. Maybe it's the weight of responsibilities. Maybe it's the compulsion to rush all the time just to try to keep up. Maybe it's the restless feeling of knowing there is more than this, but not sure how to tap in. Maybe it's the uncomfortable feeling when your identity currently feels like a pair of ill-fitting pants. Maybe it's the lack of vision when you have spent too long at a low altitude. Maybe it's the squeezing feeling of anxiety or depression.

God sees us growing in a garden, not contained in a pot on the patio. He wants to bring us to a place of spaciousness, with plenty of room to breathe and grow. He has a freedom in mind for us that requires some room. He wants us to spread out and stretch out. He wants us to open our minds and our hearts and make time for important things to sink in.

If we allow Him to, and invite Him in, He will bring us forward into a spacious place. Like wandering in a thick forest and happening upon a beautiful meadow, He wants to surprise us. He has spread a blanket on the ground and prepared a picnic for you; won't you sit down and enjoy?

Reckless words pierce like a sword,
but the tongue of the wise brings healing.

PROVERBS 12:18

It's so much easier and cleaner to ask God to watch over our words before we say them, rather than asking Him to clean up a mess we've made with a careless tongue. As a writer, you can imagine how I dearly love words. They have the power to teach, heal, connect, restore, bring laughter, and bring peace. They also have the power to inflict deep damage if we aren't careful—especially where our children are concerned. Their hearts are so tender and vulnerable while they are growing and trying to form their own concepts of identity. It reminds me of how a baby has such a tender skull with a pulsing soft spot while they are tiny—and we have to protect it. Same goes with their hearts, the soft spot is there, even if we can't see it. And we have to protect that, too.

Even when we are frustrated, we must be mindful to choose words that are life-giving and that build a child's identity, not strip it down. When in doubt of our ability to choose wisely, silence is the best option of all. We cannot afford to be careless. Knowing and saying this verse is a great way to take a moment, take a breath, regroup, and remember the power of words.

May the LORD answer you when you are in distress;
may the name of the God of Jacob protect you.
May he send you help from the sanctuary and
grant you support from Zion.

PSALM 20:1–2

Ann, my friend and mentor, was visiting me yesterday. She always brings me new verses, new ideas, and new insights.

We were talking about healing and protection. She was explaining to me how often we pray to God as if we're beggars, pleading for this or that, or trying (however inexpertly) to pray with authority to cast out the enemy. She recalled Scripture stories about Jesus healing people. Did he beg and plead with His Father in order to heal someone? No, of course He didn't! It was much simpler than that. As the Son of God, He just did His thing.

As daughters of God, we can do our things, too. Instead of begging God, and praying over every detail of a situation or relationship, Ann encouraged me to pray the power of the kingdom over that person or circumstance and *believe.* Just invoke the power of the kingdom of the living God, and watch what happens. She asked me who or what I thought the kingdom was. I hadn't really thought about it; maybe I had a picture of heaven in my mind—clouds and tranquility. But I hadn't actually pictured everyone there—all the angels, armies, saints, every loved one that has already crossed over, the Trinity in full glory: Father, Son, and Holy Spirit, the entire kingdom.

That is help from the sanctuary; that is support from Zion.

Who can discern his errors? Forgive my hidden faults.

PSALM 19:12

Oswald Chambers said it best: "There is no getting away from the penetration of Jesus. If I see the mote in your eye, it means I have a beam in my own. Every wrong thing that I see in you, God locates in me. Every time I judge, I condemn myself" (June 17, *My Utmost for His Highest*).

As we let go of judging other people, we are in a better postion to examine our own hidden faults. These are not the things we commonly struggle with and are well defined in our character assessments; these are the subtler things, the things beneath the surface. These are the hard-to-get at areas, the tiny cracks that can only be cleaned with a toothbrush. Or the dusty top shelves that require climbing a ladder. Or the invisible germs that collect on the telephone or the remote control. Or the baseboards of our being, places that mandate scrubbing from the perspective of our hands and knees. Some of our places most in need of cleaning require closer inspection to even notice the dirt. If we are so busy looking at what other people need to clean, we miss our own mess.

Ask God to shed His light into your innermost places, and be prepared that you might not like everything that is revealed. It may be time to roll up your sleeves, pull your hair back, and get to work.

May he give you the desire of your heart and make all your plans succeed. We will shout for joy when you are victorious and will lift up our banners in the name of our God. May the LORD grant all your requests.

PSALM 20:4–5

This verse is a beautiful way to intercede for our children and our friends when they are embarking on something new. Things like a new school, a new job, a new hobby or pursuit, a new relationship, or a new phase of life. We don't do this enough, support or celebrate one another enough. Perhaps it's because at some base level we all are insecure—either insecure in our faith and worried for the future, or insecure in ourselves and envious of someone else's courage or success. If someone else is bold enough to follow a dream and they succeed, what does that say to the areas in our own lives where we are afraid to step up, step out, and try?

When we truly have God's heart for our beloved, we want them to succeed. We want them to have the desires of their hearts because we aren't afraid of our own desires! We have allowed the Spirit of Christ in us to conquer our petty human nature and we can think big—for ourselves and for the people we love. There is enough love and enough blessing to go around; let's stand strong for one another in prayer and solidarity.

When any of God's children succeed, God is glorified and our entire family of believers is blessed.

The LORD is my shepherd, I shall not be in want.

PSALM 23:1

What is it you think you need right now?

A new house? That pair of shoes? A tummy tuck? Just say it, whatever it is that has your attention. Name it, and then take it to God.

We are easy prey in this immediate gratification "I'll be happy when" culture. Think about it. *When we move into a bigger house. When we have a baby, or another baby. When one of us gets that promotion.*

Sadly, we are always looking to what's next. And it always leaves us empty, because no matter what's next, we are never satisfied *right now*. An "I'll be happy when..." mind-set prevents us from ever being content.

What we are really longing for is so much bigger than the next acquisition or the next escape—it's the deeper things, the things that are harder to name and get at, like contentment, safety, faithfulness. No matter what we think we want, it always comes down to deeper things. I think I need the new outfit because I want to feel pretty. I want to feel pretty because I want to feel confident. I want to feel confident because I want to feel loved. I want to feel loved because somewhere deep inside I am afraid I'm not. I'm striving and chasing to get certain things, but I'm accepting counterfeits as substitutes.

If the Lord is our Shepherd, we shall not be in want. We already have everything we need.

My eyes are ever on the LORD, for only
he will release my feet from the snare.

PSALM 25:15

We all have certain places we get stuck. Certain pits we are prone to falling into. Certain traps in which we always seem to become ensnared. Sheer determination will not save us from these pitfalls.

We need God if we plan to prevail. I have a list tacked to the bulletin board in my office. I have learned to recognize some of my regular pitfalls—so I made a list of twelve things. It's titled, "Kristin—Avoid the Pit:"

1. I will seed God first, with all my heart.
2. I will not attempt to substitute His healing with counterfeits.
3. I will be patient and TRUST.
4. I will respond quickly to tugs of the Spirit.
5. I will pray for deliverance from evil.
6. I will foster a grateful heart.
7. I will consider the repercussions of my choices.
8. I will pursue holiness.
9. I will receive and give grace.
10. I will be very slow to judge.
11. I will be quick to forgive.
12. I will be open to love.

You can always pray about your own pits and ask God to give you your own list. I have not come close to mastering it; that's why it has to hang in my face every day.

*Accept one another, then, just as Christ
accepted you, in order to bring praise to God.*

ROMANS 15:7

Of course the Lord has high hopes and high standards for us.
He has rules He wants us to obey. He has potentials He wants
us to fulfill. He has specific tasks in mind for us. He has blessings He wants to make us ready to receive.

But we must always remember that He loves and accepts
us right now, exactly where we are today. We are already
enough.

This is the same message we must convey to our children.
The starting point is always love and acceptance; we always
begin and return there. We can encourage and instruct, but
only from a place of initial acceptance. Jesus never taught,
comforted, or healed people by degrading them; His love
drew them to a higher place. His love made people want to
seek Him and obey. That is the essence of a true and beautiful
shepherding relationship.

Are you struggling right now with things that are hard to
accept about a child or loved one? Are you having trouble coming to terms with the innate differences between you? Pray to
God and ask Him to give you His heart for that person. Soon
enough, you will find that your heart has been changed.

*When he ascended on high, he led captives
in his train and gave gifts to men.*

EPHESIANS 4:8

In church circles there is always a lot of talk about spiritual gifts. Everyone is trying to understand them, but being human, everyone really just wants to know which spiritual gift or gifts they have. Varying passages of Scripture define spiritual gifts differently, and it can get kind of confusing trying to determine if the list is short or long. I did a study about spiritual gifts with my Bible study (complete with a questionnaire to find out what yours is/are!), and at the end of all of it, I came to one personal conclusion and revelation.

We know we are "in the zone" or using our God-given gifts when doing those particular things causes us to transcend. I don't mean levitate; I mean lose ourselves. When we give of these talents, we are never depleted or irritable, never feel shy or inadequate; sharing them brings us joy. This is our way of sharing the love of God with others, when we do the things He created us to do.

Some of my friends transcend when they teach, or interact with children, or pray for others, or talk about books and ideas, or help the helpless, or hold a baby, or play a sport, or ride a horse, or sing a song. It isn't the thing so much as it is the touch of God on you when you do it. The touch of God makes you sparkle, and people get curious about where all that light is coming from so they take a closer look.

*If a man loudly blesses his neighbor early in
the morning, it will be taken as a curse.*

PROVERBS 27:14

Proverbs is typically a pretty serious book of the Bible, but for
some reason when I came across this verse, it made me laugh
out loud. God has a great sense of humor.

Have you ever complimented someone or made a comment and somehow wound up making a mess? "You look
great, really fit and healthy!" (Heard as: Oh sure, did you
think I was a fat slob before?) "If you need help, let me know."
(Heard as: Gee thanks, you clearly think I am totally inept
on my own.) "Feel free to join us if you want, no pressure."
(Heard as: I can tell you want me to stay home.)

Many times the things we intend as a blessing, whether
it is direction, discipline, advice, or a compliment, come out
crossways and are received or perceived as an insult. Just like
the irritated neighbor who just wants to sleep in, our words
can annoy or hurt instead of heal or help when we are not
mindful of our timing or the status of the recipient's heart.
In order to be well-received, our words have not only to be
carefully chosen, but also properly received. We are unable to
discern proper timing because we cannot see into the hearts
and minds of other people. But God can.

When we pause to ask him to translate and time our
words, we can rest assured that He will take over how our
heart is received by another.

I know your deeds, that you are neither cold nor hot.
I wish you were either one or the other!

REVELATION 3:15

What is more disappointing than lukewarm? Hot coffee and an iced latte are both good—but a lukewarm cup of joe sitting on your desk since morning? Ew. Passion or disdain—both are powerful in their own right, but indifference? Boring. Pro or con, it's good to take a stand; but having no opinion at all might well mean you *just don't care.*

The problem with being lukewarm or indifferent is that there is very little to work with, no conviction, no passion, no depth, and no heart. Being spiritually lukewarm is almost worse than being cold, if cold means you don't know God. Knowing God but being indifferent toward Him is a more deliberate rejection. Lukewarm is dangerous, easily misled and prone to being misleading.

If you took the temperature of your family's faith, what would it be? What can you do to turn up the heat a little? How about your own faith? Are you taking steps to ensure you are actively growing, learning, and seeking God? It's okay to tell God you are growing cold; it's easier for Him to warm your heart if you are deliberate about sharing it with Him.

*How can we thank God enough for you
in return for all the joy we have in the
presence of our God because of you?*

1 THESSALONIANS 3:9

I love Thanksgiving. It is a holiday filled with family, friends, and food, what could be better?

There are no expectations of gifts; it is a simple celebration of what we already have. Every year we (my parents, my brother, and my children every other year) spend the holiday with another family of dear, longtime friends. We have so much history together and friendships that span three generations; we are blessed.

Everyone has a role in the preparation of the meal, even the little children. Last year Luke poured wine and made homemade butter by shaking buttermilk in a jar (he passed the jar off to everyone since his arm got tired). Bella made place cards for everyone. Grace made her specialty—crescent rolls. I love how seriously the children take their responsibilities, understanding that everyone has a hand in our feast. It takes all day, of course.

As we gather around the table, we take turns sharing what we are thankful for, and it's one of my favorite moments of the entire holiday season. It's a chance for everyone to share their hearts, their struggles, their accomplishments, and their blessings of the year. This verse sums up how I feel when I look around the table, my gaze resting on my children's faces. I sometimes still can't believe they are mine to love. Do your family and friends really know how much they mean to you? Tell them.

Ascribe to the LORD the glory due his name;
bring an offering and come into his courts.

PSALM 96:8

What is your offering to the Lord going to be today? What are you bringing into His courts? It isn't necessarily a matter of doing something new or different; it's more a matter of being intentional about doing what you do *for Him*. Here are some examples of "statements of offering" with which to begin your day:

- Lord, today when I get up, I will rise and offer the gift of this day back to You. Thank You for the gift of life.
- Lord, today when I do anything physical, I will do it in gratitude for my health and the strength You provide. Thank You for the gift of my body.
- Lord, today when I use my mind, I will use it to think thoughts that will bring You glory. Thank You for the gift of wisdom.
- Lord, today when I acknowledge my emotions, I will channel them in ways that bring healing and promote integrity. Thank You for the gift of feelings.
- Lord, today when I speak, I will choose words that bring life. Thank You for the gift of communication.
- Lord, today when I take care of the people I love, I will do it with a heart for You. Thank You for the gift of love.
- Lord, today when I teach my children, I will do it with Your standards in mind. Thank You for the gift of motherhood.

One man gives freely, yet gains even more;
another withholds unduly, but comes to poverty.

PROVERBS 11:24

❧

I remember when Luke was one and I was pregnant with the girls. I was feeling emotional (big shocker, I know) and cried to my mom, worried that I wouldn't be able to love other children the way I loved Luke. My heart for him was so complete; I just didn't understand how more could fit.

My mom gave me a hug and said, "Sweetheart, love does not divide; it multiplies." She was right. I have loved those girls, each with my entire heart, from the first second I saw them. How is it that I can love three people, each with my *entire* heart? It isn't a piece of the pie; it's more pies. That is the mystery of God. He loves each of us that way, too, and that's also a mind-bender to try to understand.

But this example, one that any mother of more than one child can relate to, gives us a clue as to how we are expected to live, love, and give. If we know that love really does multiply, then we never have to withhold love out of fear that there won't be enough—for others or for ourselves. When we give love, we have more love in reserve. When we love, we are filled with love. We are constantly being replenished and restored. When our source is the River of Living Water, we are always going to overflow.

*You will be with child and give birth to a son,
and you are to give him the name Jesus. He will be
great and will be called the Son of the Most High.
The Lord God will give him the throne of his father
David, and he will reign over the house of Jacob
forever; his kingdom will never end.*

LUKE 1:31–33

I absolutely love the season of Advent. I love the time leading up to Christmas, the hopefulness, the excitement, the building anticipation. I make a purposeful choice in my heart and in my home to counter the mounting consumerism surrounding the holidays.

We all have things in our lives that we are waiting for. Many of these things have been a long time coming. It takes a special kind of faithfulness to hang in there, to not give up or relinquish the dream, to keep marching on in hope even when there is no evidence whatsoever of pending fulfillment. This requires incredible fortitude. I love the stories of people who plod along their entire lives, working diligently to be prepared, and suddenly, there it is: their chance, the chance of a lifetime. They recognize it, they are ready, they go for it, and the sweetness is beyond comparison.

I want to cultivate a spirit of hopeful expectancy in my life, working and waiting gracefully for my destiny to be revealed. Advent is a perfect time to meditate and journal on these things, the things we wait for in our own lives. Faithfulness is not found in the celebration of a blessing; it is built in the character of the waiting heart.

God is light; in him there is no darkness at all.

1 JOHN 1:5

Here we have the litmus test for every decision. We have the map for every crossroads. We have the GPS for every road trip. We have the sign and signal for every lane change. We have the marker at every trailhead. We will know where to go and what to do and say if our intended action will pass this test: Will what I am about to do (or say) stand unblemished in the light of God?

Would you be embarrassed by this decision if it was out in the open with your name next to it, for everyone, including God, to see? Would your words be acceptable, no matter who was listening in on your conversation? Would your actions be suitable, no matter who was nearby with a camera?

If the decision would sparkle cleanly, no matter where you went or who was watching you, then you can feel secure knowing you are going in the right direction.

If the choice can stand alone, without explanation or rationalization, then you can breathe easy.

God isn't just in the light; He *is* the Light. That's why if the choices we make in our lives can stand the test of light, we know we are following God.

I am now going to allure her; I will lead her into
the desert and speak tenderly to her.

HOSEA 2:14

God wins us over with His love, His consistency, His kindness, His compassion.

In the ministry of our lives, we can and should follow His example. We will not win people over for God by being judgmental, pushy, self-righteous, or demanding. Even our own children will be repelled by faith if it is introduced to them that way.

We don't push faith on people; we invite people. We are alluring. This is why I think women can be such powerful living invitations to faith—we are, or can be, by nature very compassionate and warm and nurturing. Without having to say much, we can illustrate the essence of God by our actions.

Reflect on your attitudes and actions over the past week, or several weeks. Have you been a living, breathing invitation to others? How have you shown the love of Christ in your daily, regular interactions? Have people better understood the acceptance and forgiveness of the Lord through you?

This really matters. If each of us became more mindful and prayerful about the way we are living the gospel, it would have a greater effect on our families, communities, and the church at large than any single powerful figure of faith. Think about it: a powerful sermon on Sunday is a good thing, but a powerful sermon lived out each day by women everywhere— talk about alluring! Use the gifts of your femininity and your motherhood and live your life as an invitation.

Do you want to get well?

JOHN 5:6

We are quick to say that we want healing and wholeness, but when acquiring those things requires some effort on our part (even the effort of being open), we are often stopped in our tracks.

Someone said something to me today that I can't seem to shake, and it fits well with this verse so I'll share it with you: "Do the same thing you've always done and you'll get the same thing you've always gotten." Yes, I know. Ouch. This sentence hurts, but it also has the potential to breathe life into stale places. If I keep parenting the same way, I can hope for the same results. If I keep putting the same energy into my marriage, I had better be happy with status quo. If I continue to do the same caliber of work at my job, I can expect to receive the same paycheck. (Hopefully, right? No guarantees.) If I give the same attention to my friendships, I can expect the same old thing back. If I give the same priority (or the lack thereof) to my health and fitness, I can expect to put on three pounds (minimum) a year for the foreseeable future. If I am single and do the same things with the same people all the time, I can expect my dating life to look the same a year from now.

Take a moment to consider the areas of your life that are challenging to you right now. Where is your stress coming from? What areas make you feel inadequate or ashamed? Now consider the question posed by John 5:6: Do you want to get well? Well, do you? Really?

Arise, shine, for your light has come, and
the glory of the LORD rises upon you.

ISAIAH 60:1

Opportunities come, and then they go. Your moment could be next. Are you ready? Are you present? Are you awake? Are you aware?

Ordinary times could be seen as boring, the in-betweens, or the hallways between main events. These are vulnerable times when it is easy to become restless or wander off track. Are you taking the time and making the effort in ordinary times to hone your talents, improve your spiritual reflexes, intensify your focus, and build your endurance? Are you ready to arise and shine when your turn comes up, or are you wasting time or playing small right now?

Ordinary times are perfect arenas for training. Practice your skills now, walk out your faith now, when there is less at stake. There is no emergency. There is no rush. There are no eyes on you, watching how you are going to handle this. This can be either an easy street or an on-ramp to something big. Pay attention to where you are going so you will have a better idea of what you might need when you get there.

It's one thing to miss or blow a big moment when you are single and alone. It's another thing entirely to miss it or blow it when you have little people watching you, modeling you, and counting on you. Train now; be diligent and prepared. Your moment is coming and you don't want to let down God, yourself, or your family. You are a daughter of God, and as such, you are meant for big things.

> *He touched their eyes and said,*
> *"According to your faith will it be done to you."*
>
> MATTHEW 9:29

I love this story about the way Jesus healed the blind men. I think I find it so appealing because we are so often blind ourselves. We are blind to the way God and others really see us. We are blind to our gifts and talents. We are oftentimes blind to what is going on around us. Our hardness of heart can render us blind to God and His hand in our lives.

His question to the blind men was, "Do you believe that I am able to do this?" (Matt. 9:28). A simple question, yes, but it was profound in terms of determining their level of faith. They responded "Yes," and that was when Jesus touched their eyes. Their healing, or ability to see, was not dependent upon Jesus' ability to heal or upon His power; instead it was dependent upon the depth of their belief.

Think about this for a minute. If our inability to see, our own lack of vision, our own inability to change perspective, or our inability to see beyond ourselves or our present circumstances is to be healed—it is not a matter of the Lord's ability to do it (which is unquestionable), but more a matter of our own ability to accept it. No belief, no healing, no vision.

Where are you struggling to see in your life right now? Where are your blind spots? Where are you being short-sighted? Allow Jesus to touch your eyes. But first make sure you believe.

Wounds from a friend can be trusted.

PROVERBS 27:6

Do you have the kind of friends who will tell you the truth? Will they call you on the carpet when you are playing small or being inauthentic? Will they hold you accountable to your promises and goals? Will they tell you when they think you are about to make a big mistake? Will they keep on loving you when you make that mistake anyway? Will they tell you that you have spinach in your teeth? Will they tell you that you might want to take a different approach with your children? Will they tell you when you are at fault, even if what you really wanted was just a little vent and validation? Will they call you on your laziness? Will they go deeper when you answer, "Fine"?

Friends like this are a gift from God. They will make incomparable differences in your marriage, your mothering, and all aspects of your life. They are the kind of women whose company you leave a better woman than when you arrived.

Even if what they have to tell you is painful, it is always with the intent to heal, not hurt. They will never exploit your weakness, but they won't allow it to be your excuse either. They challenge, they encourage, they love, they laugh, and they don't walk out when things get tough.

Think of the women in your life whom you love like this. Tell them, today, how important they are to you. Show them. Put time and energy into these relationships; don't let them slide. They are worth fighting for.

"What do you want me to do for you?" [Jesus] asked.

MARK 10:36

❧

Are you so busy trying to meet everyone else's needs that you have forgotten to recognize your own?

If Jesus came to see you today and asked you what you wanted, would you know what to say? If your friend, your husband, your mother, your sibling, asked you right now what you want, would you have an answer? Part of being emotionally healthy and mature is in knowing how to recognize our needs and how to get them filled.

Think about a small child before they can speak. They are frustrated! They want something and they can't ask, so they scream, cry, throw things, and can cause quite an uproar. They need language to be able to say that something hurts or that they are hungry, thirsty, or tired (okay, maybe they never will admit to being tired). We are exactly the same way when we get out of practice, which happens when we put everyone's needs far ahead of our own. We forget the language of the heart and how to express ourselves in this way. We are the equivalent of the crying toddler throwing things, only we express our needs in other ways: withdrawing, smoldering glares, snapping, nagging, or chilly extended silence. It's equally immature and unattractive.

The next time you are feeling frustrated, try to remember the last time you made your own needs a priority. If it has been so long that you can't actually remember, it's time to do something for you. You might be surprised to see how happily your family supports this bold move.

Look, he is coming with the clouds.

REVELATION 1:7

I love the idea that the stormiest or most muddled moments of our lives are when God is most recognizable on the horizon. He always shows up when things are difficult or confusing; or is it just that in those moments we are more apt to be looking for Him?

Our reaction to trials, or clouds, in life will color our children's manner of facing adversity. They will remember how we handled disappointment, how we dealt with loss, how we went about rebuilding when things fell apart. As believers, our first reaction to trouble is not to hit the panic button but to turn to God, and that is precisely what we want our children to understand. They don't need to grow up with fear as a default reaction to stress; we can help them set their default to faith, not fear. After all, every difficult moment holds an opportunity to grow in trust.

But first we have to be walking this walk. When a storm is brewing in your life, do you look up and watch for God? Where do you turn for comfort or direction? Do you share your coping methods with your children?

> *I know whom I have believed, and am*
> *convinced that he is able to guard what I have*
> *entrusted to him for that day.*

2 TIMOTHY 1:12

If we think about our burdens, worries, and responsibilities and take that thinking too far into the future, we are going to absolutely crumble. I can't think about Luke (who is ten) and consider the future all at once: if he's going to have decent friends or hang out with delinquents, if he's going to be able to withstand the peer pressure surrounding alcohol and drugs, if he will keep the faith in this carnal world, if he will be safe once he gets his driver's license, if he will keep up his grades, where he will go to college, what his career path will be, if he'll marry a girl I'm crazy about, if he will be a good husband, a good father. If I start thinking about all these things at once, I will implode. I literally can't handle it; the concerns of a mother are too much for me. My back will break under the weight of it all.

So how do we find peace? I'll give you a hint: Peace does not come from what we believe, our doctrine. It comes from *whom* we believe, an almighty God. And yes, He can handle all of it. So whatever our concerns are, as they arise, we take them immediately to God's throne and we place them at His feet. And He will remain, steady and abiding, watching over and guarding what we have entrusted to Him for that day. We don't have to concern ourselves with every day, just today, and have the faith that He is on guard.

We live by faith, not by sight.

2 CORINTHIANS 5:7

❧

You can't judge a book by its cover. Things are not always what they seem. You can't see the forest for the trees.

These are clichéd statements we have heard our entire lives, indicating that our sense of sight is often insufficient. From a spiritual perspective, this same sentiment is conveyed in 2 Corinthians 5:7. When God is busy at work in our lives, working all things together for our good, we cannot possibly make judgments based on present circumstances or our limited perspective. We don't have the full panorama, or the long-range view.

We have to trust, even when things don't seem to make any sense, that He is behind the scenes, already in the process of working things out. We have to trust that our next steps will be ordered by Him (and wait for instruction) and that those steps will ultimately take us where we should go. He may have us get there by a different route than we would consider on our own, but oftentimes His route is the more scenic. Or perhaps He is aware of a traffic jam or a potential accident directly in our path that we are unable to see. If He reroutes us, perhaps we should be grateful.

If we live by faith, we will live a life of peace, never anxious for what lies ahead, never worried about the current calamity, because we know that things are not always what they seem.

Christ's love compels us.

2 CORINTHIANS 5:14

Our own reservoirs can run low or go dry. Our personal sources of motivation can wane. Our energy levels fluctuate. Our commitments can waver. Our interest fades in and out. Our focus shifts. Our self-discipline is feeble. Our convictions can crumble in the face of temptation or fatigue. We are human, and as such, we are prone to bouts of unreliability.

But there is one thing that can draw us beyond ourselves. There is one energy Source that is never, ever depleted. There is one thing that is always reliable—and that is the love of Christ, the love of God Himself.

Christ's love can direct us in ways we would never attempt to go on our own. His love can encourage us to try things that we would never think possible for us. With Him we can go deeper, stretch higher, and last longer than would ever be possible on our own. Do you see how Christ's love compels you in your life? Do you see how you have the energy and the strength to carry on even when you know you have passed your human limit? Do you see how your conviction is sometimes bigger than you are, saving you from yourself? Do you see how, out of nowhere, you get an idea to try something and for some reason you can't seem to let it go? You are likely compelled by Christ to do something or try something new.

It's a beautiful thing to step outside our comfort zones, knowing that God's hand is upon us. We are never alone. He will guide us, today and always.

Do not lose heart or be afraid when rumors
are heard in the land; one rumor comes
this year, another the next...

Our society is riddled with rumors and gossip, from the tabloid magazines, to entertainment television, to the Internet, to our local communities. There is always someone up to something, and other people wanting to dissect and publicize it. It's a sick fascination, but a predictable and reliable way for people to turn their attention to the details of other people's lives, thereby ignoring their own—at least for a little while.

No matter how intentional we are about avoiding the rumor mill, there are times when it hunts everyone down. It will occasionally happen to us in our circles, and to our children in theirs. It's painful to watch your child feel hurt or betrayed by some social dynamic at school. But as believers we must constantly seek approval from one source only—God. This way, if we know we are working to please Him (even despite our weaknesses or failings), we are in the clear, no matter what anyone says about us. Our comfort and consolation have to come from Him. We have to be able to tune out the voices of the world and be able to listen to what God has to say about us. If He needs to rebuke or discipline us, that's one thing; but if other people are being clueless and critical, it's entirely another.

It's a good idea once in a while to ask ourselves and our children, "Whom are we going to listen to?" "Whom are we trying to please here?" If the answer isn't God, we can train ourselves to refocus and move on.

Jesus called the Twelve and said, "If anyone wants to be first, he must be the very last, and the servant of all."

MARK 9:35

✎

Being first seems to be an important thing to young children. Even something as simple as walking out to the car can bring about a race, with doors flying open, leaping in, pushing one another, shouting from the runner-up: "First is the worst, second is the best...." Being first to the table, first to finish homework, first to get dressed, first to take a bath—these things are endless and tiresome at my house. There is also the continual vying for my attention, squabbling over who gets to sit by Mom, whose turn it was last time. Sometimes I think there is mutiny caused by an unequal distribution of my eye contact. I try to make a point of looking at everyone. Good grief.

How embarrassing for the disciples to have been busted by Jesus for arguing like children, fighting over who was the greatest. No wonder when Jesus asked, "What were you arguing about on the road?" (Mark 9:35), no one answered Him. But Jesus already knew. And that's when He stated the timeless and true lesson in the verse above. When we stop trying to jockey for position or vie for first place, when we are focused on doing the best we can with what needs to be done, God will take care of our positioning. We never have to worry that there won't be enough if we aren't first in line. God always takes care of those who are busy taking care of other people.

This is a powerful lesson for people of all ages.

In fear and amazement they asked one another,
"Who is this? He commands even the winds and
the water, and they obey him."

LUKE 8:25

We spend summers near the ocean, and a couple years ago Luke asked if he could learn how to sail. I thought it was great that he wanted to learn something new, so I signed him up for a sailing camp down at the local yacht club. On the first day of camp, the kids have to take an open-water swim test. This means they start on the beach, swim out through the chop on the shore, and then swim out to a boat in the harbor, where they are tossed a life jacket. They put the life jacket on in the water, then swim back. A week into camp, I came to pick him up early so I could watch them sail back into the dock. I looked for the kids everywhere but saw only a group of sailboats far out at sea, and assumed it was a regatta for adults.

Luke later asked me if I saw him, and I said no, just some adults sailing way far out. "That was *us*, Mom! We went way out there today." I had trouble swallowing. My baby was out there, a tiny triangle on the horizon? My eight-year-old son? On a little Opti sailboat, all by himself, battling wind and waves? I didn't know whether to hug him or march him into the office and demand a refund. I looked at his face and saw something different about him, a confidence and an enthusiasm that were new. I realized my own fear had taken over, replacing my faith in both Luke and in our almighty God.

Whom are we trusting to take care of our children and keep them safe?

Wisdom and power are his. He changes times and seasons.

DANIEL 2:20–21

❧

Did it ever occur to you that perhaps time is malleable in God's hands? Do you find it interesting that an equal amount of time can seem endless or seem to pass in the blink of an eye? The last thirty minutes of a long road trip are endless. Summer months pass by in a snap. Hours can stretch out on a Sunday afternoon and yet time evaporates in the morning and we are almost late to school or work. There are painful moments where I pray to God to please fast-forward, and there are moments so sweet and sublime that I ask God to press pause and freeze time.

The bottom line is that we have to trust God's timing; He knows what He's doing. Sometimes the passage of time can trigger sadness, with kids growing up too fast, parents or grandparents seeming older, or extra lines by your eyes when you smile. We have to trust the timing of His seasons even if the transitions are hard for us. It isn't easy to admit that it's time to get rid of the crib or give the baby toys to charity. When we stop having babies, we are bidding adieu to a sweet phase of womanhood. When our kids go to kindergarten, camp, high school, or college, these events mark other seasons coming to a close. When a child moves out, gets married, or we become grandparents, these are more seasons—a passing of life's torch from one team to another. It's as natural and inevitable as spring turning into summer, but it doesn't always feel that natural.

We must remember that as every season draws to a close, there is another season beginning. God holds time in His hand, and He ushers us through the calendars of life.

*But when he, the Spirit of
truth, comes, he will guide you into all truth.*

JOHN 16:13

We have so many questions for the Lord: When will this happen? How will this be revealed? When will I know? How will I be sure? What is going to happen next? How will I get from here to there? How much longer do I have to wait? Why?

We don't always get an immediate response to our questioning. In fact, we often have to wait; sometimes we wait for so long that we are certain God has forgotten us and our questions. God reveals answers more than He spits them out, often giving us one puzzle piece at a time. As we collect the pieces, sometimes hunting quite awhile for even a single piece, we eventually start to see glimpses of His design. Just like when a three-hundred-piece puzzle is spread out on the kitchen table, piles that seem nonsensical are slowly revealed as sky, an edge, a border of trees. When, piece by piece, they start to fit together with a satisfying snap, we know we are making progress, or living our questions on the way to the answers.

We could not handle a full disclosure all at once. We would combust. We are not ready. As we grow in faith, God sees that we can handle more, and He reveals more. Understanding is a process, and with God it is revealed in relationship with Him.

*He said to me, "These are the kitchens
where those who minister at the temple
will cook the sacrifices of the people."*

EZEKIEL 46:24

Cooking is a beautiful ritual. The kitchen is a holy place in the house, where the family comes together to prepare and share meals, as well as the communication hub of the household. In ancient times, sacrifices were prepared to honor God. Today, we prepare meals to honor God. We praise Him for the gift of family, for the gift of time to spend together, and the gift of His provision as He feeds and cares for us.

In our busy lives and schedules, mealtimes can be overlooked or handled in shifts like a counter at a diner. I know how hard it is with different people going in different directions, but I also know that mealtimes are worth honoring and preserving. When we cook for our families or prepare a meal together, we are still ministering at the temple. I love an evening where my kids and I are all at work in the kitchen; Grace chopping things for salad, Bella setting the table and grating cheese, Luke getting drinks and timing the pasta as it boils.

Those moments are precious to me, building rituals and bonding together over the simple task of cooking. But it's so much more than that. While our hands are busy and our eyes are on our tasks, the conversation flows freely. We hear about one another's days, what went on at school for them or work for me. The act of cooking fosters a sense of community and fellowship. It is a celebration of who we are as a unit, each bringing our offering to make up a meal.

Jesus wept.

JOHN 11:35

This is the shortest verse in the Bible—merely one noun and one verb. And yet, short as it may be, the meaning it contains is unfathomable in its enormity.

Here we see the Lord, the Son of God, going to visit His beloved friends Mary and Martha, who are grieving the death of their brother, Lazarus. When Jesus sees the depth of their pain, the frailty of the overall human condition, He is moved to tears. Our Savior, moved to tears; we have such a compassionate, empathic, merciful, and loving God! Even though Jesus knows everything, and is fully aware of His power to heal and restore life, He still reacts to our sadness. It pierces His heart to see His people in pain.

The next time you or your child is hurting, think of this simple verse. Know that you have the compassion of Christ as your comfort. Share this verse with your children so they know they are never alone in their pain. Jesus knows what it is to ache; He walked this earth in human form and left it in sacrifice. He knows what it is to cry; His tears fell, too. He not only notices our tears, He wipes them and collects them. Not one ounce of our pain is ever wasted—He redeems and heals everything.

Meditate on His tenderness when you feel vulnerable. No one cries alone in His presence.

I hope to see you soon, and we will talk face to face.

3 JOHN 14

Ah, yes, remember face-to-face conversation? Remember when letters involved paper and ink and a stamp? Please let us never forget the old-fashioned days of communication.

Today many of our children are more adept at communicating screen-to-screen than they are face-to-face. E-mail has replaced phone has replaced physical conversation. Text messaging, with its unique forms of spelling and lingo, has become common vernacular (grammar and spelling—huh?). People stay connected via Facebook and Twitter. Complete thoughts are reduced to 140 characters or less. People spend more time updating complete strangers with "snippets" of their lives than they do connecting with the people they love. It's impossible to truly be present in the moment, say, enjoying a beautiful sunset, if you are busy taking pictures with your phone and posting them to your home page. *"Enjoying sunset!"* No, you aren't enjoying the sunset, pal; you are on your phone.

If our children are spending more time communicating with snippets and screens, how will they know how to really connect? True interpersonal skills are timeless and irreplaceable. The way you come across in an interview, or on a first date (do people still date, or just e-mail?)—these things matter. We have to insist on cultivating and maintaining some level of good old-fashioned communication. I don't know how we do this, exactly, in our rapidly advancing technological world. Maybe we should have a tech break, a hiatus one day a week, when we forgo the screens and just talk?

This child is destined to cause the falling and rising of many in Israel, and to be a sign that will be spoken against, so that the thoughts of many hearts will be revealed. And a sword will pierce your own soul too.

LUKE 2:34–35

No one travels the path of motherhood and completes the journey unscathed. When any woman makes the choice to have a child, she is opening her heart to the greatest and most unique love, but also the most exquisite pain. Not just the pain of labor and birth, but the cracking open of your heart as it willingly embraces the potential for degrees of devastation as our children hurt, falter, grow, and depart.

Motherhood is a choice to live the rest of your life with your heart wide open, exposing a vulnerability that is the equivalent of a nakedness of the soul.

There is nothing in this lifetime that can bring me immediately to tears, have me howling in laughter, cause me to climb the walls in desperation, or drop me to my knees in prayer faster than my children. I have never known love this rich; I have never been more fearful and watchful of loss or danger.

If I'd never had children, I would never have been able to fully understand selfless and unconditional love. I would not be who I am, who I was meant to be. The sword will pierce my soul, as it will at some point for every mother, but the wound will never outweigh the healing.

*He will command his angels concerning you to guard
you in all your ways; they will lift you up in their
hands, so that you will not strike your foot against a
stone. You will tread upon the lion and the cobra; you
will trample the great lion and the serpent. "Because he
loves me," says the LORD, "I will rescue him;
I will protect him, for he acknowledges my name."*

PSALM 91:11–14

I recently went on a trail run with my friend Terra up in the Santa Ynez mountains outside Santa Barbara. I hadn't seen her in a while, so we were getting caught up, talking while we ran and hiked. I didn't notice anything out of the ordinary in the terrain, just lots of sticks, branches, and rocks. Well, one of the sticks was clearly not a stick at all, and Terra screamed, "Snake!" I did a quick hop to the right and nearly knocked into her, and barely missed my next footfall landing squarely on top of a rattlesnake.

Naturally I freaked out, sprinted ahead for a bit while shrieking, but then I had to go back and make sure it really was a rattler. It took a good ten minutes for my heart rate to return to relative normalcy.

How often, are we that close to real danger—a footfall away? We travel through this lifetime with so little awareness of what is going on around us. Danger and evil lurk everywhere, disguised as the most common things. There were definitely angels watching out for me on the mountain that day, and these are the same angels I want watching over my children all day, every day.

*It is good to praise the LORD and make music to
your name, O Most High, to proclaim your love in
the morning and your faithfulness at night.*

PSALM 92:1–2

Are you familiar with those days when the sound of the alarm is jolting, and you feel like you've been shot out of bed like a cannonball? Somehow late from the word go, you scramble to wake children, find clothes, pack lunches, locate errant shoes, brush teeth, fling waffles out of the toaster, slam a cup of coffee, look for keys, holler at the kids, grab backpacks and rush out the door? Whew, I know. The day goes on at breakneck speed and you know you're going to be perpetually late to everything all day long.

That is not how it feels to begin the day in the presence of God. Seeking Him first in the morning starts everything off on the right foot. Taking time with God, even ten minutes, before the rest of the house is awake is a sacred ritual that yields peace all day long. Get quiet in His company in the morning and offer the gift of the day back to the one who created it; ask Him to ordain your time.

The same thing holds true at night. Closing the day with God is a calming ritual, a time of reflection, praise, and sometimes repentance. It allows us to go to bed with a clean heart and a quiet mind. It's totally different from falling asleep with the lights and television on, glasses halfway down your face, sprawled out on a pile of unfolded laundry. I like to read a devotional or a chapter from Psalms at night, and then think about one thing in particular about my day that I am thankful for. Think about bookending your day, morning and night, with the Lord.

David shepherded them with integrity of heart;
with skillful hands he led them.

PSALM 78:72

This verse so concisely and eloquently describes the kind of mother I want to be that I could just weep when I read it. It hits my heart in that spot. I want to live the kind of life with my children and grandchildren that would warrant this verse as part of my eulogy. If, when all is said and done, I have been a mother with integrity of heart and skillful hands, I will have done the best I can do with what God has entrusted to me.

I am a neat freak about my car and my house. Ask my friends—I like it clean. It doesn't always stay that way, but it's my preference. Now, if I am picky about my house and car, I aim to be fanatical about the state of my heart. A heart of integrity is a clean place; "You could eat off the floor in there," as my grandma sometimes says. There is no dark stain of sin, no shadowy, cobwebby, corners of deception, no trash piles of unforgiveness, no cracks of rigidity, no mildew of resentment, and no stench of reeking pride. It's healed in there—fresh, honest, open, and aired out. If we can shepherd our children with a heart like that, we will not lose them or lead them astray.

I want to raise my children with skillful hands. I want hands that are knowledgeable, kind, healing, productive, protective, capable, nurturing, strong, and soft. I want my touch to be immediately recognizable and have the power to put them at ease, no matter what their age or circumstance.

The lamp of the LORD searches the spirit of a man;
it searches out his inmost being.

PROVERBS 20:27

❧

My daughter Grace and I went through a phase where she was having trouble handling mistakes. If she made a bad choice, was unkind, broke something and I called her on it, she would burst into tears and run up to her room to hide.

One day I was in the shower and she did something to hurt Bella, then took off. When I got out, Bella was crying and Grace was nowhere to be found. I called a family meeting.

I used an example from our neighborhood, where two older boys were playing with a BB gun. One of them shot his friend in the eye, and then got so scared he ran away. We talked about how he wasn't a very nice friend, but I asked the kids what was worse—hurting someone by accident, or choosing to leave them all alone when they needed you? Everyone agreed it was worse to leave your friend. My children learned that the way we act *after* we make a mistake often says more about our character than the fact that we made a mistake at all.

I want to be a woman who is brave enough and humble enough to own my mistakes, ask forgiveness, make amends, and move on with grace.

A week or so later, Grace ran into my office to confess that she broke a candle in the kitchen. I swooped her into my arms, kissed her whole face, and told her how happy I was that she came to tell me.

A man's steps are directed by the LORD. How then can
anyone understand his own way?

PROVERBS 20:24

Let's face it, we have no idea what we're doing.

If you tried to make a diagram to explain exactly how you got to where you are today, it would be mind-numbing. There were so many twists and turns, stops and starts, characters, decisions, and variables of timing and circumstance that led you to your life today. If one imagined everything that had to line up in order for your life to be what it is, and for your effect to have rippled through other people's lives in precise ways, it would point even an atheist to the existence of God. There just aren't that many possibilities for coincidence before it becomes laughable.

God is present in everything, everyone, everywhere.

We have to trust His timing and His direction, even when it makes absolutely no sense at all. Sometimes we don't understand because we aren't meant to understand; we are just supposed to follow instructions.

If you are in a confusing place today, take heart knowing that God already has everything well in hand. He is working everything together for your good, the good of your children, the good of all His children.

Better is open rebuke than hidden love.

A friend once said something that gave me the key to understanding her. It was the Rosetta Stone to translating everything about her heart. She said, "I would have given anything to know my dad loved me like that." I dissolved into tears as everything I knew about her fell into place, into context, and became clear.

So many of us are walking around with wounds like that, the small child within us still wanting to know that she is lovable and worth fighting for. When we don't get that need answered properly or sufficiently when we are children, we spend the rest of our lives taking our questions to the wrong people. Stoic generations were taught not to share feelings, be vulnerable, or say I love you. If you ache this way, I ache with compassion for you. And now that I understand my friend, I understand you better.

Hidden love is almost like no love at all. At least with an open rebuke you know where you stand. But with hidden love you are standing on nothing, teetering and imbalanced. If you are all grown up and still have that question, ask God the Father. He will heal the places that perhaps were missed by an earthly father. He will speak words of healing.

...She wrapped him in cloths and placed him in a manger, because there was no room for them in the inn.

LUKE 2:7

❧

I love everything about the Christmas season. I love the way it smells to have a pine tree in the house. I love the carefully wrapped packages, even when the dog shreds the paper. I love baking things that smell delicious to welcome my children home after school. I love a fire in the fireplace. I love rereading the same stories every year, and telling some of the same family tales around the dining table. I love the advent candle wreath on my kitchen table, marking time.

I love all the traditions passed down through my family, in the context of the greatest tradition of all—honoring the birth of our Savior. It's easy to get caught up in the to-do's associated with the holiday and forget that the most important thing to do is be still, be watchful, be reverent, and be ready. We should prepare our hearts to receive Him with more time and effort than we spend preparing our homes for the holidays. We should make things tidy, comfortable, bright, and welcoming on the inside. Our children will remember us being prayerful and present more than they will remember the presents under the tree. Let's make room at the inn for Jesus. *Merry Christmas.*

But Mary treasured up all these things and
pondered them in her heart.

LUKE 2:19

When the shepherds got the good news from the angels that the Christ was born, they hurried to Bethlehem to see the baby. They told Jesus and Mary about the visit from the angels proclaiming news about their son, and verse 19 was Mary's response. She sat quietly and reflected on what had just transpired.

You know how it feels just after having a baby, so imagine Mary in a stable with no bed, no nurses, and no epidural, after having spent most of her labor riding on a donkey! She was likely exhausted and overwhelmed. But she remained present in the moment, soaking it all in.

We are usually exhausted and overwhelmed after Christmas. The day after can feel like kind of a lull, or a letdown. The house is a wreck, relatives are lingering, we fix one meal after another, we have a stack of items to return. If we aren't careful, the magic and beauty of Christmas can get lost in the trash bag filled with crumpled wrappings. All the time spent wrapping and readying can evaporate in a flurry of torn paper and pajama-clad children. We have to be intentional like Mary, soaking everything in and saving it to ponder later. The magic of Christmas is sufficient to last throughout the year. Don't rush the aftermath, there is no hurry to meet the new year, be present now.

> *There are three things that are never satisfied,*
> *four that never say, "Enough!": the grave,*
> *the barren womb, land, which is never satisfied with*
> *water, and fire, which never says, "Enough!"*

PROVERBS 30:15–16

Do you have any idea how happy I was not to find my name on this list? I think it used to be on there: "Five things that are never satisfied: the grave, the barren womb, land, fire, and Kristin Armstrong." I was definitely someone with an unquenchable desire for what came next. It has been a long journey to get out of that pit, and today I am happy to say I have an unquenchable desire for now.

I want to be present, fully intent and breathing in and out, in this moment. I want to realize that who I am, what I have available to me, and what I have to offer are enough, just as they are. I want to wake up and know that before I contribute one single thing, I am already valuable. Have you ever felt like a fire? Constantly consuming and moving but never content? A fire stops only when someone or something stops it or it burns itself out.

We can conjure a spirit of enough. *Enough* is a beautiful word, isn't it? It implies sufficiency, satiety, fullness, gratitude, abundance, and contentedness. We can declare a state of enough in every area of our lives. Enough is always the right amount, like eating a fine meal but stopping before you feel ill or your pants are too tight in the waist. Or sitting in the sun long enough to feel warm and get some vitamin D, but stopping before you are sunburned. Enough never leaves you in a state of longing or regret. Enough is, well, enough. Like baby bear's porridge, it's just right.

Like a bad tooth or a lame foot is reliance
on the unfaithful in times of trouble.

PROVERBS 25:19

Not only was Solomon wise, he also had a pretty good sense of humor. Too bad he's not still around, and single. But I digress....

Do you know where to go in times of trouble? Have you trained yourself well enough in ordinary times to turn to God reflexively in extraordinary times? Do you have a friend or friends you know you can count on, really count on, no matter what life throws at you?

I have a handful of friends who have seen me at my best and at my worst. The thing that stands out to me the most about them is that they have loved me equally in both instances. They are truly happy for me when life is good, and they are behind me and bolstering me when times are tough. They are not envious of the good or afraid the bad is contagious. They are just there when I need them, and even when I just want them.

Faithfulness is love and commitment proven over time. It is the essence of devotion. It's what gives nourishment to passion, which otherwise flames out on its own. It is at the core of the finest marriages, families, and friendships. It sustains emotion and transcends time and distance. It is worth finding, worth waiting for, worth working on, and worth fighting for. Know the faithful in your life.

Like a city whose walls are broken down
is a man who lacks self-control.

PROVERBS 25:28

❧

I love how Luke's kindergarten teacher would say to the children, "Sit crisscross-applesauce and keep your hands to yourself. Remember, you have control over your body so make sure it listens to you." Or the words of Bella's first-grade teacher: "Remember your self-control. Are you acting with integrity right now?" Young children need constant reminders to take ownership of their bodies and be responsible for following instructions. We need reminders as adults, too.

In ancient times, a city with a broken wall was left completely vulnerable, exposed to attack. It was easy to enter, impossible to defend. If you were to take a stroll along the property line of your character today, would you find any holes? Are there areas that are in need of repair, and as such, need extra vigilance until the repairs are complete? Where are you vulnerable right now? Are you having trouble acting with integrity? Remembering your self-control? Making your body listen to you?

Do you have a break in the wall when it comes to food? Alcohol? Caffeine? Gossip? Shopping? Worrying? Fear? Pride? Where do you feel exposed?

Our self-control is sufficient only in the context of being Christ-controlled.

I tell you the truth, if you have faith as small as a mustard seed, you can say to this mountain, "Move from here to there" and it will move. Nothing will be impossible for you.

MATTHEW 17:20–21

Apparently it isn't the size of our faith that matters, just the concentration of it. A tiny morsel of real faith has more power than we can imagine.

Whatever you are up against in your mothering right now, a sleepless baby, colic, a sick child, a toddler having tantrums, siblings at war, struggles at school, social issues, disrespectful behavior, the wrong crowd, raging adolescent hormones, lack of peace at home, issues with drugs or alcohol, a boyfriend or girlfriend you would never choose—whatever your children are facing, face it with faith. Or maybe it's about you. Are you sick, depressed, tired, feeling hopeless, stressed out, overcommitted, scattered, insufficiently equipped, or painfully alone? Whatever is going on, it's going to be okay. Together with God, you can fix this. It feels like a mountain, and maybe it is, but you can find your voice and tell it to move.

Jesus tells us that nothing will be impossible for us, and that means *nothing*. It's so important to remember that when we feel overwhelmed by it all, that it is not too much for God. It's also not too much for us when we stay connected to God as our Source. He will carry us from moment to moment, giving us the measure of strength we need for each step as we take it. He will not leave us, forsake us, or forget us. We are His children just as our children belong to us. We can't stop worrying; we are moms after all, but we can transform our worrying into prayer and our prayer into power. The catalyst is faith.

*"Many women do noble things, but you surpass
them all." Charm is deceptive, and beauty is fleeting;
but a woman who fears the LORD is to be praised.
Give her the reward she has earned, and let
her works bring her praise at the city gate.*

PROVERBS 31:29–31

⁓

This is the perfect ending to this year, this book, to the famous chapter of Proverbs, the Wife of Noble Character.

When we look back over the years of our lives and reflect on our relationships, our accomplishments, our careers, our experiences—hopefully one thing will stand out and shine— our families. Because nothing says more about someone and the legacy they have created and will leave behind than the strength of their family. Everything else will pale and wither away, and when we're old we won't care about the awards or honors we received; we won't remember how that "important" project turned out at work. We won't care how much money is in the bank, or all the places we traveled. I look at my grandparents, who have lived long lives (my three living grandparents have each made it to ninety, at least), and they care about their faith and their families. Everything else comes after that. When all is said and done, our families are who we are.

Let's love wisely and well: God first and family next. Let's surround ourselves with friends who feel likewise. Let's make choices that reflect the love of Christ, a love that is sacrificial, compassionate, unconditional, and courageous.

"Go forth in peace, for you have followed the good road. Go forth without fear, for God who created you has made you holy, has always protected you, and loves you as a mother."

—FINAL WORDS OF ST. CLARE OF ASSISI, 1194–1253